'Refreshingly honest, ... ng a path for those ready to learn how to find and nurture real, soulful love.'

SADIE FROST, ACTRESS, PRODUCER & FASHION DESIGNER

'Through Persia's blend of dirty humour, deep wisdom and girlfriend style pep talking, Love is Coming will help you understand yourself so you can find and keep a healthy relationship. Expect to be entertained, schooled and forever changed by this book.'

MEL WELLS, BESTSELLING AUTHOR, SPEAKER & COACH

'Persia is a beautiful paradox because she is effervescent with wildness, yet also has a quiet resolve for consistent love.'

CHARLIE MACKESY, ARTIST AND SUNDAY TIMES BESTSELLING
AUTHOR OF THE BOY THE MOLE, THE FOX AND THE HORSE

'Funny and profound, Love is Coming is the meeting point of Sex & The City and Eat, Pray, Love. In it, Persia embraces ancient spiritual wisdom and effortlessly applies it to a modern lifestyle to achieve real, tangible results. Life-changing.'

SEAN PATRICK, CEO OF THAT GUY'S HOUSE AND
TGH INTERNATIONAL PUBLISHING

'This is not just another dating book. Not only did I cry, I laughed out loud so many times. Persia is so deeply honest (like a young Glennon Doyle or Elizabeth Gilbert) and in Love is Coming it feels like she is telling you her stories right there with you. Read it now!'

JESSICA BENDIEN, MEDIA MENTOR & FOUNDER OF BANG TALENT

'Persia is without a doubt the best love coach of this generation. With infectious energy, she is as brilliant a writer as she is a coach, and Love is Coming will no doubt help countless women find real, long-lasting love.'

JODY SHIELD, BUSINESS COACH, MONEY MENTOR, AUTHOR & SPEAKER

'A genre defying book, Love is Coming will make you laugh, cry and rage to a place of resonance, hope and action. Whatever your love story status, this is an unprecedented and essential read.'

MAZZI ODU, AUTHOR AND CULTURAL CONSULTANT

'Love is Coming is a funny yet raw, refreshing and honest account of the complexities of losing and finding love, dating, heartbreak and recovery. I encourage anyone looking to heal their heart and find committed love to devour this book immediately!'

LUCY KEAVENY, RELATIONSHIP COACH, SPEAKER & TEACHER

'Current, grounded, funny and honest, Persia is lighting the way for a new generation of women to live more happy, more conscious lives from the inside out.'

REBECCA CAMPBELL, BESTSELLING AUTHOR OF LIGHT IS THE NEW BLACK

'Persia provides a fresh, intelligent perspective on the issues that so many Gen Y-ers face today. Her passion and dedication to her work is truly inspiring!

DR LINDA PAPADOPOULOS, PSYCHOLOGIST, BROADCASTER & AUTHOR

'Thanks to Persia, love really is coming, once and for all. As a woman who walks her talk she's trusted by people the world over to help them find and keep love. Healer of heartbreak and lighter of inner fires – she is leading the way to finding love in the modern world!'

LUCY SHERIDAN, THE COMPARISON COACH

'In Love is Coming, Persia's unique, honest and humorous way of looking at yourself and your love life will change your view of what is possible for you in romance – without you even realising.'

SUZY ASHWORTH, QUANTUM TRANSFORMATION COACH

LOVE IS
COMING

BY THE SAME AUTHOR:

THE INNER FIX
(WITH JOANNE BRADFORD)

LOVE IS COMING

PERSIA LAWSON

BookPrintingUK

Remus House
Coltsfoot Drive
Woodston
Peterborough
PE2 9BF

A CIP catalogue record for this book is available from the British Library.

The views expressed in this work are solely those of the author and do not necessarily reflect the views of the publisher, and the publisher hereby disclaims any responsibility for them.

ISBN: 978-1-913284-25-1

The author would like to thank the following for permission to use copyright material: Hodder and Stoughton and Watkins Publishing for the extract from *Conversations with God* by Neale Donald Walsch (1 Jan. 2019); and *Psychology Today* for the extract from 'The Deceptive Power of Love's First Moments' by Susan Heitler (13 June 2012). While every effort has been made to trace all copyright holders, if any have been inadvertently overlooked, the author will be pleased to make the necessary arrangements at the first opportunity.

For
Joey Wilderness
& The Soulmates

CONTENTS

GET MAXIMUM VALUE FROM THIS BOOK

I've put together some free resources for you to use alongside this book. Join me online and go deeper with *Love is Coming*:

1. DOWNLOAD MY FREE AUDIO TRAINING
'THE FASTEST WAY TO MEET YOUR SOULMATE'.

This free audio training reveals the exact process my clients and I implemented to go from being regularly ghosted, heartbroken and disappointed in love to attracting the healthiest, happiest, most soulful relationships of our lives (within three months of putting these tools into practice). Head to loveiscomingbook. com to get instant access.

2. LISTEN TO THE LOVE IS COMING
SPOTIFY SOUNDTRACK.

I've created a playlist for you to listen to as you read *Love is Coming*. Check it out over at loveiscomingbook.com

3. SPREAD THE LOVE.

I believe the message of *Love is Coming* has never been more needed in the chaos of the modern dating world. If you feel so too, I'd love you to share your thoughts and responses to the book on social media using #loveiscoming

4. ACCESS FREE RESOURCES OVER AT PERSIALAWSON.COM

My team and I are always creating more resources and tools to help our community improve their romantic lives. Make sure you sign up at persialawson.com to hear about our latest events, workshops and programmes.

Head to loveiscomingbook.com to join in now.
I can't wait to see you there!

All my love,

Persia xxx

P.S. Please note that some of the names and details in this book have been changed to respect people's privacy. Also, although I mostly refer to dating or being in a relationship with a man, as that is my personal experience in romance, the tools I share can absolutely be applied to dating women, too. I believe that although there are of course different nuances between dating men and women, being successful in love is ultimately an inside job.

FOREWORD

I have a bone to pick with Persia. I'm sure that's not the best way to start a foreword, but it's true. I've just read *Love is Coming*, you see, and, forgive me for being confrontational, but it's *so* important I ask this:

Where was this book a decade ago, when I needed it more than ever? I hand on heart believe that if it had been released back in 2011, the journey to the great relationship I'm in today would have been a hell of a lot less turbulent.

The thing is, I've always been *obsessed* with love. It has taken me to the highest of highs and the lowest of lows. It tortured me when I was dating, and tore me apart when I wasn't. Even when I hated men and learned to wear my single status like a badge of honour, I was *still* fixated on whether I was or wasn't in a relationship.

Funnily enough, it was just after a particularly bad chapter in my love story that I met Persia. If I was writing my own book, I'd call the chapter 'Heartbreak Hotel', because it's the one in which I turned up to the hotel room of the guy I was publicly dating as a nice surprise, only to get a nasty shock. It was my real-life Daniel Cleaver moment (if you're familiar with that scene in *Bridget Jones* where she turns up to his house unannounced to find out he was NOT, in fact, home alone...). This guy had nine children to three different women, FYI. If that isn't evidence to suggest someone can't or won't commit, I don't know what is. But I saw the red flags, and charged at them like a bull in a china shop.

I met Persia a couple of months later through a mutual friend, after vowing never to let anyone close to my heart ever, ever again. Some might call it coincidence, but I call it synchronicity. I think the universe tried to bring us together for a reason - what with Persia being one of the UK's most successful love coaches and me being one of the UK's biggest failures in romance, and all - but sadly, I was too shitfaced to recall much of our meeting. Oops.

Our paths didn't cross again until a few years (and yet more romantic misery) later, at the beginning of the first national lockdown during the global pandemic. I had just moved in with my boyfriend (who, spoiler alert: is now the father of my beautiful baby boy, Alfie) and was studying to be a female empowerment coach. Persia and I started following each other on social media and I asked her to be a guest on an Instagram live series I was hosting. Shortly afterwards, she asked me to be on her podcast, *Love is Coming*. It was only then that we realised *just* how much we had in common, in that we were both love addicts who'd managed to turn continuous heartaches and pains into the love story we'd always longed for. What's more, our experiences had made us passionate about helping other women turn their own love lives around - without having to make all the mistakes and go through the same suffering that we did.

When I look back at my exes now I cringe (don't you?!). Did I *really* envision my future with them? Is that actually what I thought living a life beyond my wildest dreams looked like? I wonder how on earth I let myself be treated so badly. And for so many years, at that.

When I wasn't being dumped I was being ghosted (but at least the dumpers had the common courtesy to grace me with a goodbye). I'd wonder what I'd done wrong - and, if I'm to be totally transparent, would even, embarrassingly, send texts asking (no, *begging*) them to tell me. I'd torment myself scouring through old messages looking for subtext - something, *anything* that would tell me they were still interested, and lament when, of course, they weren't.

But you know, as Persia shares in *Love is Coming*, we women *do* have a part to play in all of this. Not only do I wish I'd read this book a decade ago, I wish Persia had been my best friend back then, too. If she had been, *there's no way* she would have let me get away with some of the emotional manipulation (frankly) that I engaged in to get guys to fall in love (or stay in relationships) with me. I'd play hard to get to make men chase me. I'd also play the victim sometimes - and make them run a mile. I own that. I take responsibility. But contrary to what some other authors write, love is NOT a game. You don't have to WIN someone's heart, and meticulously orchestrate every move you make in order to do so.

I get it, you want (just like I wanted) to feel in control of your love life. To achieve at romance in the way you achieve at work. It's funny because I used to always wonder how I could be such an independent woman in so many ways, yet still feel like I needed saving. It wasn't enough that I was named GQ's woman of the week time and time again, or that I was seen on screen, in mags and rags and at red carpet events. It was as if everybody else saw my value, but not the guys I was dating (or even myself).

I'm pleased to share that I did find love in the end, but not until I learned one of the most important lessons that Persia shares in this book: that the *real* love of my life had been with me all along. It was myself. And, although it took me years to realise this - and therefore be *ready* for the right person and relationship - when my boyfriend came into my life things moved incredibly quickly (as I share on Persia's podcast, I got a boyfriend and baby inside of 365 days!). We moved in together at the start of the first lockdown, and not only do we have a five-month old, we've just bought our first house, too.

So, if your heart has been shattered, your love life is in tatters, and you're reading these words wondering whether this book is for you, trust me when I tell you that it absolutely *is*. Persia, like me (and let's be real, maybe you, too), has had a colourful history in the romance department, and in the following pages recounts her tales with rawness, realness and good old British self-deprecating humour that made me nod, laugh and cry as I remembered similar experiences from my own past. Through her tips, tools and stories, which are as entertaining as they are educational, she reveals *everything* you need to know about healing, attraction and commitment so that you can not only meet your own match (if that is what you desire), but do so far more quickly and easily than you would have done on your own. I'd even go so far as to say that this book will *save* you from yourself - from playing out the same old patterns over and over again (and dating the same type of person - e.g. the Daniel Cleavers of this world!). So much resonance, so much relatability - with Persia, you'll finally feel seen, finally feel heard and finally feel understood. She gets it. She just *gets* it.

Let me wrap this up by saying that, whether you believe it or not right now, Love *is* Coming for you - as it did for Persia and as it has for me. Don't you want to be ready for it when it does, so you don't fuck everything up? If so, read this book. Immediately. Don't waste a minute more. Your time to start... is now.

Ashley James

Presenter, DJ, Dating & Empowerment Coach

PROLOGUE

'The cave you fear to enter holds the treasure you seek.'
JOSEPH CAMPBELL

This feels like a trap. Loving you feels like a trap. But we're both too far down this road to back out now.

As I watch you take a long hit off the peacock-blue pipe and slowly slide into another reality, my impulse is to reach out and drag you back into my own.

That's how it's always been for me with men: them turning away, tunnel vision towards a personal odyssey entirely separate from us, me scrabbling to hitch my wagon to their star. (Unless I happen to be dating a nice guy. Then it's the same, but in reverse.)

Never wanting to be left behind, I take my own sloppy hit on the pipe. It tastes like burnt plastic and leather boots.

'Where are we?' I ask, as everything I assumed was real begins to collapse and fold into what appears to be a child's toy box.

There better not be any fucking clowns, I think.

As I'm pulled further away from you and the safety of what we've built together this last year, I start to panic. I feel like a mountain goat teetering on the edge of a steep cliff face; one wrong move could be fatal, but part of me wants to hurl myself into the abyss and be swallowed by it, like when you stand at the top of a tall building and imagine jumping off. *L'appel du vide,* the French call this: call of the void.

Let yourself fall and you'll fly, I hear myself whisper.

This must be my first insight. It's not the one I wanted, but we never want to hear what we most need to. Better a lie that soothes than a truth that hurts, hey?

Moments later the visions start to fade and I'm back in the room (well, yurt). I look to you and see that you're out of your trip, too. The relief is short-lived, when I realise that the water you're sitting in isn't sweat but piss. *Your* piss. I might have trouble letting go, but you certainly don't. I try to mop it up on the sly so that you don't feel embarrassed, the same way I handled all my men's messes before you came along. I can sense my fussing isn't welcome. It rarely is.

'Let him be, Persia. He's on his own journey. Stay on yours,' I'm gently advised by the leader in charge of this group healing experience.

Time for Round Two, then.

Seconds after my second hit, my limbs go numb and I'm catapulted into a kaleidoscopic nightclub that's constantly spinning, shifting, sucking me deeper into a new dimension. There's music, too, growing louder and louder as I speed through the vortexes, each more intergalactic than the last.

I've been here before.

Suddenly I have an overwhelming urge to touch myself. I run my hands up and down my body as a surge of sexual euphoria courses through me. As it does, I'm met with another overwhelming urge.

'Joe! I think I'm gonna shit myself!' I whimper in your direction, clutching at my stomach.

Once again, the visions dissipate as fast as they came and I'm a sobbing puddle on the floor. Several of the other participants form a loving shield around me and ask what's wrong, but I'm so focused on clamping my bum cheeks shut to avoid any more mess that I can't respond.

When I eventually calm down and explain my sexy-near-poo experience to the leader, she tells me this is likely a sign I have some sexual shame to heal. Makes sense, given my past.

'Next time you should wear a nappy, Persia,' she says, deadly serious. 'Maybe shitting yourself is exactly what you need to do to fully let it go.'

I look around at the rest of the group laughing and dancing and playing, and feel as much of an outsider as I have ever done.

The night ebbs on, and you continue your journey without me. I have no choice but to continue along my own, too.

As I inhale my way into my third and final voyage into God only knows where, I'm immediately met by a host of fiery-headed clowns.

REALLY?

I bury my head in my hands and cry. The only time I recall feeling this alone while surrounded by a group of people is the night I was sexually assaulted in a London strip club I was working at.

Shutting my eyes to the clowns, I hear someone retching into a bucket and wonder if it's real or part of my trip. It's impossible to know the difference at this point. I tentatively peek from behind my pillow and realise that it's you. I try to stroke your back, but you're too far away; I can't reach you.

I've been here before.

The only thing I ever feared more than not finding my soulmate was finding you and then losing you. Is this what drove me to keep picking the wrong ones for all those years – the fear of losing the right one? The fear of losing myself trying to hold on to you? The fear we'll have to one day choose between losing each other or destroying each other?

The pain of this thought makes me scream. As I do, I feel a growing warmth to the left of my body, where my childhood friend has been lying this whole time gliding through her own intergalactic odyssey. Whether my eyes are closed or open I do not know, but in whatever realm I'm currently inhabiting this friend has transformed into a golden goddess, the only happy vision I've had all night.

'*Stop fighting it and surrender,*' the goddess whispers into my left ear.

I exhale for what I'm sure is the first time in hours. A wave of calm crashes over me as a pair of pillar-like arms sprout from behind my back and wrap me in a swathe of love.

I've got you. You are safe.

Inhaling, I look back at the clowns. As soon as I do, they fade and disappear.

INTRODUCTION

'Life is a festival only to the wise.'
RALPH WALDO EMERSON

I n the summer of 2014, I went to a festival.

I'd been single for about four months following the breakdown of my healthiest relationship to date (which wasn't saying much), and had recently launched myself into a fling with someone new.

I knew this guy wasn't 'the one' from the get-go, never would be. But, with my friend and business partner eagerly planning her wedding while my thirtieth birthday loomed conspicuously on the horizon, I'd been feeling an underlying pressure to couple up, regardless. After all, it's what many of the single women I knew who were also staring down the barrel of their fourth decade on earth seemed to be doing: strapping themselves to whichever man was closest at the time, and hoping for the best.

I arrived at the festival determined to have the *time of my life* – and, ideally, meet my future husband. For as long as I could remember, my strategy for exiting romances way past their sell-by date had been to chuck myself into new ones nowhere near ripe enough for plucking, let alone consuming.

Famed for its eclectic curation of music, culture, fine food and general hedonism all set within a beautiful secluded lakeside woodland, this festival was exactly the sort of place you'd expect to find good husband material, in my defence. The problem was, instead of feeling excited by all this good stuff, I was mainly feeling overwhelmed by the magnitude of choice on offer. (And that was just from looking at the programme in the weeks leading up to the festival!)

As a rule, I've always tried to manage feelings of anxiety and overwhelm by seizing control of whatever situation is causing these unwelcome emotions to come up. In the case of this festival, seizing control looked like planning every minute of my and my friend's time there to within an inch of its life, like how I overstuff my schedule with activities whenever I'm feeling down on myself.

I'd planned where we'd eat, what bands we'd see when, what yoga classes and meditation classes we'd attend; you name it, I'd planned it. This meant there was little room for adventure and spontaneity, which I've come to learn is what a festival is really all about. As a result of trying to stick to this strict schedule, I constantly felt like I was chasing the festival, like wherever I was wasn't *quite* good enough and the real fun to be had was over there, somewhere else: watching another band, eating other food, hanging out with other people. It was FOMO at the most basic level, a manifestation of anxiety I was well acquainted with.

It didn't help that I spent most of the festival checking my phone to try to meet up with other friends who were there, but because the signal was limited (being in a field and all) and everyone was constantly on the move, I felt frustratingly hostage to my phone and its rapidly dwindling battery life. This was worsened by the bullshit show I felt compelled to put on for the folks at home via social media, showing what a GREAT TIME I was having. It didn't occur to me that perhaps I should just try to enjoy being where I was – with the friends in my actual sightline, not looking to impress the ones sitting at home scrolling through other people's carefully curated lives.

But the real humdinger of the whole experience that year was how desperate I was to pull. Like a dog with a bone, I couldn't drop my old habit of scanning the surrounding terrain for boys to kiss and distract me from how lonely I was feeling.

As a self-diagnosed love junkie, one who'd been dipping in and out of Sex and Love Addicts Anonymous over the last few years (but who was struggling to fully commit to the programme due to also being a self-diagnosed love avoidant), this had always been my favourite way to self-medicate. 'Catting for co*k', I called it. But, although this place was swarming with potential hook-ups and husbands, my desperation must have been palpable, for not *one boy* did I snog, no matter how much I tried to subtly will and manoeuvre for it to happen.

Must have lost my knack, I thought.

What I'd once relied on as a foolproof superpower for numbing out was no longer working, and this was all the more painful because, by now, I should have known better. I was writing a self-help book on this stuff, for God's sake! But I was also learning that it's one thing to know quick fixes don't work in the long run, and quite another to discard your drug of choice when, in the midst of a monstrously anxious episode, it feels like the only tonic that will snuff out your suffering. And when you've been using your drug of choice for as long as I'd been using boys and romance to self-soothe, getting clean is not going to magically happen overnight.

If anyone had evidence of this, I did, growing up as the daughter of two drug addicts who both got sober 'for good' (one day at a time) when I was sixteen. While I was so grateful for this miraculous turn around in our family (and was fortunate to have grown up in a white, middle-class household, meaning our struggles did not have to define me or my future), I'd spent the majority of my life up until my mid-teens constantly surrounded by drama and chaos. So, when that suddenly disappeared and I got the home life I'd always dreamt of having, I went looking for drama and chaos in my love life instead.

I was so terrified of being hurt like I had been growing up that I'd sabotage any chance of a happy relationship, either by cheating on the nice boyfriends I had or going out with dysfunctional bad boys so that I'd never have to risk real intimacy or commitment. The nice boyfriends fulfilled my need to feel safe and loved, while the bad boys satisfied my desire for danger and excitement. As soon as I got bored of the nice guy, I'd escape by diving straight into a relationship with a renowned emotionally unavailable player. When I inevitably got ghosted or messed around by *him*, I went looking for the closest nice guy around to try to regain all my lost confidence. A vicious cycle, if ever there was one.

This pattern continued well into my twenties, amplified by the rise of the swipe culture of social media and online dating apps that made it easier and more tempting to play away, and harder and less desirable to try to maintain a steady, long-term relationship.

Alongside all this romantic drama, it's not surprising that after university I decided to train as an actress. I was fortunate to win a place at a top London drama school, but the intense environment only added fuel to the fire of my hedonistic tendencies.

Things grew predictably more chaotic after graduating. While I had the opportunity to travel to some cool places, other than a few average credits on my CV, all I really had to show for it was a trail of messy break-ups.

Where I'd once felt like I held all the cards with men, I now felt so crap about myself that I'd settle for any guy who came along and paid me a bit of attention, no matter how poorly they treated me. It was the same dynamic again and again, just with a different face, and with every ending, my ability to cope with the normal business of living diminished that little bit more. At this point, I was experiencing regular bouts of depression and anxiety, but was in total denial that my love life was the main factor in all of this.

My rock bottom moment came in 2010. Several weeks after gaining my Master's in Acting, I started working as a hostess in a grimy London strip club in Soho. One night, towards the end of my shift, I was sexually assaulted. I remember thinking at the time that I deserved it because of how badly I'd been behaving in my love life, which is probably why I didn't tell anyone about it for so long. Shortly afterwards, the unacknowledged trauma of that event led me to put on two stone in two months while on an acting job in Shanghai. This period was the pinnacle of my self-destruction, and I started to experience regular suicidal thoughts.

However, I was blessed to have two recovering addicts for parents who were able to spot the warning signs and get me help before things got any worse. My dad decided to take me away to a health retreat in Thailand, where he gently voiced his concerns and shared a crucial insight with me that went on to change the trajectory of my life. He said:

> Focus on the insides and the outsides will take care of themselves.

Those words were the launch pad into healing the real root of all my romantic dilemmas: my relationship with myself.

After lots of therapy and reading every self-help book I could get my hands on, I decided to train as a life coach and set up a positive lifestyle movement with a friend, eventually getting a book deal that went on to become *The Inner Fix*.

However, despite my friend and I being described as 'irreverent British gurus' by *Marie Claire* magazine, I knew I still had a lot of growing to do – particularly in my own love life. This had been made abundantly clear to me after that festival in 2014, where, contrary to what my dad had taught me in Thailand several years earlier, I was back to my old tricks: obsessively pursuing a relationship I was nowhere near ready for, in the vain hope this would make me feel better about where I was (or wasn't) in life.

But a lot can happen in a year.

In an interesting turn of events, the following summer my business partner and I were invited to that same festival to run a workshop about our positive lifestyle movement's message: *focus on the insides and the outsides will take care of themselves* (the same message my dad had shared with me in Thailand). It was here, during my second time at this festival, that my wish from the previous year was granted and I met my future husband. More on that story later.

Over the last five years, this man has shown me what romantic relationships are really here to do for us: to help us grow and expand into the highest version of ourselves.

It doesn't matter where you're at in your own love story right now: whether you're sick and tired of being ghosted or disappointed in love, when everyone around you seems to be getting engaged, married or popping out babies. Or you're fresh out of a break-up and are feeling insecure and full of self-doubt. Or you've never even had a relationship and are fed up of being asked why you're 'still single' at family gatherings. Or you've had enough of the superficiality of the online dating world and want to find real, soulful love with someone you can build a life with. Or you're dating or already in a relationship, but are overwhelmed with anxiety and fear that it's not working how you think it should be. Whatever stage you're at, I believe the solution to any romantic struggle is the same:

> Stop looking *outside* of yourself for the partner you want to *get,* and start looking *inside* of yourself for the partner you want to *be.*

Because, as the late, great Dr Wayne Dyer once said: 'You don't attract who you *want*; you attract who you *are.*'

What makes this such a challenge is that none of us were taught how to have healthy relationships growing up – which is absurd to me, because look what's happening to our world as a result. The point is, if you want a healthy and satisfying love life that goes beyond what today's swipe culture has to offer, you're going to have to take full responsibility for learning how to get it.

While I know this world has bigger problems than whether you and I are romantically fulfilled, at the same time, had I not dealt with my relationship issues when I did, I would've undoubtedly ended up marrying (and divorcing) the wrong man. And that wouldn't have served anyone. In fact, I'm convinced that if we as a society spent more time and resources teaching people how to have healthy relationships from an earlier age, we'd dramatically decrease the likelihood of divorce, addiction and family breakdowns – and all the complicated crap that goes along with them. Given everything that's going on in the world with respect to the coronavirus pandemic (especially the dramatic rise in divorce filings and concern over how this global pause is reducing single women's chances to have children), romantic health and empowerment have never been more important than they are right now.

Committing to improving my relationships and becoming the best partner I can be has been my life's work over the last decade. It's the most challenging thing I've ever done and the thing I'm most proud of myself for, given that every single area of my life is significantly better as a result.

It feels fitting that the week I wrote these words, my man got down on one knee in the bluebell-speckled woods surrounding his parents' home and asked me to be his wife. What a testament to the work I've done on myself that his proposal didn't trigger all my old fears around love and commitment, like it would have done once upon a time. It was the easiest 'yes' of my life.

So, this is my question to you, dear reader: is finding real love as important to you as it's always been to me? Because if so, you're in the right place. It's my promise to you that, should you be willing to open your heart and mind to the stories and insights that follow, your love life can't fail to improve. Dramatically. Truly, it can't. You're going to learn an approach to dating and relationships that goes against most of what this world has led you to believe is true about finding 'The One'. An approach that frees you from the tyranny of arbitrary romantic timelines that make you feel like you're a failure if you don't have a diamond on your ring finger by your thirtieth birthday. An approach that stirs such excitement, hope and faith in your innate ability to attract and sustain the healthy, soulful, lasting relationship you deserve, that you'll feel compelled to shout it out from the rooftop to passing strangers (or, at the very least, to all your friends still convinced that the only way to find real love nowadays is via technology).

Trust me when I say that there *is* another way, a far simpler way to find real love in a superficial world. Stay with me and I'll show you what it is.

PART ONE:

HEAL

> 'First things first.'
>
> C. S. LEWIS

The week before my twenty-ninth birthday, my mum took me to her soul home: India. Perhaps she could sense how much I was struggling with this being my first birthday without a boyfriend in years, and knew India would serve as a good distraction. Having been single for around ten months by this point, I'd grown used to minimal interaction and attention from men. But being single on my last birthday as a twenty-something was always going to be hard.

After a quick hop, skip and a jump through New Delhi, the worst of our jet lag had subsided by the time we reached our main destination, a retreat centre near Rishikesh, the yoga capital of the world.

I'd been to a similar retreat in this part of India several times before with my parents, so was clued-up on the experience that lay ahead. There'd be sunrise and evening yoga. Meditation, massages and treatments, as well as endless cups of jasmine tea to wash down the nutritious organic vegan cuisine that had all been grown locally.

A born overachiever, I viewed our week here as an opportunity to get me an imaginary A* in wellness, rather than as the well-deserved rest I needed after a hectic few months.

'You don't have to do everything on offer here, darling,' Mum said one morning, as I hastily knocked back a green juice between two different exercise classes. Oh, but I *did* have to do everything, otherwise I'd feel like a failure. For a perfectionist like me, that wasn't an option.

A couple of months prior to our trip, I'd asked Santa for an advanced yoga book containing pictures and instructions of how to perform all the main asanas, and then some. Most mornings, I'd try out a few of the more challenging poses from the book, adamant I'd have them nailed by the time summer rolled around.

While I've always felt more drawn to yoga than most other forms of exercise, having been practising on and off since my late teens when my parents first took me and my siblings to India, it hasn't always been for the most noble of reasons. Often, it's been as much about impressing people with my bendy moves as it has connecting to the divine oneness within. On this particular trip, though, yoga had the last laugh.

A few hours after breakfast on the second day of our stay, I turned up to my first one-to-one yoga session, advanced yoga book in hand. Having said our hellos, Sumit, my yoga teacher for the week, eyed the book suspiciously.

'I wanted to show you some of the yoga poses I'd like to work on with you,' I explained as I fumbled through its dog-eared pages.

There were three poses I was certain I could master by the time I returned to London: Bird of Paradise, Tortoise and Side Crane – poses that even the more advanced yogi might find challenging.

'OK, Miss Persa,' he said, 'show me Surya Namaskara A first, and then we see…'

SUN Salutations? I thought. *Piece of cake!*

I worked my way through a couple of rounds on each side, then looked back to my teacher to gracefully accept his praise. Instead, I was greeted with a look that can only be described as decidedly… unimpressed.

4

'Please, again Miss Persa,' he said, directly.

For the remaining ninety minutes of the class, Sumit broke down each of the twelve poses that make up one round of a Sun Salutation, and showed me how I was doing every single one of them wrong. He pressed, pulled and twisted my limbs into proper alignment as we worked through the simple sequence. The next day, I was in significantly more pain than I'd ever experienced after doing advanced yoga classes.

Despite the aches, I still held hope that in our second and third sessions, Sumit might indulge me with at least a few poses that were more visually remarkable than a basic Sun Salutation. But the most advanced pose he let me attempt throughout the entire four and a half hours we spent together was Trikonasana – boring old triangle pose.

As I was rolling up my mat at the end of our final session, Sumit called to me from over by the door.

'Miss Persa,' he said gently, as I placed the mat on the shelf bedside him, 'I really enjoy our classes and it's very nice to me you want to improve your yoga so much.'

I nodded politely.

'But, one thing – may I?' he continued. 'Most important of all in yoga is we get foundation right. No run before we walk. We can to do great, hard pose one day, yes, but must to have right foundation first – and earn our great, hard pose in right way. Otherwise we hurt ourselves and fall out of great, hard pose, because not ready for it. Understand?'

Often in life, we have to hear a particular lesson, in a particular way, from a particular person, at a particular time for it to really click into place for us. This was one of those instances, and the wisdom that Sumit shared has gone on to impact far more than just my yoga practice.

Today, I'm acutely aware of my natural impulse to leapfrog the fundamental basics of a thing in order to fast-track my way to the shinier, more exciting prize that lies beyond it. Nowhere has fixating on the future at the expense of enjoying where I am right now been more detrimental than in my love life. I'd picture myself walking down the aisle towards the man I was now sat facing in a bar (on a first date, might I add), before I even knew how he took his morning coffee. I obsessed over attracting the relationship of my dreams, without first having understood why the last relationship 'of my dreams' hadn't worked out. I spent what felt like a lifetime trying to run before I could even crawl (never mind walk) when it came to romance. But the faster I tried to get to a place I had no business being in just yet, the more rapidly the walls of my unresolved pain and trauma came tumbling down around me.

We are a strange species; investing so much time, money and energy into speeding up elements of our lives (broadband, productivity, orgasms), we rarely stop to consider whether getting to an imaginary finish line more quickly actually serves us. When it comes to dating, rather than waiting for someone we're actually compatible with, we settle for relationships that feel fun and pleasurable in the moment, but don't have the qualities required to be healthy and sustainable in the long run.

Having grown so accustomed to getting our desires and whims met in an instant (hello, junk food, online shopping and digital porn on command!), we've forgotten that in most cases, good things take time. And if you want to experience real love, there's no getting around the fact that it demands patience, commitment and the ability to be present in the moment with yourself and another person.

Given hindsight, I'm not sure if meeting my future husband,

making lots of money or having big career success in my early twenties would have done me any favours, even though I wanted all these things at the time. In fact, if I'd been given most of what I wanted when I wanted it, it would have been a disaster; I would have ended up sabotaging it all, for sure.

The truth is that we can never outrun grief, trauma or heartbreak. We must feel it to heal it, and heal it to be free of it. It took me four and a half years from the day I started working through my many relationship-based issues before I met the man I've now committed to spending the rest of my life with. That's how long it took me to learn the lessons I needed to learn, to heal the wounds I needed to heal, and to become the person I needed to become if I wanted to get (and to keep) the kind of relationship I'd always longed for, but didn't know how to be inside of.

Like yoga, romance is a journey – not towards getting all the moves right and gaining status amongst your peers, but towards unravelling the infinite potential of the human mind, heart and soul in collaboration with another sentient being. It is an ever-unfolding experience; there is no final destination to arrive at. There is, however, always a starting point: wherever you are right now. From this place, you must be willing to look at the beliefs, patterns and behaviours that have blocked you from receiving and expressing love in a way that actually feels *good* to you and the other person. You must be willing to release the pain, before you can let in the pleasure. You must be willing to heal your heartbreak, before you can attract your soulmate.

1. HOW TO FIX YOUR BROKEN HEART

SQUEEZE

'Do not squander the hour of your pain.'
MARIA RAINER RILKE

know you're hurting.

I know you can't sleep, eat or adult.

I know it feels as though a gigantic slab of lead is pressing down on your chest; that facing a whole day at work is inconceivable; that everything which exists outside of you and him is grey and irrelevant.

I know every song makes you think of him.

I know you've forgotten what it's like not to be consumed with thoughts of how to get him to contact you, get him to want you, get him *back*.

I know *you* know you can't burden your friends with this *again*.

I know you've fantasised about your own death; oblivion feels like paradise compared to this living hell. (Also, you wonder how much pain *he'd* be in at the funeral…)

I know you're less than an inch away from sliding back into all those self-defeating behaviours you've worked so hard to shake off:

- Hacking his social media.
- Calling him incessantly.
- Texting your ex.

What no one tells you about the road to transformation is just how tempted you'll be to jack in all your progress in exchange for the familiar shackles of your comfort zone. Because shit stinks, but it's warm.

Listen. You're in the depths of withdrawal. Like a shivering junkie locked in a dank and dusty basement, you're detoxing cold turkey. This was never going to be easy. So, when you're tempted to throw in the towel and pick up the crack pipe that is him, remember that the high is never as good (and the comedown infinitely worse) once you've started on this path to recovery.

The juice just ain't worth the squeeze anymore. Time to stop squeezing.

DESPERATE

'Nothing grieves more deeply or pathetically than
one half of a great love that isn't meant to be.'
GREGORY DAVID ROBERTS, *SHANTARAM*

When I was twenty-two, I lived in Moscow for the summer. As part of our Master's in European Classical Acting, my peers and I were required to train and perform at the prestigious Boris Shchukin Theatre Institute, an experience that turned out to be one of the most brilliant and bizarre of my life so far.

Upon our arrival at Moscow's Domodedovo airport, we were divided into groups of four or five and taken to various apartments in the city, none of which appeared to have seen a lick of paint since dead, pickled Lenin was plonked into a mausoleum in Red Square in 1924.

'By the way, there won't be any hot water for the first few weeks,' our translator told my British flatmates and me as we scrambled to bagsy the least sagging mattress for ourselves. 'Annual maintenance. Be prepared when you shower. The water will be very cold.'

Fantastic.

Our three-month stint here was to culminate in a performance of scenes from various Chekhov plays in front of a predominantly Russian audience. To prepare us for this final show, we took a series of Stanislavskian acting masterclasses with one of the most beloved professors of the school. This professor was affectionately referred to by the Russian students as 'Slohn' (meaning 'elephant') on account of his big flappy ears and nose, and his ability to remember vast amounts of Russian acting trivia. An elephant never forgets.

'Today, we explore the theme of unrequited love,' The Elephant told our group via the translator at the beginning of our first session.

He went on to explain how, when we fall in love, our energy is channelled into four separate 'circles of attention'. The first circle is established when we look at the object of our affection and acknowledge our own feelings of adoration towards them. The second emerges when we try to gauge whether or not this person feels the same way about *us*. If they don't, we move on to the third circle: deciphering who they *are* into, if not us. In the final circle, we seek to discover who else is after our beloved, besides us.

To experience this phenomenon for ourselves, The Elephant set us a practical group exercise. He directed us to walk around the room and mentally 'pick' one of the other members of our class, who we were to imagine ourselves being madly, deeply, obsessively in love with. We then had to try to work out if they 'loved' us back (circle two). If they *didn't*, we had to try to discover who they'd chosen to love (circle three), and who else had chosen to love them (circle four). And we were somehow to do all of this without giving ourselves away to the person we'd picked – or to anyone else in the room.

As we continued to move around the space, the atmosphere grew thick with suspicion and insecurity, with each of us trying to mask our desperation while simultaneously vying for the attention of our chosen person.

Well, this feels familiar, I thought.

It reminded me of an unrequited love dynamic from my teenage years. The wrenching, relentless ache for someone completely oblivious to the extent of my infatuation. That someone who had no clue that I knew precisely where he was in every single second in every single room we inhabited together. That someone who was the centre of my world, but to whom I mostly felt invisible.

We'd grown close while my dad was in rehab during my GCSEs. It's only looking back I can see the significance of this: I was trying to distract myself from reality by catapulting myself into a love story I knew had an expiry date (if it ever even got off the ground in the first place). Illusory romance is always the safest.

My love interest went to a school nearby, and every day we'd meet outside the train station at 4 pm with our respective gaggle of mates. Like Pavlov's dog, I'd come to associate the ringing of a (school) bell with the anticipation of seeing this boy, who probably hadn't thought about me once since we last spoke. I, on the other hand, could think of little else.

I made a fool of myself in front of him and our mutual friends time and time again. Mostly during ill-advised attempts to impress him when blind drunk. Still, I couldn't drop this fantastical love that refused to fit me, no matter how much I tried to squeeze and stretch it into my shape. Like an archaeologist, I'd sift and search for signs of his love in the most banal of circumstances. A lingering gaze. An irrefutable dig at whichever boy I was parading around in front of him. A message loaded with subtext, invisible to the untrained eye.

'He's just scared of the intensity of his feelings,' my friend Amber and I would kid ourselves during double chemistry, trying to minimise the intensity of my own.

So entrenched was my denial about this total non-starter

that I wrote this poor teenage boy letter after handwritten letter, each one heaving with not-so-cryptic clues as to how I felt. He either didn't respond, or worse, texted me a simple *'thanks Pers x'* (which I, of course, still found a way to read into).

Why did no one ever tell me that if it's true love, you shouldn't have to work so fucking hard for it?

But I did not love him truthfully. I loved him desperately. And desperate love is just about the furthest thing from true love there is.

Then, one day, he found the girl that did fit him. Or rather, *I* found the girl that fitted him (if I couldn't be chosen *by* him then at least I could choose *for* him). The problem was that in trying to win his favour like this, I'd foolishly cast myself as *Les Misérables'* Éponine to his Marius and her Cosette, forgetting that the only thing Éponine gains from the set-up is a bullet in the boob.

Years later, I stumbled across the Greek myth about the unrequited love affair between Narcissus and Echo in Ovid's *Metamorphoses*. Ovid describes how, after Narcissus rejects her advances, Echo's 'great love increases with neglect' – similar to Desdemona's words in Shakespeare's *Othello*, when she says that 'His unkindness may defeat my life, but never taint my love.'

What *is* it with humans? Why do we want the ones who treat us badly or don't want us, and reject the ones that do? I'll tell you why: because it's the template of love we grew up with.

If a child is brought up in a home in which love is either inconsistent or conditional (for example, if one or both of the parents struggles with addiction or mental health, or the couple are navigating a difficult divorce), the child may grow up feeling compelled to try to win the love, attention and affection of their parents. Or the child may have observed their parents in an unrequited love dynamic themselves, and gone on to mirror that in their own romantic life later on. Either way, they stay stuck in that old, familiar pattern of loving someone without being loved back.

I've been on both sides of this predicament myself, and would opt for being the rejecter over the rejected every time. While I was ghosted on numerous occasions throughout my early twenties, I've only been on the arse-end of unrequited love twice. And twice was quite enough torture for one lifetime.

Isn't that how unrequited love feels, though: *torturous*? Why, then, don't we just wake up out of this fresh hell of our own making and walk away? Because the only thing more frightening than love unrequited is love requited. Requited love means intimacy. Vulnerability. Commitment. All those things we're so certain we want – until we're given them. The moment that happens, those of us who grew up without witnessing intimate, vulnerable, committed love via our parents or main caregivers won't know what to do with it.

So we'll run. We'll run to food, to booze, to work, into the arms of another lover. We'll run towards the predictable refuge of self-sabotage, so that we continue to play out the same old story we're well aware doesn't serve us, but at least we know the ending. As kids, we liked best those stories we already knew, and it's no different as adults.

How do we take a risk on a new story, one that hasn't yet been written or experienced by us? How do we stop kidding ourselves that love predominantly infused with jealousy, disappointment and yearning is somehow going to magically transform itself into the opposite? It's simple: we take responsibility for the fact that it's not the unrequited lover that's rejecting us; it's *us* who's rejecting us. Because people who love, accept and respect themselves do not chase someone who cannot (or *will* not) meet them

14

halfway. People who love, accept and respect themselves know that what misses them was not meant for them, and what's meant for them will not miss them. And, most importantly, people who love, accept and respect themselves are willing, even though it may be terrifying, to walk into the void for a period of time, without having one iota of romantic validation or obsession over another to distract them from what they really came here to do: to learn to love without condition. Starting with themselves.

BACON SAVER

'When a train goes through a tunnel and it gets
dark, you don't throw away the ticket and jump
off. You sit still and trust the engineer.'

CORRIE TEN BOOM

The Serenity Prayer, which was originally written by Reinhold Niebuhr, is spoken out loud at the end of every Twelve Step meeting by the meeting's attendees. It has saved my bacon too many times to count over the last decade. Never more so than at the end of a romance that I wasn't ready to be over.

Say the extended version of it below out loud every time you need talking off the ledge. If you find the word 'God' triggering, substitute it with something else. 'Universe' works. So does 'Love'.

(God),
Grant me the serenity to accept the things I
cannot change,
The courage to change the things I can,
And the wisdom to know the difference.

Grant me patience with the changes that take time,
Appreciation for all that I have,
Tolerance of those with different struggles
And the strength to get up and try again,
One day at a time.

MONTH ONE

'The art of losing isn't hard to master;
so many things seem filled with the intent to
be lost that their loss is no disaster.'
ELIZABETH BISHOP

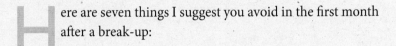

ere are seven things I suggest you avoid in the first month after a break-up:

1. Rebound sex with the back-up boy.

2. Any contact with your ex whatsoever, including: texting, calling, following/stalking him on social media, meet-ups, break-up bonks. Going 'no contact' will feel like you're coming off crack, the withdrawal will be that godawful. But it's the only way.

3. Nights out with your party friends. Don't even entertain this idea for the first month. You're too tender right now.

4. Looking at old photos, cards, letters, messages or gifts from him. Put these well out of sight and reach until you *know* looking at them won't trick you into thinking this break-up has been a terrible mistake and he must still love or want you back. Take him off the pedestal. Put yourself up there instead.

5. Online shopping. Dangerous.

6. Tormenting yourself with what you did wrong and scouring through your memory bank for signs that the relationship was doomed from the outset; then tormenting yourself *again* for having missed what must have seemed so obvious to everyone else. In time, you'll be ready to explore both of your parts in all of this. But today is not that day.

7. The hairdressers. *Very* dangerous.

LABYRINTH

'If you look the right way, you can see
that the whole world is a garden.'
FRANCES HODGSON BURNETT, *THE SECRET GARDEN*

A year into our relationship, Joe and I were leaving a restaurant near Embankment Station in London, when I caught sight of a man selling his handwritten poems by the side of the street.

On closer inspection, I realised that this was the same man that my ex-boyfriend, Tiger, had purchased a poem from the day we broke up in the summer of 2012. That poem, which Tiger had given to me when I left his East London warehouse for the final time, was called 'Farewell Blessing'. It had moved me so much that I'd included it in one of the chapters of *The Inner Fix*.

Since then, I'd always kept an eye out for this street poet whenever I passed through Embankment Station, but with no luck. He'd signed his name on the poem simply as 'Joseph M', so I couldn't even track him down on the internet (a rarity, nowadays).

Which is why spotting him with Joe four years on was such a welcome surprise. First, because it meant I could get his details to send him a copy of our published book with his poem inside. And, second, because it meant I could treat myself to a new creation of his that would hopefully be as poignant and relevant to me today as 'Farewell Blessing' had been back then.

His full name was Joseph Marinus. Just as I recalled from last time, he sat on a foldable garden chair beside a frayed blanket laden with brightly coloured envelopes. The colours of the envelopes, he told us, indicate the feeling of the poem inside: yellow for joy, pink for love, blue for peace.

Joseph was delighted to learn of his poem's inclusion in *The Inner Fix*, and equally delighted to supply me with a new one. Part of his genius seems to lie in selecting the most appropriate poem for its recipient. 'Farewell Blessing' had been spot-on for the ending of my and Tiger's relationship in 2012. This time, Joseph said he felt called to give me a blue envelope marked with the words 'Invitation to a Journey'.

The poem inside read:

> As you know I came
> By discontent to the wall.
> A door materialised
> And I went through it
> Into larger space
> Where led another door:
> So without intention
> I left my country
> And arrived elsewhere.
> In the human stumbling
> Who easily discerns
> Call of Providence?
> Yet exhilaration
> Of unimagined wings,
> Sense of youth recovered,
> Cannot entirely deceive.
> There is no movement of advance

without loss,
Wound of sacrifice,
The shed skin by the road
Precious with memory
Holds me anguishedly.
Laden with the ache
Of its abandonment
I turn, and hurry on
The road which is myself.

The poem summed up the journey I'd been on in love for the last four years. I had indeed come by discontent to a kind of wall: the brutal discontent of heartbreak, the wall otherwise known as 'rock bottom'.

A rock bottom is so-called because when you hit it, there's nothing left for you to lose. But having nothing left to lose is subjective, and looks different for each of us. For some, having nothing left to lose means just that: no money, no job, no family, nothing. One rung up from death – and that rung may well be a lifetime jail sentence.

Regardless of the circumstances, you know you've hit your own rock bottom when the pain of staying the same outweighs the inevitable pain involved in changing. Thankfully, a broken heart was all it took for me. (Actually, that's not entirely true. In the same week that I was dumped by Tiger, I lost my acting agent, as well as all my savings when the American visa company I'd hired to obtain a US work visa went bust, meaning I had to move back in with my parents for what I thought would be five months, but turned out to be five years. However, in comparison to the agony of my break-up, that all felt like a relative inconvenience.)

One of my favourite films growing up was Jim Henson's *Labyrinth*, which revolves around a teenage girl's quest to reach the centre of a huge and bonkers maze to rescue her baby brother from David Bowie's Goblin King.

When Sarah first enters the Labyrinth, the corridors of the maze seem to go on forever, and no matter how far or fast she runs, she never gets anywhere. Collapsing against one of the walls in exhaustion, she hears the voice of what turns out to be a little worm with a bright blue mohawk and a serious case of red eye. When she bemoans the lack of turns and openings in the maze, the worm tells her: 'You ain't looking right! It's full of openings, it's just you ain't seeing them… There's one just across there, it's right in front of you!' It continues: 'Things aren't always what they seem in this place, so you can't take anything for granted.'

With that, Sarah gets up and slowly walks towards the wall that the worm's referring to. When she reaches what first appeared to be one continuous mass of brick, she realises that the middle section of the wall extends further back than the side sections, meaning that she can walk straight through to a new corridor. A way through emerges out of what had only moments ago seemed like a dead end, because when her perspective shifted, so too did her reality.

When heartbreak first brought me to my own wall at age sixteen, I hadn't seen a way through, either. Instead, I spent ten futile years running up and down the wall, lamenting my lack of options, just like Sarah in the Labyrinth.

A decade later, another heartbreak brought me back to that same spot. This time, though, instead of trying to clutch on tightly to a way of doing things that clearly wasn't working, I sat down, I shut up, and I surrendered. Almost immediately, I was met with a surge of relief. Maybe I couldn't figure this out on my own, because I wasn't supposed to. In the stillness, my inner wise worm directed me to look at the wall in front of me from a different vantage point. In doing so, a door materialised where before there had been none. That door led to a new road, and four years later that new road led to me standing in the middle of a muddy field at one in the morning beside the man who was to guide me towards the next door along my journey.

If you're battling through heartbreak right now yourself, my advice to you is this: choose to see that wall you're banging your head against not as a dead end, but as a portal to something better. Because it is.

BUNNY BOILING

'I'm not gonna be ignored, Dan!'
ALEX, *FATAL ATTRACTION*

I hope you enjoy shagging your craggy-faced girlfriend. I wouldn't.'

… Is what my friend Belle texted her ex after learning he was in a new relationship just a few short weeks after dumping her. To be fair, it was a damn sight more sophisticated than when I was in a similar situation in my late teens, and found myself outside my ex's parents' house at three in the morning on my hands and knees, screaming bloody murder.

We've all been there: losing every last ounce of grace and dignity at the mere *thought* of our former (or even current) lover hooking up with someone else. So, when our worst fears inevitably become a reality, it's only natural that the pain it triggers causes us to act irrationally, inappropriately – and sometimes, even borderline insanely.

If you've seen the film *Fatal Attraction* starring Glenn Close and Michael Douglas, you'll be familiar with the term 'bunny boiler'. (If you haven't seen it, then consider it mandatory homework for this chapter.) According to the *Collins English Dictionary*, a bunny boiler is: 'A person, esp. a woman, who is considered to be emotionally unstable and likely to be dangerously vengeful.'

While I'd never encourage bunny boiling for obvious reasons, the reality is that we've all engaged in varying degrees of it at one time or another, and then felt mortified afterwards (or not, depending on the context) when we inevitably get branded the 'psycho ex-girlfriend'.

In my years working as a love coach, I've been privy to some extraordinary (and frankly hilarious) examples of bunny-boiling behaviour. Whatever your moral standpoint on it, this behaviour comes about because a wronged woman is in pain and desperate to be heard. So let's hear from some of them.

> My bunny-boiler moment was bagging up my now cheating ex-husband's things and dumping them outside his girlfriend's house. The bags split and all his stuff was in the road. I then calmly got in my car, turned it around and ran over all his things. My friends and family were mortified; I, however, regret nothing.

> A guy I had a fling with decided to get into a relationship with another girl. I was hung up on him so got my friend to prank call him, pretending he was from an STI clinic and telling him to send a stool sample in.

> Called up an ex's employer and informed them he was working under a fake name and underage. #zeroregrets

> Rang up and reported my ex's passport lost, knowing full well he had a work trip the next week. *Muhahhahahahaha* – who me?! No idea, darling.

> Started visiting an old cousin I hated because they

lived on the same street as someone I was dating; even started walking their cat – I fucking hate cats.

I found out my ex was cheating on me, I knew he was away for the weekend and I (luckily) still had a key to his flat. I brought some fresh salmon from the Tesco fish counter, asked the fishmonger to cut it up into small pieces. Taking the cut-up salmon bits away with me, I go to my ex's flat. I hide the salmon bits all over his flat, in his couch, under his mattress, under his rug, in cupboards – and I put the heating on to full. Now he was away for seventy-two hours with his heating on full! When he got back, he rang me and was so angry – but not with me, as he didn't know I had done it. He didn't even suspect it was me. He said the smell was horrendous and it was that bad he thought an animal had died. #sorrynotsorry

My recent ex… we were together three years before he told me, 'I'm never marrying your ass.' He never locks his back door – stole his Viagra for my new guy… didn't work for either of them.

NEW GIRL

'Nothing is so essential as dignity…Time will
reveal who has it and who has it not.'
ELIZABETH GILBERT, *THE SIGNATURE OF ALL THINGS*

et me share an alternative (slightly more graceful) approach to navigating your ex or current partner shacking up with a new girl prematurely. This is what I did in the summer of 2012, when I learned that my ex had moved the girl with whom he'd cheated on me into his East London warehouse – only two weeks after I'd moved out of it. It was the most painful break-up I'd ever had, but I was determined to come out the other side with my dignity still intact, regardless of how he was choosing to behave. Here's what worked for me:

1. DON'T CONTACT THE NEW GIRL

What do you actually hope to gain from speaking to the new girl? Unless they happen to be one of your best friends (in which case, ignore this point completely and release the kraken on the bitch), she really is none of your business, and contacting her will only leave you feeling worse. Your focus right now needs to be directed solely towards nurturing and healing yourself, not aggravating the wound.

2. DON'T USE IT AS AN EXCUSE TO
GET IN TOUCH WITH YOUR EX

'He just needs to know how hurt I am by this!' is what clients have told me after finding out their ex is with someone new.

Listen to me: *nothing you could ever hear from him or her will EVER make you feel any better.*

I know it's painful, but it's not your ex's job to soothe your pain anymore. The only person who needs to know how hurt you feel is YOU, because you're the only one who has the power to heal this pain.

Now, I absolutely *do* advocate expressing your feelings towards your ex in order to release them, but do it in an email or letter that you DO NOT SEND. Right now, your emotions and modes of expression are going to be much more extreme than usual. Tell yourself you can send it to your ex in a month's time. I can almost guarantee that by the time a month rolls around and you re-read your letter, you'll cringe and wince and be over the moon that you didn't send it.

3. DON'T STALK EITHER OF THEM

Social media has become the world's most socially accepted addiction these days, and as such can be seriously detrimental to our mental health. Never more so than when using it to digitally stalk an ex and his new girl. I think the reason we all fall into this trap is that it gives us a weird (and very short-lived) sense of power to know exactly who this new person is, and how we match up.

But this I know for sure: the less you know, the better. Remember: you are powerless over their relationship, so why keep beating yourself up by obsessing over what you can't change?

What's worked for me is simply to remove the temptation to stalk by blocking both of them as soon as possible. Who *cares* if they realise? This is about doing what's right for YOU, regardless of what they think about it.

4. DON'T GO ROOTING FOR INFO FROM YOUR MUTUAL FRIENDS

One of the hardest things about break-ups is how they can divide a friendship group. And I've certainly made the mistake of trying to get my and my ex's mutual friends to dish the dirt on his new relationship. (In fact, I even went so far as to go on *holiday* with them in order to do so.)

Again, knowing all the intimate details of their relationship is only going to delay your healing process. Plus, it's going to put your mutual friends in an awkward situation, and you really don't need any more difficult dynamics right now.

In the first three to six months after the break-up, I suggest giving yourself a bit of space from those mutual friends so that you can process all of this stuff without involving anyone too heavily linked to your ex. You can always reconnect with them when you're in a better place (or even a new relationship) further down the line.

5. DON'T CREATE A SCENE WHEN YOU BUMP INTO THE EX OR NEW GIRL

I've always been a bit of a drama queen, so bumping into an ex (with or without his new girlfriend) tended to end up with me crying in a corner all night, flirting with other boys right in front of them or making a dramatic exit. The sad reality is that when you behave like this, *you're* the one who ends up looking like the plonker; people always tend to remember the person who acts immaturely, not the reason for them doing so.

My advice? First, do all you can to avoid those places your ex and his new partner are likely to be – at least for a few months.

When you can't avoid them (at weddings, funerals, etc.), behave as maturely and gracefully as you possibly can. Ideally, meditate beforehand and visualise yourself seeing them together and being OK with it. If you can stomach it, I'd suggest briefly saying hello to them at the event, too, and then spending the rest of the time with your close friends trying to have a good time (but without getting too drunk or making a point of how *fine* you are).

Don't give your ex or the new girl *any* fuel to bitch about you. Go in there with your head held high. Be kind. Be gracious. Smile. Then get the hell out of there. Having something nice planned for afterwards always helps.

These five tips are goals to aim for, but let's be realistic – they are *bloody* difficult to stick to in the wake of a painful break-up. If you slip up, don't worry. Pick yourself up, dust yourself off, and start over.

One of the most helpful things I was told when I found out my ex had a new girl was that, however painful it was thinking about him falling in love with someone else, it didn't actually change my current reality. He was no longer in my life anyway, so what difference did it make whether he was single or not?

The only thing that matters now is that you devote all your time and energy into becoming the happiest, healthiest version of you, not into obsessing over your ex. And, soon enough, when you're ready, you'll meet someone to whom you'll be irreplaceable.

TULIP

'In a pandemic, self-isolation is called quarantine.
In Buddhism, it is called retreat.'

LAMA WILLA MILLER

8.30 pm, Monday, 23 March 2020.

The UK Prime Minister, Boris Johnson, has just announced a national lockdown in response to the coronavirus pandemic that's ripping through the planet like a tidal wave. The world as we know it is on hiatus, and it's forcing each of us to confront some uncomfortable home truths about who we are and how we've been living our lives, both individually and as a collective.

As scary and uncomfortable as all of this feels, we needed this wake-up call. Our earth has been crying out for change, and the time has finally come for us to face her music. And I believe we're ready to. As a species, we're being given another shot at treating this planet as though it were our home. Because it is. As individuals, we're being given another shot at treating ourselves and each other as though love were the only viable option for our survival. Because it is.

So, like the caterpillar who bids farewell to her current life so she can metamorphose into something better, we must cocoon. We must cocoon as individuals, and we must cocoon as a species. We have no other choice.

It strikes me how similar this experience feels to heartbreak. The shock of it. The loss of appetite. The bargaining. The crushing loneliness and burning rage. The anxiety. The frantic urge to climb out of your skin and numb out with anything and everything. The fatigue compounded by the insomnia. The piercing grief as withdrawal sets in. The baffling uncertainty, a wasteland without borders.

But we're built to survive hard times, we humans. Which is why I find myself navigating Armageddon 2020 the same way I steered my way through the worst heartbreak of my life. It helps, so I share my suggestions with a few of my clients who are struggling.

1. Stop fighting reality. Swim against the tide, and you'll go under. Surrender to it, and the current will carry you.

2. Avoid technology where you can. Submerge yourself in nature instead.

3. Take life one day at a time. If a whole day feels insurmountable, scale it back to an hour, a minute, a moment.

4. Don't rush to distract yourself from your fear and pain. You'll have to face it someday; may as well get it over with.

5. Surround yourself with the people who make you feel safe. Gently step back from those who don't.

6. Remember that life is no less uncertain now than it ever was, it's just that the illusion of control has been stripped away. Soon, you will normalise to this new way of being. Heartbreak is not permanent.

7. Do something nice for someone worse off than you.

8. Choose to believe that you will emerge from this like the tulip, the only flower that can be cut and continue to grow.

2. HOW NOT TO BE A HEARTBREAKER

THE BOYFRIEND-STEALERS

'Well, there were three of us in this marriage, so it was a bit crowded.'

DIANA, PRINCESS OF WALES

Matt was the first boyfriend I ever (knowingly) stole. When we met during my first year at Exeter University, I also had my own boyfriend back home in London. However, six months of long-distance love was starting to take its toll. My London boyfriend and I had already had a rough time of it as a couple after his dad passed away the previous summer, following a long and torturous battle with cancer. That's a lot of pressure for a teenage relationship. Too much, evidently.

Matt was three years into a relationship with a girl from his year when we started rehearsals for *Macbeth*: him, the title character; me, his opportunistic wife. As so often happens on sets and stages, life soon began imitating art, and before we knew it, the two of us were passionately kissing in the wings between scenes on opening night, while his girlfriend sat mere metres away in the second row of the auditorium.

Matt and I spent the rest of that summer meeting up for dangerous liaisons somewhere between his hometown of Oakham in the Midlands and mine of Kingston in the south-east. Each time, we would lie to our families about where we were going and who we were seeing.

On 7 July 2005, the web of deceit we'd been spinning eventually caught up with us. Deceptive webs have a habit of doing that.

We'd been enjoying one of our secret sojourns in a random village in the middle of the Cotswolds when we discovered – via the news that was on in the background of the rickety little pub we were in – that London had been hit by a series of terrorist attacks.

To cover my trollopy tracks, I'd told my parents that I was in London with friends that day. However, because all the phone lines were down, I wasn't able to let them know that I was well out of harm's way until much later that night.

Watching the shocking images on the news and not being able to contact my family to check they were safe, I'd felt a sharp sting of remorse as it dawned on me what needless worry my lies would have caused them all. Still, it wasn't enough to reform my behaviour; I still had another six years of recklessness ahead of me before I even *considered* taking responsibility for how I was treating myself and the people I claimed to love.

The next few years saw me cheat on Matt over and over again (if you want to see how a relationship will end, look at how it started). The beginning of the end for Matt and I was a mirror image of my previous relationship: I'd moved to Vancouver Island in Canada for my second year of university, meaning we were (very naively) trying to make long-distance work. *Again*. When it inevitably got too hard, one drunken night I hooked up with my best male friend there, which quickly morphed into yet another affair. Then, one morning, I got the news that Matt's father had died. From cancer. Just like my previous boyfriend's had.

If ever there was a perfect moment for redemption, that should have been it. However, although I had enough good sense to terminate the affair, cancel my plans to travel around Canada with my group of friends (including the one I'd been cheating with) and instead return home to my grief-stricken boyfriend, the damage had already been done. Over the following year, our relationship continued to disintegrate until there was nothing left to fight for.

A while later, this pattern was repeated when I hooked up with another guy I'd been at uni with in Canada. He'd been with his girlfriend (who I knew, albeit not well) for four years when I came on the scene. When she hacked his emails and discovered a ton of incriminating messages between us, she spent an entire day – very understandably – defacing my Facebook wall with words like 'whore', 'aids slut' and my personal favourite: 'slack-jawed swamp donkey'.

All addictive behaviour is progressive, and my love addiction (and the compulsive lying I relied on to try to hide it) was no different. Evidently, the cheating-on-my-boyfriend fix was no longer sufficient validation that I was attractive and desirable to the opposite sex; I now needed to actively *steal* other people's boyfriends to get the same hit. I'd tricked myself into believing that if these guys had picked me over their own girlfriend, then I must be worth something. That's how low an opinion of myself I had back then. As I'd done with Matt, whenever I'd start to feel any guilt, shame or remorse, I'd drown it out with the anaesthetisation of alcohol or drugs, and set about finding someone new to obsess over. I was completely addicted to the high I got from falling in love.

During those turbulent years, I accumulated a handful of girlfriends who shared the same tendency towards this vice. Like me, they craved romantic attention and validation so much that, if chatted up on a night out, they refrained from mentioning that they were already in a relationship, because they didn't want this new guy to try his luck with someone else. Also like me, when it came to cheating on their doting boyfriends (or nabbing someone else's), their conscience seemed to have gone AWOL.

We were often told by our morally superior friends that we were 'just like a bloke': seizing what and whomever we wanted the moment desire took a hold of us, without a care in the world for the consequences. Much of the time, we took this as a compliment.

'Why is it one rule for them and another for us?' we'd say, trying to justify our antics.

While we genuinely felt bad when an unfortunate girl got caught in the crossfire, we were mostly ambivalent towards causing men pain, our argument being that we were only treating them like they had been treating women since the dawn of time.

Of course, this warped morality was just a childish attempt at masquerading the truth: we were hurting badly, and men had become our drug of choice to temporarily numb the ache. Unfortunately for their girlfriends, if these guys happened to be in a relationship, the high was all the more intoxicating precisely *because* it was taboo. Also, it doesn't take a psychologist to deduce that, having all had particularly rocky childhoods, we were terrified of intimacy and commitment, and affairs offered us all the fun bits of romance with none of the dreariness.

The thing is, no one gets away scot-free when it comes to addictive and dysfunctional behaviour. No one. It doesn't matter if your obsession resides in Jack Daniels, online shopping or cream puffs, there will come a time when you won't be able to sweep the consequences under the carpet of self-delusion any longer.

And so it was that I and my merry crew of boyfriend-stealers were each brought to our knees by karma, eventually. Like dominoes, one by one we toppled into relationships with men who ended up doing the dirty on *us*. The sense of betrayal, coupled with the guilt of our own behaviour in past relationships, was so acute that this time we couldn't run away; it kept catching up and dragging us backwards until we had no choice but to grow up and face ourselves.

So, if you've ever wondered what became of the girl your high-school boyfriend cheated on you with, trust me when I say that she will have paid the price for her offence, at some point.

THE GENTLEMAN

'We must be willing to let go of the life we've planned,
so as to have the life that is waiting for us.'
JOSEPH CAMPBELL

I met The Gentleman over by the gin bar at my friend Fleur's
wedding, in the summer of 2014.

A very charming and very intelligent film producer, he asked
for my number after sharing a delightful smooch on the dance
floor. A couple of weeks later, we managed to sync our chock-
a-block diaries and met for a casual drink. I wouldn't say it was
fireworks exactly, but we definitely clicked. I liked him, and I was
looking forward to seeing him again. He seemed to mirror my
feelings, as he booked me in for a second date while we were still
on the first (always a good sign).

The second date was what did it for me. The ice had broken
by this point, and, after a couple of cocktails, The Gentleman
grabbed and kissed me as I was stepping away from the bar. We
barely came up for air the rest of the evening. It was one of those
rare, magical dates where you just couldn't imagine it having
gone any better than it did. Which is why I was so excited for
our third date. (He'd booked me in for that one while still on our
second, too.)

This is it, I told myself. *This. Is. IT.*

Bit hasty to make that call, I know, but I just *really* wanted it to be true. I was twenty-eight at the time, and the majority of my friends were already living with, engaged or married to their partners and I didn't want to be the only single one left.

A few days before The Gentleman and I were due to meet for our third date, I received the following message from him:

> Hey Persia,
>
> Hope life is good :)
>
> I thought I'd write you a message as I know we're planning on seeing each other in a few days.
>
> Someone who I had a story with earlier this year has unexpectedly come back into my life in the past couple of weeks, and things have moved quite quickly with her... As a result, I think it probably wouldn't be fair for me to then still see you tomorrow.
>
> I know that's a bit of a bummer, as we were having a really fun time, but I hope you understand. Not an easy situation and I want to be honest with you, given we got on so well, and also I guess before anyone gets hurt. I know etiquette might have dictated that telling you in person would be more the done thing, but thought better to let you know sooner rather than wait.
>
> Sorry for such a serious message! I hope we'll still see each other around, and would love to stay in touch. Hope all continues to go gloriously for you xx

Although part of me felt like I'd been sucker-punched (and it was obvious we weren't likely to 'stay in touch' while he was dating someone else), I was grateful for the way he'd handled the situation. He had definitely made the right call to text me before the date, as it would have been awkward as hell to have had this conversation in person, and then have to sit there twiddling our thumbs until we'd finished our drinks.

I was also grateful that The Gentleman didn't bullshit me with the 'I'm just so busy at work right now' diatribe (although I knew he actually was), or make up some other lame reason why we couldn't meet – and keep on doing the same thing until I eventually got the hint. He had owned, in a kind way, the one inconvenient truth that most of us are simply too terrified to admit to the person we are dating: *I've met someone else, and I like them better than you.*

I'd put money on this being one of the most common reasons as to why people *really* start ghosting or avoiding the person they've been seeing. It certainly was my main reason for doing so.

I have broken up with around fifteen people in my life. Most were casual, a few were serious relationships. I would back out of these dynamics in all manner of cowardly ways: cheating, sexting someone else, long-term affairs, bizarre lies, and straight-out vanishing into thin air. With each person, I failed to remember that this was a human being I was dealing with. An actual person with feelings and emotions, just like me. So, if I was willing to treat *them* this poorly, then I'd kind of lost my right to bitch and moan when Karma brought that same treatment back to me. (Which, as you know, she did.)

At the time of writing this (August 2020), divorce rates have skyrocketed across the globe, thanks to the national lockdowns initiated to help prevent the spread of the coronavirus. With nowhere to hide and limited ways to distract ourselves, existing animosity between couples has been amplified, and denial over the true state of our relationships is now virtually impossible. If it's bad and one or both partners are not willing to take drastic action to improve it, separation or divorce are going to be inevitable realities for many of us.

According to the *Financial Times*, more than a dozen cities in China have reported a surge in divorce filings since March of this year, when marriage registration agencies returned to work following the lunar New Year holiday. 'Covidivorces', they've been coined. For every divorce, there will likely be hundreds of non-marital break-ups, ranging from the termination of a casual fling, to the separation of couples who lived together throughout quarantine – only to discover they weren't all that compatible, after all.

In the bigger picture, I believe this is a good thing. As individuals and as a collective, we are staring mortality in the face and being reminded just how short life is; why on earth would we waste time in a relationship that simply doesn't work?

So if divorces and break-ups are an unavoidable part of the Great Awakening of 2020, it makes sense that we should take a leaf out of The Gentleman's book and just be honest and direct about our reasons for wanting to walk away from the dynamic; and that includes when there is someone else on the scene. The truth always comes out sooner or later anyway, and it's far less humiliating for the person being broken up with if they hear it from the horse's mouth, rather than seeing it via a Facebook status, or hearing it from a mutual friend at a party.

There is a silver lining in all of this, though. At the same time I went on those few dates with The Gentleman, Joe happened to be working as a runner on one of his films – which was exactly a year before Joe and I met.

If only I could've known when I was being dumped what I know now. If only any of us could.

3. HOW TO HEAL FROM BAD SEX

SAUSAGE

'Everything in the world is
about sex except sex. Sex is about power.'
OSCAR WILDE

When I was eleven, I was convinced I was destined for stardom. With a handful of TV and child modelling gigs under my very teeny belt, and having won a variety of lead parts and solos in my primary school's highly revered end-of-year productions, I felt ready for a role I could really sink my teeth into. I was sure my new secondary school would feel equally elated to have such a consummate young performer joining their ranks, too.

The First Year play that year was to be *The Grimms' Fairy Tales*. 'Hansel and Gretel' was the only tale I was familiar with, and I figured that either Gretel or the witch would be perfectly adequate parts for me to prove my talent and kick-start my glittering acting career at this school.

I turned up to the audition room early to show the director (aka my English teacher) that I was very professional and serious about my craft. She was busy writing names on scripts and didn't notice me, but I refused to let that knock my confidence; the audition itself would be my time to shine.

Soon, the room was swarming with nervous eleven-year-olds, several of whom looked like they were on the brink of throwing up.

Amateurs, I thought smugly.

One by one, we were called to the front and handed a script. Naturally, I was asked to read for the part of Gretel, and gave what I believed to be a dazzling performance, brimming with nuance and empathy.

Several days later, the much-anticipated cast list was pinned up outside the school hall for all to see. During break time, I casually made my way over to the list with my friend Sophie. Mentally preparing for my best 'oh-my-gosh-I-can't-believe-it-I-thought-I-was-*terrible*' face, I noticed some of the first years who were stood in front of the board start to smirk and snigger as we approached.

Poor Sophie, I thought. *I wonder what crappy part she's been lumped with.*

I looked at the sheet of paper. The names of eight different tales from the Grimms' collection were listed in alphabetical order, and beneath each title were the names of the characters and the students who were to play them. I didn't recognise any of the tales on the top page, so I scanned down the list for 'Hansel and Gretel'. I looked at the spot where my name should be, but there, it was not. Instead, next to Gretel was written 'Amber Lamari', an irritatingly pretty girl from 1L. Next to the witch it said: 'Rosy Latham'.

I've never even heard of HER, I seethed.

Now I was feeling panicked. I continued to scan down the

44

rest of the list, but I could not see my name for love nor money. Realising I must have somehow missed it, I started reading back through the list, this time from bottom to top.

It was then that I saw it, clear as the wart on the nose of the witch from 'Hansel and Gretel'. The second-to-last play on the sheet of paper was called 'The Mouse, the Bird and the Sausage'. Next to the character of the Sausage was written 'Persia – 1P'.

No.

There must've been some kind of mistake. I was a child *actor*, for God's sake, a professional – and they wanted me to play a SAUSAGE in a play that I was pretty sure had been conjured up by one of the teachers so that every kid who'd auditioned could have a part.

Two months, two thousand tears and tantrums later, it was opening night. At the ten-minute call, I dashed to the bathroom for one final costume check. As I went in, Amber Lamari came out. Dressed in a cute blue pinafore with her hair twisted into two pretty plaits, she looked like a toy doll. I turned towards the mirror and gave myself one last look-over. Dressed in a brown leotard, brown swimming cap and with my entire face smeared in brown face paint, I looked like a human shit.

The tales were being performed in the round. As I stood in one of the darkened corners, waiting for the tale before ours to finish, I noticed that all the cool boys from my class were sitting together on one of the front rows. If ever there was a moment I wanted the ground to open up and swallow me whole, this was it.

The lights went down, leaving a single spotlight on centre-stage. The narrator of our tale stepped into it.

'Once upon a time, there lived a mouse...'

The lights came up and the girl playing the mouse scurried onto the stage, nibbling a piece of cheese.

'A bird...'

The girl playing the bird glided in majestically from the corner opposite me, and took her position by the mouse.

'And a sausage.'

I flopped on to the stage and rolled my way between the two of them.

Howls of laughter erupted throughout the audience, but all I could hear were the cruel sniggers from the cool boys in my class.

As I lay there motionless, a stream of tears carved skin-coloured pathways down my poo-smeared face. I wanted to die, but the sausage had to stay alive for another fifteen minutes, when it was to be 'eaten' by a pre-pubescent boy dressed as a dog.

It was a moment that will remain permanently etched in my mind, mainly because the school decided to immortalise it in a large framed picture that I believe is still hanging outside the drama room to this day. Talk about childhood trauma.

When I think of that moment now, I can still recall in technicolour detail the searing stab of humiliation I'd felt lying there on that stage floor. It was like that nightmare where you find yourself naked in public, with nowhere to hide.

I've experienced this same sensation many times since, not from playing a sausage in a school play, but from being a young woman trapped in an inappropriate situation with an older man who's established himself as the hunter, and me as the prey.

One of the most memorable of these incidents happened at drama school when I was in my early twenties. I'd been selected to read Cleopatra's final monologue from Shakespeare's *Anthony and Cleopatra* in a special performance that was to be directed by a mature male student from the Directing BA as part of his coursework.

Something had felt off from the start. Perhaps it was because the director had picked me after watching me play a prostitute in another show, or perhaps it was because prior to our first rehearsal together he had emailed me the following:

> Please do not say a word or even try while we are experimenting. For the whole time. Use your other senses, all of them. Hearing, seeing, touching, taste...
>
> Bring in with you some clothes Cleopatra-You might like to wear. Come in with some food or fruits you might like to eat. Come in wearing Chanel No. 5...
>
> Queen, ruler, passion, impulse, vulnerability, sex. These are the words you used in your description and these are the words we will start to explore tomorrow. You have to come prepared for everything and ready to take in a lot. Not to fight any emotion or sensations which could come up from tomorrow.
>
> We shall try to find Cleopatra physically, we shall try to recreate her senses, her inner, Her–You. We shall begin finding how far are you willing to go...

While these words struck me as being quite suggestive, I didn't give it too much thought. That is, until the rehearsal itself.

I entered the candlelit space to find the director dressed in shorts and T-shirt, tying a piece of material around his head, Rambo-style. He explained that for the next few hours, we would be using music and movement to explore the physical and emotional dynamic between Anthony and Cleopatra, with him playing the role of Anthony. By the end of the rehearsal, he wanted me to have stripped out of my rehearsal clothes, put on the costume I'd be wearing for the performance in a few weeks, and taken my seat on Cleopatra's 'throne' – a wooden chair he had placed in the middle of the studio.

'Let's see how far you're willing to go,' he said again, echoing the closing words from his email the day before. Then he pressed play on the CD player, locked the studio door, and placed the key in the bottom of a zipped pocket in his bag.

For the next few hours, this stocky, hairy, six-foot-five man chased me around the space, brandishing his leather belt high in the air as a mark of his power. He cornered and pinned me up against a wall by my throat, ripped at my clothes and taunted me with insults – all the while calling me 'Cleopatra', as though to make his violent and at times sexually coercive behaviour seem justifiable... because *we were in character*.

Like a frenzied animal being baited by an iron-handed poacher, I tried my best to defend myself against his advances by any means necessary. At one point, having jumped onto a table (which promptly collapsed under my weight), I grabbed the belt out of his hand and thwacked at him repeatedly to try to get him to back away. But my retaliation just seemed to rev him up more.

I remember feeling afraid of him physically, but the shame and humiliation of being laughed at by him were worse. This was partly because I couldn't goad him back, having been recently diagnosed with nodules on my vocal chords and told by my doctor that if I wanted to perform in our class production at Shakespeare's Globe in a month's time, then it was crucial I upheld strict vocal rest for the next few weeks. Trying to stay silent while being pursued by an aggressive fully-grown man felt so counterintuitive that it was almost comical.

At some point in the chaos, I somehow remembered to change out of my rehearsal clothes and into my costume, which means I must have been running around that studio in my underwear for at least a few minutes. Maybe I blocked it out, I don't know. Either way, at the end of the two-hour stint I was sitting on the 'throne' dressed as Cleopatra, but looking like a poor man's Alabama from Quentin Tarantino's *True Romance* when Tony Soprano beats her to a pulp (before she stabs him in the foot with a bottle opener).

When I finally left the studio, two of my classmates were waiting to go into rehearse a duologue with this same director. I'll never forget the horrified look on their faces when they saw me. I ran to the toilet upstairs and immediately understood why: my hair was wild, my face caked in thick, black, streaky mascara, my eyes bloodshot and my bare arms covered in red marks that were rapidly turning into bruises from where he'd grabbed at me.

I later found out that the director had tried to use a similar rehearsal approach with my classmates, but they had shut him down within ten minutes and refused to carry on, reporting him to the head of our year.

It hadn't even occurred to me to stop the rehearsal. I thought that to be taken seriously as an actress, I had to be willing to go wherever the work took me, no matter what the cost to my mental, physical or emotional wellbeing. This is what I thought was meant by 'sacrificing for your art'.

The next day, I received the following email from the director:

Hi Persia...

You have had very eventful week, haven't you? Loss of voice which almost cancelled your rehearsal with me. Then the Tuesday, which went outstandingly well. It went so well, the **scratch** on my nose is still visible after you smashed it. The **bruise** on my back can still be felt after you hit it with a belt. It went so well, I still remember your eyes when you were **hidden** in the corner and cried. I also remember the **broken** expression of your face. I definitely remember the way you didn't care less after the table on which you stood **collapsed** and you were so close to causing yourself a serious injury. At that point one would think you would not want to carry on, that it was careless and dangerous. But it was not really you anymore. You were halfway through your **mesmerising** transformation, which was completed by your walk to the **throne**. It was someone else walking down that **path**. I am not a sentimental being and I don't care for pathos. But there right in front of me I saw a bit of **magic**. I was stunned by the quality and nature of your work. Later on in the week I saw you again. **You**, not Cleopatra. You were sitting with your phone glued to your ear and **crying** your heart out. Something beautiful but broken was going on, just like on Tuesday.

I am sure you understand the reason for this paragraph. Did we get it all?

M.

I was alarmed by the words he'd chosen to highlight in bold, yet I couldn't help feeling a tiny bit flattered by his praise of my work (although there was zero actual acting involved). Unsure if my concerns were legitimate, I showed his emails to my boyfriend and mum. Both were shocked and felt like he had been grooming me.

I sent the following message to my head of year:

> Simon,
>
> I've received this rather weird message from Manny and I showed it to my boyfriend, who suggested I forward it on to you, as we both think it is a little disturbing and I'm not sure how to respond to it. Please don't tell Manny I've forwarded the message. I just wanted to let you know before my next meeting with him.
>
> Our rehearsal on Tuesday was quite disturbing and I don't want to create any trouble, but there were several boundaries crossed that scared me a little and I'm not sure are acceptable between a director and actor. Because I did get quite a lot out of the rehearsal in terms of character, the more I've thought about it, the more I feel that I achieved certain results because I was provoked and, to be honest, a little terrified. I really do not want to stop doing this part as I've done so much work for it and it's a dream role. Am I overreacting?
>
> Regards,
>
> Persia

Reading my words back now, while I'm proud of myself for speaking up at all, I'm sad that despite being subjected to a major abuse of power by this director, I didn't want to 'create any trouble' that could sully my reputation or have a negative impact on my career.

While my head of year did acknowledge that the director's emails were 'way too weird' for his liking, nothing much else happened.

The next memory I have is of performing the monologue in front of the drama school and getting my boob out at the end of it, when the stage directions instruct Cleopatra to place a venomous snake on her breast. (Funny that the director should pick this speech for me to perform out of the entirety of Shakespeare's canon.)

What happened shortly after this incident makes me wonder if word had somehow gotten out about it and painted me as an easy target. Either way, I'd already gained a reputation for sleeping around at drama school by this point and unfortunately that came with its own consequences. It always does when you're a woman.

I lived alone in a sweet little one-bed loft flat a brisk three-minute walk from my drama school, which meant that my pad quickly became the go-to party hub. This made me feel popular and important. One Friday night, I had a group of students over from different years. Midway through the evening, one of the drama school's visiting acting coaches showed up with a couple of guys from the BA acting programme. I didn't know this man personally as he didn't teach my group, but I'd heard several rumours circulating about him hooking up with female students in the past.

At around midnight, I found myself sitting on my bed with this man, asking him questions about the acting methodology he taught. Initially, there had been a handful of others in the room with us too, but in my drunken haze I only noticed they had all left when this teacher lunged and kissed me.

I was so shocked that it took me a moment to register what was actually happening. As soon as I did, instead of asking him what the hell he was playing at, kissing a student, I got up and left the room without saying a word.

I have no recollection of what happened after that. The next memory I have still makes me shudder when I think about it.

It's morning time. The sun is streaming through the bedroom blinds, and my head is pounding. As I reach out to the bedside table for my phone, I realise someone is in the bed with me. They sigh and nestle in closer. I place my hands under the covers and realise I'm not wearing any underwear. I feel sick to my stomach as I think back to my last memory of the night before.

I'm now certain I know who is in the bed with me, but I'm too terrified to look. Looking would make it real. I slowly pull myself over the side of the bed, put on last night's skirt, which has been tossed on to my vanity dresser, and tiptoe out of the room like a cartoon villain. I don't look back to the bed once.

The flat is a mess, but that's the least of my worries. I peek into the kitchen and see my friend Clio lying face down on the floor, surrounded by empty crisp packets and cans of cider. My living-room rug has been pulled over her like a blanket. I creep over and shake her awake, grab a bottle of water from the shelf and drag her into the bathroom. Locking the door, I explain what I fear has happened and we try to fill in the gaps in both our memories of last night, but can't come up with anything conclusive that proves who is lying in my bed.

'Just poke your head around the door quickly!' Clio says.

'No way.' I shake my head. 'What if he's awake?'

I refuse to let either of us leave the bathroom until over an hour later, when we hear the door to my flat open and close, signalling that the coast is clear. I usher Clio out of the bathroom first to double-check we're definitely alone, before I feel safe enough to come out myself.

The following week at drama school, a rumour spreads that I slept with the acting coach at the weekend. Judgmental glares follow me down every hallway, but this is nothing I haven't dealt with before. I swallow down the shame and throw myself into my acting work and, soon enough, yet more boys' beds. It's like I'm trying to tape over a bad movie with a new recording, but the label on the video keeps reminding me of the story that came before: you can record over it, but you can never forget that it happened.

In both these instances, I was more afraid of my acting career being ruined than anything else. My life was a mess, and my career was the one glimmer of hope I had left that I could turn it all around and make something of myself.

There was also the painful reality that I probably wouldn't be believed or taken seriously, anyway. (You need only look to the Harvey Weinstein scandal to see how long it took for the many allegations against him to come to light.)

Laura Bates, who founded the movement Everyday Sexism, says that: 'When women do report sexual harassment, the outcomes are terrible. Over two-thirds of young women are experiencing sexual harassment in the workplace now, today. Eighty per cent of them felt unable to report it, but three-quarters of the ones who did said that nothing changed afterwards, and sixteen percent said that the situation got worse.'

When the odds are stacked *that* heavily against you, why bother speaking up at all? This is why I didn't take the Cleopatra incident any further. Neither did the teacher I shared it with, which was evidence enough for me that there would be little point in opening up about what happened with the acting coach at my party. It seemed far easier just to bury it and let it slowly eat away at my self-worth.

But what happens when you fail to speak up against any form of abuse is that it keeps on happening – not just because your silence enables the perpetrator to get away with it, but because you start to internalise the abuse. Worse still, you come to accept and expect it as part and parcel of being a woman.

I'd experienced sexual misconduct many times before in my life, particularly in my teenage years. When I was sixteen, a homeless man came and sat next to my group of friends and me in a Wetherspoon's pub in Wimbledon and proceeded to jack off while looking directly at us. That same year, while on holiday in Malta with my friend Salena, the two of us were followed home one night by a masturbating teenage boy who seemed to find our outrage hilarious. Not long after that, a middle-aged man sat opposite me on a train with his willy very casually hanging out the bottom of his shorts. (I have no idea whether or not he realised, but seeing as the train window beside us was wide open, you'd think he'd have felt the breeze on his nether regions, surely?)

In addition to these overtly lewd examples of sexual harassment, I encountered a different kind of violation that seemed as much about a display of power as it did the act of sexual gratification itself.

When I was in sixth form, I went to the Blue Bar in Knightsbridge's Berkeley Hotel with a male friend. While Mike was in the toilet, I was asked by a middle-aged American stockbroker to have sex with him in his chauffeur-driven car around the corner – for £1000. This proposition happened just after he had ordered my friend (whom he thought was my boyfriend) and me a round of very expensive cocktails, and precisely one minute after he had shown me pictures of him with his wife and kids. When I politely (!) declined his offer, his affable demeanour instantly melted into vitriol.

'Look around you,' he said bitingly, as he gestured towards a couple of glamorous women sat at the bar. 'Most of the women in here are turning tricks – what makes you so special.' It wasn't a question; it was a statement.

With that, he necked his Scotch, waved to the waiter to bring over his bill, signed it and left.

'What happened?' said Mike, when he returned from the toilet to find me swallowing down tears in between sips of my extortionate mojito.

'He thought you were my boyfriend and he wanted to pay me to have sex with him in his car anyway,' I replied.

That particular experience was the closest I'd had to the two at drama school six years later, because in all three instances the violation was instigated by older men who had more power in the situation than I did. One of these men was my director, one an acting coach at my school, and one a man my father's age, who had made a point of distinguishing himself as the richest, most important (certainly most obnoxious) person in the room.

This dynamic continued to show up throughout my early twenties. One time, the billionaire father of a fourteen-year-old girl I was tutoring sent me inappropriate text messages – while sat across the table from his daughter and me. Around that same period, my friends and I spent an entire evening batting off the salacious comments and wandering hands of some of the richest and most powerful men in the UK at a men-only charity event, where we were waitressing. (Interestingly, this event and charity got disbanded in 2018, after the *Financial Times* sent two female undercover reporters to work as hostesses at the dinner. The #MeToo movement was in full swing at this point following the

Weinstein scandal, and the Presidents Club annual dinner, which had been running for thirty-three years, was – quite rightly – next in the firing line.) Not forgetting all those nights I was repeatedly propositioned for sex by a rich Australian businessman who frequented a London strip club I was hostessing at. He would buy me expensive bottles of champagne (which I was supposed to tip down the bathroom sink on the sly, though I never did) and make me sing duets with him while we were stood over by the bar. Then, at around 11 pm, when he had gotten all the ladies in the club sufficiently hammered, he'd whisper into my ear, 'Tonight is our lucky night.' Each time I declined his offer to join him in his chauffeur-driven car (yup, another one), he would slink off out the club in a foul mood, only to repeat the whole charade move for move several days later, as if for the first time.

'The men who do this do it because they have the power and wealth to get away with it,' said writer, feminist and human rights activist Joan Smith in relation to the Weinstein scandal. 'They deliberately pick on women who are less powerful than themselves.'

When you are in the unfortunate position of being a target for one of these men (which I'll bet you have been at least once), the humiliation you feel in the moment is immense. Almost like being an eleven-year-old human sausage, flopping on to a stage at the feet of a gaggle of laughing schoolboys, wishing the ground would swallow you up.

BASIC INSTINCT

'We are healed of a suffering only by
experiencing it to the full.'

MARCEL PROUST

When I was in my late twenties, my friend Jess took me to see an energy healer. We were both recently single and working hard to heal our unhealthy patterns in relationships. While I had done a ton of therapy, Twelve Step work and coaching by this point, I hadn't done much body work before other than my regular yoga practice, and was keen to find out what all the fuss was about.

The therapy centre was situated in Covent Garden. It offered a broad range of treatments, ranging from acupuncture to clairvoyant readings to body stress release – and everything in between. After a few minutes waiting in a tiny foyer that smelt of patchouli, our practitioner, Bill, a kindly older gentleman who was the dad of one of Jess's friends, came out to greet us.

'You're welcome to stay in the room for one another's treatments, if you like?' he said warmly. Not normal practice for a therapy treatment, but given what happened over the next hour, I'm glad we accepted his offer.

Jess went first, while I sat in a chair adjacent to the bed to watch Bill work his magic. While she lay fully-clothed and flat on her back, Bill slowly and delicately pressed his hands on to different areas of her body. It looked a lot to me like a hands-on version of reiki, an ancient Japanese method of energy healing that my mum had trained in and performed on me several times, and that I learnt myself years later.

As Bill worked around her stomach area, Jess became quietly emotional and I could see tears cascading down the side of her left cheek. I assumed this meant she was releasing some trauma or pain from her past.

When her time was up, she calmly rose from the bed and switched places with me. I expected my experience to be similar to Jess's, especially as I didn't think I was particularly responsive to energy work. However, from the moment Bill's hands made contact with my solar plexus area, it began pulsating with what felt like an electrical charge so intense that I erupted into laughter, like a greyhound bursting out of its starting box at the beginning of a race. It started as a small tremor in the pit of my tummy, before reaching a sudden crescendo in an almighty cackle that was probably about as welcome to the people enjoying relaxing treatments in the rooms either side of ours as having death metal played as ambient background music.

I could sense Jess squirming in her seat, but I could not shut myself up. Then, without warning, my cackle morphed into the most harrowing howl of pain I had ever witnessed exit my body. Tears and snot gushed out of me, as my whole frame started to shudder involuntarily. Less than a minute later, and the howl had transformed back to the witch-like cackle.

It went on like that for the remainder of the treatment: *cackle, howl; cackle, howl.*

I wasn't in some kind of trance; I knew exactly what was going on. And my body wasn't reacting to sad or funny thoughts or memories. I can't recall thinking anything, other than how weird this all was. It felt as though my body needed to physically expel these emotions in the same way it needs to evacuate the bowels after a dodgy curry.

The last time I'd had such an intense physical reaction to body work was after a session with a chiropractor when I was fourteen. While I was watching TV at home a few hours after the treatment, I started coughing up mouthfuls of phlegm so thick it had formed into a kind of ropey cord that felt as though it was still attached to my lungs, meaning that when I tried to spit it out, I promptly started choking. It was terrifying, especially as I was alone in the house at the time. Thankfully, I somehow managed to dislodge the phlegm without bringing up a lung with it, but I've felt wary of chiropractors ever since.

It was only when my treatment with Bill had finished and Jess and I were on the bus back to her flat that I recalled phlegm-gate from more than a decade earlier and, significantly, what had happened a few weeks beforehand that I think may have triggered it.

In *The Inner Fix*, I described the time I ended up in hospital, having taking twenty-five caffeine pills at school in a bizarre quest to win back my ex-boyfriend after he'd found out I'd been cheating on him. The weekend before that, I and the guy I'd been cheating with had wound up in a drunken tryst that had culminated in me blacking out. When I came to, he was nowhere to be seen. Several hours later, I was nearly arrested for smashing up a house party with the boys from my year.

It was a turbulent time for me, mainly because my dad's alcoholism was at its peak, and I was projecting all that pain and anger towards the other men in my life. Sometimes it's easier to distract ourselves with self-created drama than it is to feel the grief of situations beyond our control.

As I shared my recollections of this period with Jess, I started to have visual flashbacks of what I think may have occurred during my blackout.

In the midst of a violent or sexually traumatic experience, the prefrontal cortex of the brain can become impaired (sometimes even shutting down) by a surge of stress chemicals. In some instances, it can feel near-impossible to make sense of what is happening to us, meaning that later on we are less able to recall the ordeal in a clear way.

In the 2018 trial between American psychology professor Dr Christine Blasey Ford and Supreme Court judge Brett Kavanaugh, whom Ford accused of sexually assaulting her back in the 1980s, her inconsistent memories of the incident resulted in her testimony being dismissed and Kavanaugh being appointed a lifetime seat on the Supreme Court – just a month after the trial. But when it comes to recalling something as traumatic as a sexual assault, of course you're not going to remember every single detail accurately (especially when it took place some thirty-six *years* ago). Shock may distort the truth, but this doesn't mean you're a liar.

Another thing that happens during a traumatic experience is that, because our bodies can't tell the difference between physical and emotional danger, they automatically go into 'fight or flight' mode. This causes symptoms such as sweaty palms, shortness of breath and a rapidly beating heart. So, no matter how much talking therapy we do, full healing can only be achieved when the body is brought into the process too, because that's where the pain and fear are stuck.

Before addressing the physical effects of these past traumatic events, I'd never fully understood why I could be having sex with my boyfriend quite happily one minute, and then all of a sudden feel my body tense up and go into total panic, which would cause me to scream at him to stop while beating his chest to try to push him off. When he'd ask what was wrong, I wouldn't really know what to say other than, 'I'm sorry, I got scared.'

I didn't talk about this pattern to anyone for years, but after the session with Bill, I started recalling other instances from my past where I had hazy memories of sexual encounters that hadn't felt entirely (sometimes barely) complicit. By this time, I was working in the wellness industry and had a great support structure around me, which gave me the confidence to open up about these memories to friends and colleagues.

The responses shocked me. Most of the women I spoke to had experienced something very similar. However, like me, they hadn't felt there was any point in telling anyone because they were drunk at the time, so couldn't remember all the details clearly. Except for this one crucial fact: they are absolutely certain they'd said 'no', or been asleep when it started, which is the same thing.

Since I began taking responsibility for my behaviour in my love and sex life (which includes not getting into such a messy state that I don't know what's going on), I haven't had any more of these ambiguous sexual encounters. Maybe it's because I'm no longer an easy target. Maybe it's because those sort of men aren't drawn to me anymore (or know I wouldn't keep my mouth shut this time around). Maybe I'm just lucky. Either way, while I do think it's crucial that both women and men take ownership of how we're showing up in the romantic and sexual arena (not least because it makes our lives a hundred times easier and more enjoyable), this is the bottom line:

If a woman wants to sass her way into a party in the shortest skirt she owns, proceeds to get blind drunk on shots of Patron and pass out atop the pile of coats on the bed in the spare room, the next morning – while she may want to question her reasons for getting so slammed – she should never, ever have to wonder whether or not something sexually sinister happened during her blackout.

Enough now.

4. HOW TO LET GO OF YOUR ROMANTIC BAGGAGE

RUBBLE

'A snake didn't mourn when it had to shed its skin.'
LEONARDO DONOFRIO, *OLD COUNTRY*

When the artist Michelangelo was asked by the pope how he created the statue of David, considered to be one of the greatest sculptural masterpieces of all time, Michelangelo responded: 'It's simple. I just removed everything that is not David.'

So it is when it comes to healing our blocks around love and relationships. Our work is not so much about adding more good stuff, but stripping away the unhelpful stuff that doesn't serve us.

It is about becoming who we already are underneath all the rubble.

RENT

'No other road, no other way, no day but today.'

JONATHAN LARSON, *RENT*

What I remember most about visiting my parents in rehab was the smell. I could recognise the scent of The Priory Clinic in south-west London from a mile away, it was that distinctive. Old carpets and musty books.

My mum was the first to go in. We would visit her once a fortnight, and with every first hug I'd notice how she'd shrunk a couple more inches. I guess that's inevitable when you're drying out alongside famous models and actresses in what's effectively a boarding school for unruly adults.

By the time Dad went in, I could recite the canteen menu like it was the two times table. As we'd turn left up the driveway – the white, Grade II listed building looming ahead of us like a dystopian Disneyland – I'd decide what to have for our bi-weekly family dinner. Small rituals like this gave me something to be sure of in a sea of uncertainty.

The soundtrack to this period of our family life was the nineties' hit musical, *Rent*, which had become a global hit during my parents' respective stints at The Priory. A classic tale of redemption, *Rent* was the life raft that helped us find beauty amidst the bleakness. It had the drugs, the drama and, most importantly, the promise of a happy ending (for the survivors, at least).

And my parents did survive. Not only did they survive their addiction, they went on to thrive because of it. They poured all the energy that it had once hijacked into rebuilding everything from the ground up. Mum trained as a massage therapist, Dad sold his London estate agency and became a successful property developer, and together they flipped houses to help fund their sober pilgrimages to south-east Asia, their soul home. They are my heroes.

If you're not familiar with love stories rooted in addiction, you should know that this is not a common one. Roughly 30 per cent of addicts who make it to rehab actually finish it. Between 40 to 60 per cent of those who finish will relapse within a year. Couple those unfavourable odds with the added challenge of trying to stay clean alongside a partner you once used with, and you'll get why my parents' love story soon replaced *Rent* as the ultimate tale of redemption for me.

It took nearly a decade to learn that the success of their love story was not enough to ensure the success of my own. I had assumed that because they had got their shit together, I'd been spared from having to sort through mine; as though their mutual recovery could somehow eclipse all the debris their co-addiction had left in its wake.

But no one gets away from the effects of addiction unscathed, least of all the family of the addicted. Dysfunction gets passed from generation to generation, until someone is brave enough to disrupt the pattern and take the road less travelled. My parents took that road and our family life became infinitely better as a result.

However, although their recovery had provided a new

reference point for me for what a healthy relationship could look and feel like, what it couldn't do was banish all the skeletons that were racking up in my own closet. Mum and Dad had given me a map to the solution, but it was up to me to put rubber to the road.

Redemption is a solo gig. A lonely one. From my experience of coaching hundreds of women, I can guarantee that the painstaking work of transforming an ineffective romantic blueprint will cost you tears. Plenty of them. No matter what support you are able to accrue along the way, no one else can cry those tears for you. They are the non-negotiable price of admission to the kind of love that will heal you, not steal from you.

JUNKIE

'The trouble is, humans do have a knack of choosing
precisely those things that are worst for them.'

J. K. ROWLING, *HARRY POTTER AND THE PHILOSOPHER'S STONE*

I n 2010, I spent many a night scouring London bars, looking
for a boyfriend like a junkie scoping out their next hit. I just
couldn't seem to drop the belief that acquiring a romantic
relationship would somehow fix my life. But there was an ever-
present uneasiness in the pit of my stomach that maybe it just
wasn't meant to happen for me.

In an attempt to stifle this thought, I became chief cheerleader
of my own ridiculous romantic escapades, all of which were
doomed to fail from the get-go. Humour and self-ridicule were
temporary tonics to distract me from my loneliness. And they
worked. For a while. But Loneliness doesn't tend to let you off
the hook that easily; she'll always claw her way back into your
consciousness eventually (usually around dawn, when the birds
start tweeting, the bin men start binning, the smug early morning
runners take to the streets, and there's no escaping the fact it's
time to call it a morning).

The main problem, as I saw it, was the type of guys I was
attracting – and attracted *to*. They were typically heavy substance
users, serial philanderers and almost always emotionally
unavailable. I hopped from destructive fling to destructive fling

with these kinds of men, frantically trying to find some kind of magical key in them that would unlock the door to a happy life, but always coming up short.

Inevitably, these relationships never worked out. Yet I often found myself stuck between a rock and a hard place, believing that I was destined only ever to fall for men who would eventually do the dirty on me; they were 'just my type'. As far as I was concerned, my love life was essentially out of my control, because I couldn't help who I fell for. (I'd tried dating nice guys, but they bored me; I always wound up treating them the same way the bad boys treated me.)

It never occurred to me that I was actively *choosing* to be attracted to these toxic relationships as a way of avoiding having to look at what was really going on inside of me underneath all the romantic drama. Because it *is* a choice, who we give our hearts to. Infatuation and obsession are decisions like any other, but we tend not to perceive them this way because we're regularly bombarded with the Hollywood-ised perception of true love as being all-consuming and full of obstacles, suffering and heartache.

However, there came a point, having experienced one crushing break-up too many, when I decided that this addictive form of love was just too painful and exhausting to fight for any longer. There had to be another way to navigate romantic relationships.

Turned out, there was. Many ways, in fact. But having had two parents go down the Twelve Step route of recovery to heal their own addictions, this felt like the most obvious place for me to start. Specifically, the two fellowships Al Anon (for families and friends of addicts and alcoholics) and SLAA (Sex and Love Addicts Anonymous).

Choosing to attend these meetings regularly back in 2011

was transformational for me. They helped me refocus all the energy I'd once used in obsessing over doomed romances into obsessively learning to love and respect myself instead. After all, I'd been more than willing to become addicted to my previous love interests, knowing full well it would only end in pain; so why not permit myself to become equally addicted to my own healing, safe in the knowledge that it could only benefit my life? Without that other person to fix on, something needed to fill the void; it may as well have been me.

As I made my way through the Twelve Steps in both programmes – which took a hell of a lot longer than I'd anticipated – how I related romantically to others slowly started to change. Whenever new love interests turned up on the scene (as they always tend to do when things are going well), I wasn't completely thrown off course by them, as I always had been before. My new-found self-worth was too precious a thing to discard for what I'd once naively considered *true love*.

Instead, I took my time, assessed whether these potential suitors would help or hinder my life, and made the decision to proceed only when I felt sure the man in front of me valued me as much as I now valued me.

In today's world, there seems to be even more stigma around sex and love addiction than there is around food, drugs or alcohol-related addictions – especially when the sex and/or love addict in question also happens to be a woman. Women aren't meant to struggle with this kind of thing. If they do, they certainly aren't meant to talk about it.

I have yet to see a person, man *or* woman, celebrate a sobriety milestone from sex and love addiction on social media. Not one. It's this stigma that makes it so hard to admit we have a problem in this area, let alone seek help with it. But, nothing can be changed until it's first acknowledged. The more open we are about taboo topics like sex and love addiction, the less power they have over us. (Just look at how much attitudes have changed around mental health in recent years.)

Being a love coach, I have people come to me with all sorts of struggles around their love lives, and while many of them wouldn't necessarily identify themselves as being a sex or love addict (again, mainly due to the stigma), most of them *do* relate to the characteristics associated with sex and love addiction.

Before I share these characteristics with you, it's worth mentioning that, unlike substance-related addictions, individual patterns of sex and love addiction tend to vary. I've never had an addiction to porn, for example; while another sex or love addict may not have the same predisposition to codependency in relationships that I do. So, as you read over the following list, just be aware of what resonates for you personally. Most importantly, don't panic or judge yourself; most of us will identify with at least a few of these characteristics. (I've related to every single one at some point.)

Also, as mentioned earlier, don't be off put when you see the word 'God'. Twelve Step fellowships often use this as a stand-in for the concept of a spiritual connection or 'Higher Power'.

THE CHARACTERISTICS OF SEX AND LOVE ADDICTION

(SOURCED FROM: HTTP://WWW.SLAAUK.ORG)

1. Having few healthy boundaries, we become sexually involved with and/or emotionally attached to people without knowing them.

2. Fearing abandonment and loneliness, we stay in and return to painful, destructive relationships, concealing our dependency needs from ourselves and others,

growing more isolated and alienated from friends and loved ones, ourselves and God.

3. Fearing emotional and/or sexual deprivation, we compulsively pursue and involve ourselves in one relationship after another, sometimes having more than one sexual or emotional liaison at a time.

4. We confuse love with neediness, physical and sexual attraction, pity and/or the need to rescue or be rescued.

5. We feel empty and incomplete when we are alone. Even though we fear intimacy and commitment, we continually search for relationships and sexual contacts.

6. We sexualise stress, guilt, loneliness, anger, shame, fear and envy. We use sex or emotional dependence as substitutes for nurturing, care and support.

7. We use sex and emotional involvement to manipulate and control others.

8. We become immobilised or seriously distracted by romantic or sexual obsessions or fantasies.

9. We avoid responsibility for ourselves by attaching ourselves to people who are emotionally unavailable.

10. We stay enslaved to emotional dependency, romantic intrigue or compulsive sexual activities.

11. To avoid feeling vulnerable, we may retreat from all intimate involvement, mistaking sexual and emotional anorexia for recovery.

12. We assign magical qualities to others. We idealise and pursue them, then blame them for not fulfilling our fantasies and expectations.

I know this list can be a daunting read. It certainly was for me when I first read it back in 2011. If, like me, it resonated so much that you just did a mini-sick in your mouth, know that I've been where you are and I promise there *is* a light at the end of the tunnel. If I'm now able to have a healthy, happy relationship, I genuinely believe anyone can – so long as they are willing to get the help and support they need.

Attending a Sex and Love Addicts Anonymous meeting (which you can do in person or online) might feel like the next right move for you. If so, you can find out more in the resources section at the back of this book. If that feels like too much of a leap, just continue reading these pages instead. I wrote them for the version of me that felt how you are feeling right now.

CAN YOU?

Can you trust you're meant to be here?
Can you trust this pain will pass?
Can you trust this pause is serving you?
Can you trust the grey won't last?

Can you trust it will get easier?
Can you trust you need to heal?
Can you trust this will feel worth it?
Can you trust real love is real?

Can you trust the best is coming?
Can you trust you're going to thrive?
Can you trust the stars are aligning?
Can you trust the timing of your life?

EXCLUDED

'People enjoy things more when they know a
lot of other people have been left out.'

R. BAKER

The experience of university was a mixed bag for me. Having been part of the 'cool' clique at school, when I first arrived at Exeter University I was dismayed to discover that the lion's share of social power and popularity belonged to the 'Rahs': those that had been to boarding school, lived in the home counties and had a penchant for pearls and pashminas. This was not me.

The Rahs' assumed superiority over the rest of us lowly commoners (or at least the superiority I projected on to them) infuriated me, never more so than when one of the rugby boys nicknamed me 'New Money' on account of my (admittedly) rather dramatic entrance to freshers' week. My dad had dropped me off at halls in a Range Rover with blacked-out windows and Bob Marley blaring out of the stereo at full volume. Amidst a sea of Hunter wellies, Ralph Lauren polo shirts with upturned collars and younger siblings with nicknames like Bumpy, Bitzy or Muffy, we stood out like a couple of sore thumbs. Still, the nickname was a bit harsh – and ironic, given that Dad lost most of that 'new money' a few years later in the Great Recession of 2008. First appearances rarely reveal the whole picture.

Considering that I hadn't gone to boarding school, had no intention of ever picking up a lacrosse stick and my family didn't own a stitch of tweed between us, I came out relatively low in the social ranking during that first term. It didn't feel good. Which is why by the end of my third year, I'd mastered the art of affecting my voice to sound posher than it actually was, and dulled down any part of me that didn't fit in with the Jack Wills-clad clichés that ruled the campus roost, including the fact that I was the daughter of two recovering drug addicts.

This feeling of being excluded reappeared while I was at drama school, too. First, during a foundation course in Musical Theatre at one of the world's best schools for MT. Second, during my Master's in Acting at the drama school in London. And third, while at the drama school in Moscow. In all three cases, the students on the Bachelor of Arts courses, which the schools were famed for, openly looked down on students from any of the other courses, assuming them to be less talented.

One time, a now-famous student even went so far as to hang an invitation to her annual Christmas party in the main corridor, on which was written the coda: NO MA STUDENTS ALLOWED. SORRY. Considering myself to be a good actor (never mind a fun friend!), being excluded for such a banal reason really got to me. I felt small and humiliated. Which is probably how a lot of the kids who were on the outskirts of my popular clique at school felt, too. Funny how we only tend to notice exclusion when it's us who are being excluded.

Instead of doing the adult thing and focusing my attention towards my work and those who actually *did* think I deserved to share the same air as them, I put 100 per cent of my energy into trying to impress the BA students into liking and/or fancying me. In the first term alone, I must have hooked up with a good handful of the third-year boys, who made no bones about being higher up the social chain. There is just something so gratifying in (temporarily) winning the attention and affection of someone who has up until now graced you with nothing but ambivalence, if not mild disdain.

This pattern of being drawn to those who oscillated between hot and cold with me (and shunning those who were consistent and loyal) had also played out in my romantic life before university and drama school, and it continued well after I'd graduated from both. Although it wreaked havoc on my self-worth, it was the only relational dynamic I knew.

By the time I started dating Joe in 2015, I was the healthiest and most emotionally stable I had ever been. This made it safe for me to explore where my hypervigilance towards feeling excluded had come from.

In a hypnotic regression session with a therapist, I recalled my first ever memory as a baby or young child, lying in my cot in the house where I grew up. I remembered the cotton sheets being covered with bobbles that itched my delicate skin, and I remembered screaming at the top of my lungs as I arched my head to see the hallway light on, and no one coming up the stairs to rescue me. That's where the memory stops. I have no idea exactly how old I was, but young enough to still be in a cot. I know now that my parents would have been struggling in their addiction at this time (but then again, leaving a child crying in bed is hardly something only addicts do – it's even recommended in many parenting books). Either way, in years to come there would be many instances when my parents seemed to be in a totally different place from my sister and me, even though we were all in the same room.

That feeling – of being with someone physically and yet in two different worlds – that is what I hated the most. It felt dark and unsafe. That's why I checked out of relationships via cheating before the other person had a chance to: I self-excluded so as not to feel forced into exclusion by them. It's also why passive-aggressive behaviours and other people's mood swings have always affected me so much, and why I've repeatedly called on both as a tactic to win the power back in a relationship when I feel it's being taken away from me.

Today, I can still feel pulled towards those who have little to no interest in me, and am sometimes tempted to withdraw from those who give me their undivided attention, love and respect. It's one of the main reasons I resisted committing to Joe in the first few months of dating. The difference now is that I am no longer willing to abandon myself in order to avoid being excluded by someone else. Because when you are committed to showing up for yourself, being excluded by others no longer feels like a death sentence. It's just a sign that these are not your people.

5. HOW TO STOP PANICKING YOU'LL BE SINGLE FOREVER

CHECKMATE

'The thing that looks most ordinary might be
the thing that leads you to victory.'

MATT HAIG, *THE MIDNIGHT LIBRARY*

For as long as I can remember, I've felt the need to be seen as special. Different. The *Best*.

Although this has given me motivation and drive (and helped me accomplish many things), it's not something I'm proud of. Because it's a bottomless pit, this quest to be the top of all leader boards. There's never enough likes, followers, attention, money or love to make you feel like you're winning.

In my twenties, this need to be The Best looked like always having to have some guy chasing me to feel like I was ahead of the game. I wish I'd realised then how much time and energy I was wasting trying to win at something I was in no way ready for. I wish I could have valued the space and solitude I'd been gifted with, rather than frittering away every spare moment trying to close the gap between where I stood and my next relationship so that I wouldn't feel like a failure. I wish I'd known just how good I had it.

Yes, I was single. But I was also healthy, solvent and loved. That's more than can be said for the majority of the world's population.

The hardest thing about not having a partner (especially if you're a woman around the age of thirty) is the feeling that without a plus one and two names on the tenancy instead of just ours, we're somehow being left behind by the tribe. But left behind from what, exactly? Where is everyone else going?

Love is not a race. There is no finish line, except for the imaginary ones we conjure up in our mind:

- *Relationship?* Check.
- *Engaged?* Check.
- *Married?* Check.
- *Mortgage together?* Check.
- *Dog, baby, second baby, breakdown?* Check, check, check… CheckMATE.

No matter what you successfully manage to tick off the arbitrary timeline associated with romantic relationships, you never feel like you've 'arrived' when it comes to love. There's always the illusion that another baby, house renovation, a new car, holiday, a better therapist will be the secret key that unlocks the door to lasting romantic bliss. But they never do. Not for more than a hot minute, anyway.

Whether it's nature or nurture that drives this compulsion of mine to be The Best, I'm tired of it, and I'm ready to let it go. Because the happiest people I've ever met don't need to win at love – or anything else. They don't need to beat their friends to the altar. They don't need constant attention, or to be seen as special. They don't need to be The Best. And they are free.

COVET

For every woman you covet for her happily-
ever-after,
There's five who'd (nearly) kill for your latest career
achievement.

For every time you bemoan your lack of a plus one,
There are many more moments when your solitude
is your most treasured luxury.

For every stomach-churningly hideous first date,
There's a third so electric your married friend
would sell her firstborn
To switch places for the night.

For every Christmas without that extra gift,
There's a birthday that's not your job to stress about.

For all those nights you panic you're being left
behind in love,
There are dozens of days when you lap your peers
in productivity and purpose.

For every man you wish was yours,
There's another woman who wishes he wasn't hers.

For every romantic city break you long to book,
There's an annual girls' trip you'd miss over your
dead body.

For all the love you're currently not making,
There's a pocket rocket that never fails to satisfy.

For all the times you'd give anything to be married,
There's another woman who'd give anything not to be.

For all the dinners, flowers, candles he isn't treating you to,
There's a soul sister who surprises you with VIP tickets to the Spice Girls.

For every lonely evening without a Netflix and Chill bedmate,
There's a magic morning where starfishing, farting and morning breath go unjudged.

For all the times you dream of being held by your soulmate,
There's the possibility they could walk into your reality that very same day.

So stop convincing yourself there's something missing from your life.
Stop assuming all your coupled-up friends have it so much better than you do.
And stop overlooking the magnitude of love that's already present.
Millions would give everything to be in your shoes.

THUNDER-STEALER

'Look, I am so... so happy for you guys, but
you getting married just reminds me of the
fact that I'm not. I'm not even close.'

RACHEL GREEN, *FRIENDS*

Several years ago, a close friend of mine got engaged two weeks after I got dumped. While I was happy that she had found someone to share the rest of her life with, the year between their engagement and wedding was a massive rollercoaster of emotions for me. Try as I might, I just couldn't seem to shake the contrast between where she was in her love life, and where I *wasn't* in mine.

It had amplified a contradiction I'd felt trapped by for a while now, along with many of the other single women I knew: on the one hand, we resented our culture's obsession with labels and relationship statuses as the predominant measure of a woman's worth. On the other, we had a deep longing for a great relationship with someone we could envision sharing the rest of our lives with.

As the inevitable barrage of hen-party WhatsApp messages began rolling in, I found myself obsessing over the dreaded seating plan at the wedding reception. Was I going to be plonked next to some random cousin no one had seen in two decades, just because, without a plus one, there was nowhere else to put me?

On the morning of the wedding, when my stunning friend stepped out in her dress for the first time, her hair and make-up impeccable, I felt a sudden stab in my chest that I may never get to experience that iconic look of adoration from the women closest to me.

During the groom's speech, my mind started conjuring up images of my most recent ex. *Should we have tried harder to make it work? Would he have said such lovely things about me in a speech? Would anyone... ever?*

I hated that I felt this conflicted, and I tried to mask it as best as I could (because, you know, THE DAY WASN'T ABOUT ME). But I wasn't the first woman to feel envious of a close friend's happily ever after, and I certainly wouldn't be the last.

Today, having been a bridesmaid several times while single or heartbroken, and having gotten engaged on the same weekend that one of my best friends got dumped, I know all too well how triggering engagements and weddings can be. I also know how much pressure we women put on ourselves to try to hide the fact we're feeling triggered, for fear of being deemed a *bad friend* to the bride-to-be. It doesn't even occur to us that we might extend the same compassion towards ourselves in this situation as we would if we were attending the wedding of one of our exes. Because in a way, we kind of are – especially if we grew up with the bride-to-be through our childhood, teenage years and/or twenties. As so potently (and hilariously) portrayed in the rom-com *Bridesmaids*, female friendships that have a long and complex history can often be as intimate – certainly as enmeshed – as our most significant romantic relationships. All that's missing is the sex. Most of the time.

Even when we are genuinely happy being single, all the drama that surrounds engagements and weddings can make it virtually impossible *not* to reflect on our own relationship status, especially when it feels like it's happening for everyone in our peer group except us; we're not even close.

Marianne Williamson once wrote that 'love brings up everything unlike itself'. In my humble opinion, so too do weddings. Yes, we know it's meant to be all about the happy couple. But, believe it or not, it *is* possible to feel two emotions at the same time: joy for the bride and groom's happiness (and the hope their union inspires within us). And sadness that we don't have what they have. Yet.

If you're struggling through this internal conflict yourself right now over a friend's impending nuptials, I implore you not to beat yourself up over it. It doesn't make you a bad friend, it makes you a very human human. And, from one very human human to another, I invite you to do what I did and choose to see this situation as an opportunity: an opportunity to heal and release any old limiting beliefs about what is possible for you in romance. An opportunity to fall in love with yourself and your life so deeply that you won't even care about your position in the table plan (because either way, you'll still get to sit with YOU). And an opportunity to get clear about what type of partner *you* would want to see waiting for you at the other end of the aisle one day.

PERSPECTIVE

> 'As far back as slavery, white people established a social hierarchy based on race and sex that ranked white men first, white women second, though sometimes equal to black men, who are ranked third, and black women last.'
> BELL HOOKS, *AIN'T I A WOMAN: BLACK WOMEN AND FEMINISM*

While I've experienced a fair amount of misogyny from men over the years, I've never had to deal with the bitter sting of racism on top of that.

Never had to try my luck at online dating, knowing that as a black woman I'm statistically less likely to receive matches and responses than any other ethnic group.

Never had to wonder if my white boyfriend's family will reject me for having a different skin colour to their son. It's important I remember this every time I complain about how hard and unfair the modern dating world is. I have it easy.

As a white woman, it is only until embarrassingly recently that I have acknowledged my place of privilege in the dating arena and how this might have subconsciously impacted my choices in the past. Of course, I have had my fair share of escapades with black and brown men, but did I ever consider myself with a life partner who was anything other than white? Did I ever consider that, short of being up against Naomi Campbell, I would always be considered the prize by a system that puts white and blonde at the top of the pile, no matter what, and how this is just not right?

This is not about wallowing in guilt or shame. However, if we are doing the work and showing up for our love lives, everything should be up for examination, including our internalised prejudices.

I challenge you, whatever your colour, to consider the attitudes you grew up around and how they might be influencing and limiting your choices on the apps. Do you filter colour consciously, for example? And if so, why – or why not? Because love is love, regardless of age, race or gender. And we all deserve it in our lives.

CHÂTEAUNEUF-DU-PAPE

'The beauty of a woman with passing years only grows.'
AUDREY HEPBURN

I used to think that because I was about to turn thirty and didn't have a partner to bring to weddings and family events, I was failing at life.

Today, I know this is absolute hogwash, but it's understandable why so many of us women feel this way, given that society promotes the belief that after the age of thirty a woman's value goes down, whereas a man's goes up. With insipid subliminal messages like this being thrust at us 24/7, no wonder we feel pressured to hunt down a husband.

But there comes a point when you just cannot accept this sort of crap a moment longer. Not if you want to stay sane.

When I hit thirty, I came to the conclusion that, actually, I just get better with age. (Trust me, you'd rather be dating thirty-four-year-old Persia than twenty-four-year-old Persia.)

So, if I'm getting better with every year that passes, then so are you. Because we are fine wines, baby. We are Châteauneuf-du-Pape.

FUCK THE TIMELINE

Fuck the timeline, you gorgeous thing –
You're far too prodigious to be defined by a ring.
Who cares if you're married by your thirtieth birthday?
I'll tell you: just dull people with nothing to say.

Fuck the timeline, my sweet honey pie,
This pressure you're feeling is all just a lie.
Men are called 'bachelor' while we're rendered 'spinster' –
It's this kind of bullshit that drives one to Tinder.

Fuck the timeline, you absolute babe,
Your identity's solid, it doesn't need to be changed
By titles or surnames or anything else;
You're winning at life if you've still got your health.

Fuck the timeline, my baby doll
And fuck ticking boxes over growing your soul.
A woman who's older is like a fine wine –
Full bodied, exquisite, delicious, divine.

Fuck the timeline, you angel face,
This time on your own really isn't a waste.
You're learning, evolving, becoming anew
So that one day your soul's mate will recognise you.

Fuck the timeline, my beautiful friend,
Love isn't a race but a dance in the end.
Go travelling, adventure to far distant lands
And trust that you're right where you're meant to be now.

FLEUR AND WILL

'If we could untangle the mysteries of life and unravel the energies which run through the world; if we could evaluate correctly the significance of passing events; if we could measure the struggles, dilemmas, and aspirations of mankind, we could find that nothing is born out of time. Everything comes at its appointed moment.'

JOSEPH R. SIZOO

The first time I went to my friend Fleur's family home in Devon was in the spring of 2013, straight after a holiday in Beirut where my then-boyfriend Sam had spontaneously decided to get a nose job which, unfortunately, marked the beginning of the end for us. I hear nose jobs sometimes do that.

Devon that year was equal parts wonderful and depressing. Wonderful because this house, nestled in a secluded valley overlooking an estuary, was the perfect setting for Fleur's loved ones to celebrate her thirty-first birthday in style. The group included Will, her charming and besotted boyfriend of only a few weeks. Depressing, because I could see the way Will looked at Fleur and Fleur looked at Will, and I knew without a shadow of a doubt that Sam and I had never and *would* never look at each other in that way. It was a most unwelcome realisation, and not one I was ready to act upon just yet. In fact, it was nearly a year before either of us was willing to confront this inconvenient truth, a year of trying my hardest to revive a relationship I had once been so convinced was 'it'. But you can only kid yourself for so long.

Two weeks after Sam and I eventually called time on our love story in April 2014, I wound up back at the Devon house, this time for Fleur's hen party. Her and Will had gotten engaged six months after our last trip here. Mercifully, there were only five of us attending the hen do. Even more mercifully, there was to be zero organised fun: no annoying creative workshops, no cringeworthy stripper, and no naff nightclubs. That wasn't Fleur's style. Instead, we would simply be enjoying one another's company while indulging in lots of great food, wine, and countryside air. So, although a hen weekend wasn't at the top of my list of desirable activities so soon after a break-up, what the universe had actually lined up for me was a rural mini-retreat (minus the curfew and smoking ban). It was exactly what my sore heart needed.

In the days between the break-up and departing for the hen do, a book had serendipitously landed in my lap, the way self-help books tend to when you are on the precipice of a major life-change. The book was *Conversations with God* by Neale Donald Walsch.

This book had come about during a low period in Walsch's life, which found him writing an angry letter to God, asking questions about why his life wasn't working. After writing down all of his questions, he heard a voice over his right shoulder say: 'Do you really want an answer to all these questions, or are you just venting?' When he turned around there was no one there, but Walsch received inner answers to his questions and decided to write them down. The resulting content was so powerful that it eventually became published into one of the bestselling self-help books of all time.

Having seen me flicking through the pages of the book in the car en route to Devon, Fleur assured me its arrival in my life was right on cue.

'Game-changer,' she'd whispered with a wink.

Between long, invigorating walks, delightful dinners and *Sex and The City* binges with the girls, I spent much of the weekend snuggled under my duvet gobbling up the book's profound insights and teachings. Inevitably, I was most drawn to what the book had to say about romantic relationships, in particular, this:

> Most people enter into relationships with an eye toward what they can get out of them, rather than what they can put into them. The purpose of a relationship is to decide what part of yourself you'd like to see 'show up,' not what part of another you can capture and hold.

Reading these words, it occurred to me that I had entered into all of my previous relationships for one of two reasons: I was either looking to fix the other person, or looking for the other person to fix me. Both reasons were effective distractions from fixing myself and taking responsibility for the results I was getting (or not getting) in my love life.

After this revelation, on the second evening of the hen, something bizarre happened. Inspired by Neale Donald Walsch's communion with 'God', I was lying in bed meditating, when I started to connect with an energy that I could identify with absolute certainty as being the man I would one day marry. I know it sounds bonkers (and it was), but I could genuinely hear and feel this person as though they were in the same room. The reason I trusted this connection as being more than just wishful thinking is that during our exchange, this person told me that I wasn't yet ready for them to enter my reality, and neither were they. We both needed to spend a period of time falling in love with ourselves and our lives first. This was required preparation for the kind of relationship I had watched blossom between Fleur and Will.

Impulsive as I am, these are not words I would have ordinarily wanted to hear. But I knew they were words I needed to hear. As such, instead of feeling panicked at the prospect of having to spend an unspecified amount of time on my own, I felt excited. I finally understood that being alone wasn't a punishment, but an opportunity. And I was ready to make the most of it.

When I shared all of this with Fleur on the last night of the hen she smiled and said: 'I wouldn't have been ready for Will to show up in my life one second before he did.'

A year and a half later, when I met Joe, the physical manifestation of the energy I'd been conversing with during Fleur's hen, I understood what she'd meant.

CELEBRATE

'Sooner or later we all discover that the important
moments in life are not the advertised ones.'

SUSAN B. ANTHONY

My biggest achievement was not meeting the love of my life. It wasn't travelling the world with this man. It wasn't getting engaged to him, nor planning our dream wedding.

The biggest achievement of my life was pulling myself out of rock bottom and into recovery. This is how I ended up being in the right head and heart space to meet him in the first place. This is how I've managed to keep my side of the street (reasonably) clean for the last five years and not sabotage our relationship, like I did all the ones before it. And this is how I can genuinely say that, today, I live a life beyond my wildest dreams.

But no one threw me a party for this transformation. There were no balloons, no cake, no champagne (although there *was* a shit ton of tea and biscuits).

So I made a promise to myself that I would celebrate this transformation every single day with me, myself and I. And I made a promise to the world that I would celebrate all girls when they accomplish other things besides those that involve weddings, babies and diamond rings.

I hope you do the same.

PART TWO:

ATTRACT

'The secret is not to run after butterflies, but to take care of the garden so they come to you.'

MARIO QUINTANA

Jumping out of a plane was only ever pencilled in lightly on my bucket list. While I would occasionally ruminate about how euphoric and liberating it must feel to glide above the earth like a bird on wing, my fear of falling was always that little bit more potent than my curiosity.

In order to experience something new in life, you first have to be willing to shed your identification with where you are standing right now. But when it came to overcoming one of my most primal phobias, falling, I was reluctant to take even the first step. It was just too damn scary.

Yet in January 2019, I found myself strapped to a handsome twenty-something Argentinian skydiving instructor called Keko, peering out of an open plane door at the 15,000 feet between the two of us and the western coastline of Costa Rica.

I hadn't chosen to jump out of a plane so much as I'd been plopped into circumstances that had made it nearly impossible for me *not* to jump. That, I discovered, is the most effective way to transcend those fears and limiting beliefs that block us from achieving something our soul longs to experience, but our mind and our body absolutely do *not*.

Joe, my partner of three and a half years at this point, has always been an adrenalin junkie of epic proportions, just like my dear old dad. There were few extreme sports Joe hadn't (or at least wouldn't) try. So when we were invited to travel around Costa Rica with his Costa Rican work colleague, Camille, her husband, Dan, and a few of their mutual friends who were equally dare-devilish, I knew I was going to be challenged. They were all just so very *brave*, you see. Nothing seemed to phase them. For this crew, jumping out of a plane was akin to riding a rollercoaster: thrilling, but no big deal. To say I was intimidated by the monumental gap between my psyche and theirs would be the understatement of the century.

The resistance I felt in the days leading up to the jump was debilitating. So bad, that the day before it I contracted a beastly bout of cystitis, no doubt a psychosomatic response to my anxiety, one I secretly hoped would get me out of jumping. But the group were having none of it. Camille whisked me off to the nearest doctors, warbled off some Spanish punctuated with a lot of Penélope Cruz-esque hand gestures, and got the meds I needed down my gullet before I could think up any more excuses. As the symptoms began to dissipate, it became clear that come hell or high water, I was going to be jumping out of a plane within a matter of hours.

The ascent, in the teeniest plane I have ever seen, was surprisingly tranquil. Costa Rica is stunning from the ground, but from lofty heights its beauty is hard to do justice to in words. Although I've always been scared of flying, compared to what was about to come, this part felt like a breeze (a sign that just by boarding the plane, my comfort zone had already expanded significantly).

My one non-negotiable was that I got to jump first. The idea of watching our friend Ruby disappear off the ledge into the abyss was one more obstacle I didn't need to overcome today. It helped to know that Joe was waiting in the drop zone several miles below us, a welcome incentive to get my arse out of that aircraft and into the sky. But nothing could've prepared me for the deafening rush of air that hit my face when Keko opened the plane door, nor the sickening anticipation of the jump itself as he began to shimmy me towards it.

When your legs are hanging out the side of a plane at 15,000 feet, shit becomes very surreal, very fast. It becomes even more surreal when seconds later you're suddenly tumbling through the air at 160 miles per hour. But it's crazy how quickly you become normalised to something that, only moments beforehand, filled you with inconceivable dread.

As soon as Keko distracted me from the shock of the jump by pointing out towards the horizon, I was no longer afraid. Because I was not falling, I was gliding. I was free. I was euphoric. Not just because of the view (although it was breath-taking), but because, as my consciousness started to catch up with my plummeting body, I realised that I had just conquered one of my biggest fears, despite all the excuses and subconscious attempts to keep my feet safely on the ground, in the prison of my comfort zone.

Within a matter of seconds of jumping, my identity had transformed entirely. I was now a person who had jumped out of a plane. I was a different Persia to the Persia who had boarded it. I had leapt, and the net had appeared.

The following week, I got a tiny tattoo of a plane on my left wrist as a permanent reminder of this new identity: the woman who had felt the fear to a colossal extent, and jumped anyway.

The twists and turns of this whole experience could not have been more similar to the journey I'd been on when I'd committed to majorly upgrading my identity – that time, in relation to love. It had taken an agonising break-up to show me that if I wanted to one day have a lasting relationship, I was going to have to show up in my love life in a way I had never done before. Because the kind of man I wanted to ultimately end up with was not going to be attracted to the immature antics I'd been demonstrating in the romantic arena up until that point.

The single greatest block that prevents us from making our dream romantic scenario a reality is that our current identity is not yet a match for that level of relationship. Think about it: if you were in a healthy, happy partnership with the love of your life, would you be wasting your time analysing lukewarm WhatsApp messages from a guy you've only been on two dates with, mining for non-existent subtext? Would you spend too many hours scrolling through dating apps (instead of being present in your other relationships or work life), manically willing someone to match with you so that you can feel that transient jolt of validation, one that will evaporate as fast as it materialised? Would you have sex with a stranger you don't even fancy, just to remind yourself that you're still desirable? Would you make a real song and dance about being 'the only single one left in the ENTIRE WORLD' every time you saw a post on social media announcing a new engagement? Would you get wasted and barrage your ex with texts and calls because you'd rather suffer the inevitable humiliation than the sting of loneliness? No, you would not.

You cannot get an adult relationship by behaving like a love-struck teenager. Convincing yourself that you'll show up differently in love once you have a partner is not only naïve, it's selfish. A romantic partner is a *human being*, not a magic pill to fix your lack of self-worth. You've got to do that all by yourself.

A solid relationship requires patience, self-awareness and maturity. It's a result of two whole beings coming together and recognising that they do not *need* one another, they *desire* one another. And, to be blunt, if you're not willing to put in the work it takes to become ready for the great relationship you say you want, then you don't really deserve it. I know that sounds harsh, but in a culture that fetishises motivational smack-downs in the form of #realtalk and #noexcuses and #hustleandgrind when it comes to our career, in the field of dating and love, we seriously need to grow a backbone. We need to stop saying that getting a relationship means EVERYTHING to us, unless we are *actually prepared* to take responsibility for the results we're currently getting in our love life. Unless we are *actually prepared* to get out of our comfort zone and start cleaning up the unhelpful thought processes and language we use to describe our romantic status. Unless we are *actually prepared* to stop looking outside of ourselves for the partner we want to get, and start looking inside of ourselves for the partner we want to *be*.

Make no mistake: attracting a great relationship is not a question of luck. It's a question of whether or not our identity is a match for it.

6. HOW NOT TO ATTRACT A MAN

SNUBBED

'A boo is a lot louder than a cheer.'
LANCE ARMSTRONG

Dating has always been hard. Back in ye olde days (aka my teenage years – pre-social media and dating apps), I recall the heady hit of adrenalin that would course through my veins every time the landline rang. Remember those?

PLEASE let it be him! I'd think, picturing the face of whichever guy I'd just started seeing.

Disappointing as it always was when the caller turned out to be someone with far less sex appeal, at least in those days I didn't have the option of spending the next three hours trying to track down the object of my affection online, like some kind of love-crazed detective.

Nowadays, we're not so fortunate. Not only has modern technology made the stalking of and obsessing over a new love interest so much more accessible, it's facilitated a whole host of new ways to reject and be rejected by potential partners. Here's a list of the most common examples:

1. THE BREADCRUMBER

This person gives you tiny titbits of contact or affirmation via text or social media to keep you hooked in and interested, while at the same time positioning you at a far enough distance so they can keep their options wide open.

2. THE GHOSTER

Your typical Ghoster suddenly disappears from your life/ text/dating app exchanges for no apparent reason, leaving you clueless as to what went wrong and desperately scouring your past interactions for clarity (or a sign of hope that they *do* care about you, really).

3. THE HAUNTER

The Haunter still watches all your Instagram stories, but they make zero effort to interact or engage with you beyond that; they care enough to want to keep tabs on you and your life, but not enough to actually want to be part of it.

4. THE BENCHER

The Bencher treats you like a substitute football player: when their main preference is unavailable (or not that into them), they'll randomly get in contact with you for a boost of validation, or to make the person they actually like jealous. Late-night booty calls or last-minute invitations tend to be a signal you're on the bench, not the pitch.

5. THE SLOW FADER

Similar to the Ghoster and Haunter, the Slow Fader is probably the most common emotionally unavailable culprit of them all. When I asked several guy friends how they've ended things with girls they weren't that into in the past, slow-fading was the most popular option by far. If his responses to your texts are vague and general (e.g. 'I'm really busy at the moment, but drinks soon?') this is a sure sign he's trying to let you down gently.

Most of us, understandably, take this kind of behaviour personally. We think it means we aren't good enough for the person who is rejecting us when, if anything, the reverse is true: if the person you are (or were) in a romantic dynamic with is not mature or respectful enough to communicate *why* they've backed away, this is not a person deserving of your attention. (And, in any case, if they're being this fickle and flaky when you're supposed to be in the honeymoon phase, how do you expect them to behave if you were in an actual *relationship* with them?)

The real problem here is that romantic rejection is a notoriously potent aphrodisiac. Throughout history, it has incited countless otherwise dignified and self-respecting humans to try to win back the attention of their rejector in a myriad of embarrassing ways. In today's digital world, this looks like posting soft-porny pictures on Instagram to get the rejector to notice you again, spending hours stalking the rejector online, or scouring through streams of old messages between you to try to understand the reason for their vanishing act. In particularly dire cases, it looks like drunk calling or texting the rejector up to 187 times in one sitting, as a former client of mine once did (*before* we worked together, might I add).

Why do we do this to ourselves? Because we all love a challenge. It makes victory all the more sweet when we eventually win the rejector back. Unfortunately, however, winning them back is unlikely, because working so hard to gain the attention of someone who has made it clear they don't want to be with us just isn't sexy.

Not every guy you date will be a compatible life partner for you, in the same way not every shoe you try on in a shop is going to fit. Doesn't mean there's anything wrong with your foot. It's not personal, you just need a different size. So, for the love of your own sanity, don't waste one more second of your precious time and energy trying to win back someone who doesn't want to be won (not by you, anyway). With around eight billion people on this planet, there are so many others out there who you won't *need* to try and win back, because they wouldn't dream of disappearing in the first place. Here's the catch, though: they'll only show up once you value yourself enough to shut the door on the ones who can't even be bothered to reply to a simple fucking text.

DEAR MEN

Dear Men,

We love you, BUT… in the same way you want us to stop with the nagging, controlling and drama, we'd be ever so grateful if you'd stop with the ghosting and general avoidance of anything that brings up uncomfortable emotions.

We're big girls. We can handle you telling us you're *not that into us* (or our friends will help us handle it, at least). What we *can't* handle is you wasting any more of our time because you're too cowardly to have an adult conversation.

We know we have shit, too. We know we can be nightmares. We're working on it. And the more we work on it, the stronger we become in ourselves. Meaning that our days of putting up with this ghosting nonsense are coming to a very speedy end.

So don't expect us to welcome you with open arms when you inevitably slide back into our DMs after your next vanishing act, like the predictable, emotionally unavailable f*ckwit you are. Got it? Great.

All the best to the family!

Love,

Women x

THE WET BANDIT

'They cannot take away our self-respect
if we do not give it to them.'
MAHATMA GANDHI

My third year of university was the first time since lower-sixth form that I'd officially been single – even though I'd cheated on the two boyfriends I'd had within that period. A lot.

So now that I was free to bed whomever I wanted, whenever I wanted (without having to usher my conquests out of my student digs before the rest of my housemates woke up), needless to say, I didn't hold back.

One Saturday evening, while downing ghastly shots of what we called 'apple sourz' at the equally ghastly student union bar, I glimpsed a very pretty posh boy to my right who was waiting to be served. I instantly recognised him as one of my housemate's boyfriend's rugger-bugger brethren, and I used this piece of information to spark up a dialogue.

About seven more shots later, the rugger bugger and I were en route back to mine. So horny were we that we didn't even bother to stop en route for cheesy chips, a staple part of every Exeter University student's night out.

Being half-cut myself, I didn't notice that this rugger bugger was completely fucking shunted. So shunted, in fact, that the sex itself was pretty much a non-event. Which is why I was surprised to awake several hours later to bed sheets sodden with his perspiration.

Rugby boys must just sweat a lot, I told myself.

As dawn came and the room began to lighten, I felt his warm, musty breath on the back of my neck nearly as fast as I smelt it. His chiselled, naked body wriggled against mine and before I'd even had a chance to bid him a good morrow with my own rancid apple sourz-soaked breath, he was inside me once more.

Our fresh sweat mingled with the already sodden bed sheets to create a most unbecoming scent. But feeling grateful to have the undivided attention of such a good-looking and popular boy, I put it to the back of my mind. And, apparently, so did he, for neither of us mentioned the sheets once.

When he left, I toyed with the idea of washing the linen – as any self-respecting woman would do, following a one-night stand. But considering there was less than a week until the end of term (and hygiene featured alarmingly low on my list of priorities back then), I decided to leave it until the day before I was due to head back to London for the Easter break.

A few days after my romp with the rugger bugger, I went over to my friend Nicky's for a girly dinner party. Two bottles of Jacob's Creek in, we tipsily toppled into our latest boy sagas. These girls had been privy to all my naughty shenanigans over the last few months, so were expecting some top-notch content from me. I did not disappoint, but alas not for the reasons I'd imagined.

I told the girls all about the rugger bugger and the sweaty sex we'd had a few days earlier.

'What's his name?' Sara asked as she refilled our glasses.

'Uh... Tom, I think? Don't know his surname.'

With furrowed brow, Sara got up from the table, ran upstairs and returned a few moments later clutching her laptop. She opened it up and logged straight on to Facebook.

'Is this him?' she asked, turning the computer to face me.

'Yeah, that's him,' I replied, clicking through his profile pictures. 'Fit, isn't he,' I said smugly.

Sara pursed her lips, stifling a laugh. 'You *do* know who that is, don't you, Pers?'

'No… but, I feel like you're about to tell me.'

Sara sighed as she pointed back to the computer. 'That's The Wet Bandit,' she said, 'he's famous here for getting wankered, taking girls home and then pissing in their bed.'

Oh, for fuck's sake.

When I got home later that night, I pulled my duvet cover off the bed to reveal a large, circular, yellow-green stain in the middle of the sheet.

For fuck's SAKE!

I must have subconsciously known it had been wee, not sweat, that me and old pretty boy had been romping around in, but had refused to admit it to myself until Sara had ripped away the sheets of denial through her revelation. Which means that I'd opted to have sex and sleep in someone else's *piss* over telling this guy to get his urine-soaked arse OUT OF MY FUCKING BED. I'd put up with some crass behaviour from men in my time, but this took it to a whole new level.

You would think I'd have learnt from this incident. If so, you'd have thought wrong.

A few years later, while on an acting job in Shanghai, I fell asleep in the corridor outside my hotel room after a heavy night on the razz with a Russian boy I'd flung myself at in a bar hours earlier. I awoke to a warm stream of liquid trickling down the side of my torso, and soon realised that the source of this liquid was the unconscious Russian boy's flaccid penis, which was poking through the flies of his shorts. Horrified (not to mention covered in piss – *again*), I ran into my hotel room, locked the door, took off my damp dress and shoved it in the bin, before jumping into the shower to try to wash away both the evidence and the memory. When I emerged from my (mercifully fresh-as-a-daisy) bed sheets hours later, I quietly opened the door to my room and peeked into the corridor. The Russian was gone, but a big wet patch remained, an unwelcome reminder that, no, it had *not* all been a bad dream.

Extreme as these two tales may sound to you, I do hope they've shed some light on the ways you may have settled for your own version of piss-soaked linen in your love life over the years, because crumbs of romantic attention seemed better than *no* romantic attention.

Maybe you've found yourself justifying or rationalising why all communication and interaction between you and the guy you're dating tends to be on his terms only. Or why he makes a concerted effort to hide his phone from you whenever messages come through, and is generally evasive, secretive and vague about what he's been up to since you last spoke. Or why he constantly makes little digs or jokes at your expense. Or why he cancels plans with you at the last minute and doesn't call when he says he will. Or why he openly flirts with other women in front of you. Or why he does everything to avoid having a serious and meaningful conversation about where your relationship is headed. Or why he doesn't show any interest in your life and minimises your feelings because he's just so very *busy*. Or why his mood is so unpredictable that there's a permanent ball of anxiety in your stomach whenever you're in his presence.

And yet, just to keep hold of this man who treats you with not one iota of dignity or respect, you find yourself blowing off dates with your friends when he calls you for a last-minute rendezvous (and then lying to your friends about it). And you dress and behave in ways that are not really you, but you hope will make him like you more. And you plan your entire weekly schedule around when he *might* want to see you. And you ignore him when he tells you early on that he's not ready for a relationship and is just looking to have fun. And you convince yourself that the mad-hot sex and physical chemistry between you must mean that he *does* want to be in a relationship with you, really. And you lose yourself entirely in this person and dynamic that have done not *one thing* for your life, apart from drain it of all its luminosity.

In romance, as in life, you get what you tolerate; you make the bed you lie in. So, if those bed sheets happen to be covered in piss and you continue to lie in them anyway, you've only got yourself to blame.

SUBTEXT

'Indecision is a decision.'

NITYA PRAKASH

The last guy I dated before I met Joe definitely fancied me and enjoyed my company, that much I knew for sure. Didn't mean he wanted a relationship with me, though. That was a bitter pill for me to swallow, considering what great chemistry we had and how perfect he seemed on paper.

This guy had told me on our first date that he was recently out of a long-term relationship, a fact I'd conveniently pushed to the back of my mind – until it became glaringly obvious that no matter how much he may have been attracted to me, he just wasn't ready to commit. And if a guy's not ready to settle down, there ain't a thing you can do to hurry him along. Trust me, I've tried everything in the book (and many things outside of it, too).

When that romance ended, I made a pact with myself to do the challenging inner work required so I could one day attract a guy who *was* ready and willing to be in a committed relationship with me. It worked, because a few months later, along came Joe. I'll explain how shortly.

The point is, men don't tend to overcomplicate romance in the way so many of us women do, complex creatures that we are. So, if you're scouring your text messages from him looking for subtext, if you're constantly checking your phone while out with your friends hoping he's tried to get in touch, if you're spinning plates to maintain his attention… you're working too hard. Because if a guy really wants to call/see/move in with/marry/make babies with you… he will.

I know this is hard to hear, especially if you really care about (or even love) this person. But, just because you may not ultimately end up with him, that doesn't mean he wasn't a key part of the journey towards your 'forever' partner, like the guy before Joe was of mine. Stop clinging out of fear this is your last chance for a happy ending. It's not.

THE WIFE OF BATH

'Deceiving others. That is what the world calls a romance.'
OSCAR WILDE

For the first five years of my career shift into coaching, I worked as a part-time tutor to keep the pennies rolling in while I tried to figure out how the hell to run a profitable business.

My qualifications meant I was a good fit for teenage girls doing GCSEs or A-Levels in English Lit, Classical Civilisation and Theatre Studies. What was so great about this gig was that I got to practise my coaching skills on these teens at the same time as re-familiarising myself with many of the great works of literature I'd studied back at school and university.

The fun part came when I had to somehow find a way to transfer my very uncool passion for this literature to a fifteen-year-old girl whose focus was 100 per cent directed towards her Instagram feed, and who could have cared less about 'the extent to which *Tess of the d'Urbervilles* demonstrates how the suffering experienced by tragic protagonists evokes pity in readers and audiences alike'. So I used the one tool I had at my disposal which, fortunately, I knew was guaranteed to pique any teenage girl's interest: the fact I was a love coach, and had a thousand times more experience than they did when it came to understanding the mystifying mechanics of a teenage boy's brain.

One of my most beloved (and tricky) tutees was a Russian

girl named Katya. Beloved, because this feisty Russki took no prisoners. Tricky, for the same reason. Katya hadn't gelled well with the tutors before me, so I knew I'd have to find a way to gain her respect and attention quick-smart, if I ever hoped to get her the good grades the tutor agency and her parents expected me to. This was easier said than done, given that one of her set texts was *The Canterbury Tales* by the medieval poet Geoffrey Chaucer, and that English was her second language.

The Canterbury Tales is a collection of twenty-four stories presented as part of a story-telling contest by a group of pilgrims en route from London to visit the shrine of St Thomas Becket in Canterbury Cathedral. Basically, it's about as far away from *Gossip Girl* as you can possibly get. However, as we settled in to Katya's Easter holidays study period, it occurred to me that while Chaucer and his medieval language may have held zero resonance for Katya, one of the characters from his tales was sure to spark her interest.

The Wife of Bath is up there with one of the sauciest female characters ever depicted in literature, especially when you consider that the tales were written in the late 1300s, a time when women were doomed to live out a cloistered existence under the most extreme constrictions of patriarchal law. Yet despite the odds being stacked against her, the Wife of Bath introduces herself and her tale with arguably more power and gusto than all the other pilgrims put together. She openly admits that she married much older men for financial gain four times (they kept dying on her), and explains that she doesn't think it necessary to enter marriage a virgin. Refusing to pigeonhole herself into the submissive role expected of women back then, she shamelessly describes her insatiable sexual appetite, as well as her skill at using sex, money and her words to control her husbands. This is mirrored in the message of her tale, which stipulates that what women *really* want is power over the men in their lives. I think she was on to something.

To better help Katya understand the character of the Wife of Bath, I realised I was going to have to take these themes out of medieval England and plonk them into a context she was a lot more familiar with: the world of modern dating. It didn't take long for us to draw parallels between the two eras. In both cases, there's a blatant battle for power between the genders when it comes to sex and love, and the most effective strategy to win this power, it would seem, is to manipulate the other person into believing that they need or desire you more than you do them.

While the Wife's modes of manipulation in romance may be extreme, our approach to modern dating can be just as subversive. Let's take the 'seduction community' of pick-up artists first initiated by Ross Jeffries in the eighties and later made infamous by the *New York Times* bestselling book *The Game* by Neil Strauss. Pick-up artistry is a movement of men (and now some women, too) whose one and only goal is quick sexual success with whatever prey they set their sights upon. Some of the tools and techniques they use to achieve this goal are downright dreadful. For example, 'negging': the practice of giving a woman a back-handed compliment to weaken her confidence and make her more susceptible to seduction; or 'pawning', which means trading or discarding an unwanted woman as proof of the pick-up artist's own social value. Gross.

At the less offensive end of the spectrum are bucket loads of YouTube videos called things like 'The 5 Best Text Messages to Make Any Man Obsessed with You' and 'The Secret to Winning Back Your Ex Fast'. While I'm all for a catchy title to get your message out there, if the content itself fails to adhere to the most basic standards of treating other people like human beings (rather than prizes to be won), then it's not content worthy of consumption, in my opinion. Because let's just be real for a moment: while this smoke-and-mirrors approach to dating may work in the short term to hook in a romantic partner, it's never going to work in the long term. Of course it isn't.

I can say this from first-hand experience, because I used to be really good at manipulating men through seductive trickery. The problem was that it didn't get me anywhere close to what I *actually* wanted, which was a genuine, intimate, committed relationship where my partner and I could support each other to grow and thrive in all areas of our lives. This is the type of relationship I have today, and let me tell you, I didn't get it by playing power games. I didn't get it because I looked hot in my social media pictures, or had a brilliant dating-app profile, or nailed playing hard to get. I got it by healing my relationship with myself.

When I met Joe, it was the first time a man had been so clear and direct about his feelings for me so early on in a courtship. No games. No subtext. No drama. I'd gotten to a point in myself and my life where I just wasn't willing to entertain a potential partner who couldn't (or wouldn't) be straight with me about where their head was at. If the man before me wasn't able to match my desire for a committed relationship, then instead of trying to manipulate him or the situation to my favour, it became my cue to walk away. Not only did this spare me from a lot of needless heartache, it meant that I soon stopped attracting timewasters in lieu of men who wanted the same things I did in romance.

7. HOW TO BE AS SUCCESSFUL AT LOVE AS YOU ARE AT WORK

ROYAL FLUSH

'A woman's sensuality makes the best of a man.'
LEBO GRAND

To the eyes of the world, she had it made: beautiful, intelligent, successful; a regular Heather, if ever there was one. Which is why her Instagram DM begging me to coach her came as such a surprise.

My love life's in crisis, she'd said. *I don't know why it's such a fucking mess, but if something doesn't change really fucking soon I'm in serious fucking trouble.*

The surplus of 'fucking' told me she meant business. I later discovered it was also part of the problem: too much fucking, too little discernment.

Once I'd got her on the phone for a compatibility call to see if I was the right person to help her, it didn't take long to decipher what the underlying issue was. Like many of the high-achieving women I'd worked with, she'd been duped into drawing the logical conclusion that a great relationship could be obtained by following a simple (albeit strict) formula:

1. Decide you want a man.

2. Look around you and find a man close enough to fitting the bill of what you want.

3. Do everything in your power to make said man yours.

4. If/when you've achieved Step 3, do everything in your power to turn this man into a version of himself that's more acceptable to you.

Qualities required to ensure the success of this 'foolproof' strategy:

- focus,
- action and goal-orientated,
- determination.

What applying these qualities looks like in practice:

1. Woman instigating the lion's share of communication (calling/texting first).

2. Woman manoeuvring for dates (either directly or indirectly), and then taking the lead by planning them to within an inch of their life, too.

3. Woman using sex as a tactic to gain man's intrigue and (fingers crossed) devotion.

4. Woman forcefully driving the direction of the relationship (i.e. initiating the 'commitment' chat ASAP, directly or indirectly).

5. Woman eventually breaking up with man because he's a useless shit, and she has no cards left to play.

It doesn't take a brain surgeon to spot the vital flaw in my new client's approach to romance. By relying on her more masculine traits to 'win' the game of love, this woman was quite literally working against nature.

I could relate. These masculine qualities had served me well in the pursuit of my own work and life goals, but when it came to romance, they were steering me away from my God-given superpower: my femininity.

I'd wrongly assumed that employing my more feminine qualities in the advancement of my love life would somehow render me passive and weak (to be fair, when you live in a patriarchal society, it's an easy assumption to make). This is laughable to me now, when I consider that women are the gender who've been entrusted with birthing an actual human being (which, in case you missed the memo, is a process that's anything *but* passive and weak). Vaginas are to humanity what lightsabers are to the Jedi Order: a force to be reckoned with.

It took me a long time to realise that, when it comes to romance, it's actually the woman holding all the cards. But, because we're so busy trying to work out what cards the man opposite us is playing, we fail to see that we already have the winning hand ourselves.

Stepping into our inherent power as a woman creates space for a man to step into his inherent power as a man. Inevitably, that feels really good to him. When we women operate from a more masculine approach to dating and relationships by trying to manoeuvre and control the dynamic at every turn, we give the man no choice but to assume the feminine position. This tends not to go down so well – unless the man is looking for someone to take his mother's place, in which case... *RUN.*

BOTTOM LINE

'You get what you settle for.'
LOUISE SAWYER, *THELMA & LOUISE*

Although channelling the same masculine energy that helps us get ahead in our career rarely works when directed towards our love lives (not for long, anyway), the flipside is that too many of the high-achieving women I come across these days accept the sort of shitty behaviour from men that they would *never* tolerate from clients, colleagues or bosses.

I get why. No matter how proud I felt of the life and success I was creating for myself, it was often still painful to watch the majority of my peers ticking their way through the arbitrary romantic timeline: falling in love, moving in, getting engaged, married, pregnant, etc. This, coupled with society's insistence on measuring a woman's worth according to her relationship status, never mind being constantly reminded that our fertility is dwindling with every passing year, makes it easy to see why so many brilliant women cling to men who seem to value them even less than Gwyneth Paltrow values gluten.

If this resonates, you need to understand that the real issue here is not, in fact, these men who are treating you like dirt. The real issue is how YOU are showing up (or not showing up) in a romantic context, which is not only determining the quality of men that you're attracting, but also the level of respect these men have for you – and, subsequently, how they behave towards you.

If you want to feel as empowered and successful in love as you do in work, then you must demonstrate the same level of self-respect in romance that you do in your career: you need to decide what your bottom line is. If or when that bottom line is crossed, rather than trying to negotiate your way through what is clearly a no-win deal, you must have the dignity and courage to walk away. That's what a good CEO would do.

RISKY BUSINESS

'Love cannot be had without the risk of being wounded.'
JOHN MARK GREEN

Believe it or not, it ain't a bad time to be a woman. We've got more freedom, choice and opportunity available to us than ever before, and the ability to create success and wealth on our own terms looks like it's set to continue on an upward trajectory.

The female employment rate is the highest it's ever been. According to the Department of Labor's Women's Bureau, mothers are the primary or sole earners in 40 per cent of households with children under the age of eighteen (compared to 11 per cent in 1960). In 2019, 29 per cent of senior management roles were held by women, the highest number ever on record. Yes, there's still a bullshit pay gap between the genders, but it *is* closing (albeit slowly).

What's fascinating to me is how this escalating success in our work lives is affecting our love lives. The proportion of women who never have children has doubled in a generation (a good thing in my opinion, considering our planet has a serious population crisis: a century ago there were 1.9 billion people; today we're at 7.9 billion and counting). We all know that marriage rates are rapidly declining, as divorce rates are doing the opposite.

The question is: are these dramatic shifts purely a result of a greater social acceptability of a marriage and childfree lifestyle? To a degree, of course. But having surveyed and coached thousands of women all over the world about what they really desire for their romantic life, I've learnt that these statistics don't necessarily reveal the whole story. Statistics never do. When we asked the women we surveyed what their dream romantic scenario for their future was, the majority simply put: *Marriage with kids* (or a version of this).

Many of these women cited the negative effects of online dating as being a leading cause of their romantic frustration. On the one hand, apps like Tinder, Hinge and Bumble have given us much more opportunity to meet potential partners, but on the other, they seem to encourage a non-committal 'grass-is-greener-elsewhere' attitude – from both sides.

What's been most surprising to me, when examining the data we've collected over the years, is the undeniable correlation between career success and a lack of romantic fulfilment. Here are a few examples of the types of answers we receive from women who describe themselves as 'high-achieving':

> *'I'm successful in my career, friends, family etc. and am generally a bit of a boss, but my love life feels embarrassing and is my Achilles heel.'*

> *'I'm nailing work, but romance is a DISASTER.'*

> *'I feel I'm successful in friendships, family, career, but in terms of a romantic relationship I seem to struggle and I'm out of answers. I'm obviously missing something.'*

What this last woman was 'missing' is what so many of the single and high-achieving women I encounter also seem to be missing when it comes to dating and relationships: the approach and qualities that help a woman succeed at work are not the same approach and qualities that will help her succeed in love.

Often, when a woman is thriving in her career, her identity naturally becomes predominantly wrapped up in what she *does*, not who she *is*. Through both my coaching practice and my own experience, I've seen first-hand how a high-achieving woman's tendency to focus on what she's achieving over who she's being then leads her to behave in her love life in the following detrimental ways:

- Impressing/auditioning when on dates (aka 'peacocking' – a male behaviour).
- Hiding behind her work success to try to conceal her sadness around the lack of romantic connection.
- Devoting the majority of her time, energy and finances towards her career progression, not her love life.

While it's fantastic for a woman to be both driven and successful at work, contrary to popular belief, this does *not* have to be at the expense of romantic success. Dating coach Sami Wunder said it best in an interview with *Business Insider Africa* in 2019:

> *A man doesn't fall in love with you because you've led so many meetings, and been on TV, and travelled the world and can speak five languages. He falls in love because of the connection he feels for you.*

This brings us to another unhelpful (and untrue) school of thought: that all men are intimidated by successful women. What *some* men may actually be intimidated by is the lack of connection and vulnerability that a woman's success may appear to suggest (and vice versa, by the way). This inability to be open and vulnerable in your love life often looks like:

- Holding back from sharing your desire for a committed relationship when on a date, because you're afraid you'll be rejected or look desperate.

- Not clearly stating boundaries out of fear those boundaries will either be ignored by the other person, or cause your date to ditch the dynamic altogether.

- Projecting a façade to the world that you've 'got it all together' (when in reality it feels like the opposite).

- Hiding behind constant banter and aloofness with the guy you're dating as a way of feeling in control/avoiding deeper feelings that could lead to rejection.

You don't need me to tell you how important vulnerability is when it comes to cultivating meaningful connections with others; Brené Brown has already done a sterling job of that. But what you perhaps *do* need reminding about, especially if you identify as being a high-achieving woman yourself, is that if you fail to make vulnerability an active and consistent part of your romantic life, you don't have a hope in hell of attracting (let alone sustaining) a great relationship in the future. Let me tell you why.

A woman thriving in her career is usually well practised in feeling confident, certain and in control in her work environment. That's why she's successful. But when it comes to romance, there's a whole other person with a whole other agenda to take into consideration, meaning she's no longer solely in charge of her success or experience. Ay, *there's the rub.*

It doesn't matter how beautiful, sexy or magnetic a woman may be; when it comes to love, she'll still have to face the possibility that she may be rejected or have her heart broken by the other person. The crazy irony is that the best chance any of us will ever have of *not* being rejected in love is to show up authentically, imperfectly, vulnerably as ourselves, warts and all. That's the only way we ever fall in love: through a mutual revealing of who we really are, underneath all the bells and whistles.

What's so terrifying is that if we're brave enough to show up as our full self, we still may wind up getting rejected, anyway – and the pain will be that much more acute because it won't just be our performance being rejected, but the real deal.

That's the thing about love: there are no guarantees. Even when it seems to be going all hunky dory for two people in a relationship, one day one of them is going to have to deal with the loss of the other, and there ain't nothing more vulnerable than grief.

What I know for sure is that if you want to experience real intimacy and connection in your love life, then vulnerability is a non-negotiable part of the deal. Without vulnerability, intimacy isn't possible. Without intimacy, real love can't be born, let alone grow. Vulnerability is a muscle that needs regular exercising. The more you work at it, the easier it'll be to open up to (potential) romantic partners in the future. Only then will you experience true intimacy and open the doors for real love to come rushing in.

Healthy romantic dynamics are a collaborative energy exchange. Give and take. Ebb and flow. You *can* be both fiercely independent and part of a team (that's ultimately the secret to lasting happiness in all relationships, after all). But to be part of a two-person team means to risk one day losing your teammate in a way that neither of you can possibly know nor prepare for.

The question is, is real love worth taking that risk to you? It abso-fuckin-lutely is to me.

8. HOW TO GET READY FOR LOVE

THE BUMP BUMP ROAD

'If you have built castles in the air, your work
need not be lost; that is where they should be.
Now put the foundations under them.'

HENRY DAVID THOREAU

When my sister and I were kids, our dad used to drive us down a private road near where we lived to look at all the beautiful big houses this road was known for. We called this road 'The Bump Bump Road' on account of all the speed bumps along it.

'One day, I'm going to build us a house as amazing as these ones,' Dad would tell Evie and I, as we pressed our little noses up against the backseat windows, giddy with awe at the Gatsby-like mansions that stood proud and tall on the other side of the glass.

At the time, we were living in a cute but small townhouse in the suburbs. Our family had been on the brink of bankruptcy several times, which is why Dad's vision felt like a lovely but impossible pipe dream.

Yet Dad continued to hold that vision firmly in his mind until one day, many years later, it became a reality.

On a handful of occasions, I've been stood outside the house my parents created together when a passing car has slowed down to let the kids in the backseat catch a closer look, their mouths agape in wonder. One of those full circle moments, you might say.

What I learnt from my parents' journey towards creating their dream home (as well as overcoming their addiction) is that you can achieve whatever you want in life if: 1: you're clear on your vision; 2: you consistently work and move in the direction of that vision; and 3: you find a way to stay very, very patient around how and when that vision will come into fruition. Because, as I shared earlier, good things take time to grow.

ONE LOVE

'Music acts like a magic key, to which the
most tightly closed heart opens.'
MARIA VON TRAPP, *THE SOUND OF MUSIC*

Growing up, I was obsessed with the musical *Les Misérables*. Whenever things were tough at home, I'd whip out my chunky red Sony Walkman and lose myself in the bracing drama of a fictional reality that was preferable to my own. Disappearing into music as a way to evade painful feelings soon became a lifeline for me. In addition to my budding obsession with musicals and angsty teenage anthems, it wasn't long before I was writing my own songs and singing solos on my primary (and then high) school stage. All through my higher education, I headed up the vocals in varying local bands and continued to etch out lyrics about my most recent romantic melodrama in my tattered Moleskine notebook.

The love junkie in me had always been fascinated by Shakespeare's opening lines of *Twelfth Night*:

> If music be the food of love, play on;
> Give me excess of it, that, surfeiting,
> The appetite may sicken, and so die.

Like Duke Orsino, who speaks these lines, I guess I'd subconsciously hoped that an excessive indulgence in music might cure (or at least stifle) my obsession with relationships, just as binging on food soon dissolves the appetite for it. In theory.

Alas, it didn't work; for the more Linkin Park I listened to as a forlorn teen whose latest crush could not have been less interested in me, the worse I'd feel about my sorry state of affairs. (A little tip for you… if you're suffering from a hellish bout of unrequited love, then blasting yourself with depressing music that matches that emotional frequency won't relieve the angst. It'll amplify it.)

That's the thing about feelings: we're as addicted to the painful ones as we are the pleasant ones. And, aside from drugs and the experience of falling in love itself, music's the fastest way to ignite or heighten both. I'm sure that's why I've always been so drawn to singing: it takes the heady high (or low) from listening to music one stage further, stirring our soul on a primal level.

Every known human culture practises some form of singing, regardless of how remote or isolated that culture is. When performed as part of a group, singing has been proven to reduce stress, promote a healthy immune system, increase feel-good endorphins and foster social bonding. No wonder that for our ancient ancestors (the Egyptians, Greeks, Romans etc.), music and singing were a vital part of all religious, social and healing rituals. Arguably, the equivalent today would be football chanting, festivals and pop culture. In these instances, the communal singing may not seem overtly spiritual in nature like it was way back when, but consider how we instinctively raise our hands to the heavens when the music moves us: we're reaching for the divine, even if we don't know it.

As I've grown older, those years of bludgeoning my aching heart with sad songs are now but a distant memory laced with bittersweet nostalgia, and my relationship with music has become way simpler: today, it's a tool I use to help me feel better, not worse. This isn't to say I steer clear of all lyrics or melodies that could be deemed melancholic (Fleetwood Mac are one of my most beloved bands); I'm just more discerning about when I choose to indulge. For example, if I'm feeling shit, I avoid the sad stuff and blast myself with tunes that I know will help elevate my mood.

The most effective music for getting me out of any funk or bolstering my already good vibrations (cos I'm always up for getting higher) is reggae. I swear those carefree calypso beats could comfort the most cheerless of souls. (I heard recently that apparently even dogs find reggae soothing – along with classical music.) Emerging in Jamaica in the late sixties out of the ska and rocksteady genres, reggae may be infused with a spirit of fun and freedom, but it's not without depth. The reason I love it so much is that even when exploring gut-wrenching pain and systemic injustice (I'm looking at you, 'Redemption Song'), it still finds a way to align itself with a message of hope and love.

The more I've explored less well-known reggae music (from the likes of Burning Spear, The Slickers and Blue Bells), the more interested I've become in the messages and insights of the Abrahamic religion of Rastafarianism that's associated with reggae music. Developed in Jamaica in the 1930s as a kind of counter-culture to British colonialism, Rastafari was made more visible by the global popularity of reggae, which became a kind of soundtrack for the social movement. Unlike the majority of religions, there's allegedly no dogma (praise be!) and, while Rastas do believe in one God – 'Jah' – and revere the Bible (especially the book of Revelation), it's their reliance on personal experience and intuition that I find most appealing and useful. I also like the simplicity of their values: they promote natural living and focus on the 'two great commandments': love of God and love of thy neighbour, which can definitely be felt through the relaxed and inclusive vibe of reggae music.

Unfortunately, the only characteristic of the religion that I'm strongly averse to is also the most significant, given my gender: Rastafari deems women inferior to men, a frustrating reminder that if something sounds too good to be true, it probably is. That said, I'm a big believer in the Twelve Step philosophy of 'take what you like and leave the rest' when it comes to spirituality (and most things in life, actually).

What has this to do with attracting love, though? you may be thinking. EVERYTHING, my friend. Everything.

The Sufi poet Rumi once said that, 'Your task is not to seek for love, but merely to seek and find all the barriers within yourself that you have built against it.' The biggest barrier to love always, always comes back to fear. Fear of rejection. Fear of abandonment. Fear of commitment... The list goes on. There may be varying nuances and layers depending on your personal context, but fear is what always lies beneath them.

You can spend years and years in therapy trying to snuff this fear out. You can analyse, acupuncture and transcendentally meditate until the cows come home. And... you can also whack on your favourite reggae tune, dance around your kitchen naked while singing into your hairbrush and shaking that gorgeous tail feather of yours. If you choose the latter every once in a while, I can almost guarantee you'll feel better, if only for the duration of two verses, two choruses and a bridge.

So, here's a truth my ever-evolving love of reggae has revealed to me over recent months: when you make an active decision to spend less time and energy talking about your issues and problems, and *more* time revelling in the spirit and energy of celebration – in the savouring of what a magnificent thing it is just to be alive right here – right now… guess what? You become a fucking delight to be around. And you know who'll adore being around someone fucking delightful? The person who'll one day get to dance around your kitchen naked with you to your favourite reggae beats, as you sip on sangria and wonder why you were ever so afraid to love and be loved like this.

At least, that's been my experience.

HEARTBEAT

'In black ink my love may still shine bright.'
WILLIAM SHAKESPEARE

I was once told by an acting teacher that the best way to attract more romance into your life is to first romance yourself.

'And, the best way to do so,' she explained, 'is to spend a few minutes every day speaking language that feeds your soul. Read a sonnet a day and just watch all the boys come out to play,' she finished with a wink and pantomime flourish, before tootling off to teach her next class.

I'd written my English Literature dissertation on the sonnet form while at university, so her suggestion actually made a lot of sense to me, given that romantic love is a prominent theme throughout the sonnet tradition.

The sonnet originally appeared in Italy in about the thirteenth century (the Italian word *sonetto* means 'a little sound or song'); then it made its way over to England in the sixteenth century. At just fourteen lines long and bounded by a very strict rhyme scheme, there are two main types of sonnet: the Petrarchan (Italian) and the Elizabethan (English – and more commonly referred to as Shakespearean), which are mainly differentiated by their structure.

However, what makes sonnets such powerful love poems is that they are always written in iambic pentameter. Iambic pentameter is a poetic meter with ten beats per line made up of alternating unstressed and stressed syllables. When spoken aloud, the rhythmic effect sounds very much like a heartbeat. Let me show you what I mean.

Below is Shakespeare's most famous sonnet, Sonnet 18: 'Shall I Compare Thee to a Summer's Day'. Try speaking the first four lines of it out loud, and, as you do so, hit your chest with your right hand (palm flat) on each syllable, lightly on the un-bolded bits (unstressed) and a little harder on the bolded bits (stressed):

> Shall **I**/ com**pare**/ thee **to**/ a **sum**/mer's **day**?/
> Thou **art**/ more **love**/ly **and**/ more **tem**/per-**ate**:/
> Rough **winds**/ do **shake**/ the **dar**/ling **buds**/ of **May**,/
> And **sum**/mer's **lease**/ hath **all**/ too **short**/ a **date**;/

Repeat that exercise a few times until you really feel that heartbeat, and then try it again, this time just speaking the lines naturally (without tapping your chest or intentionally stressing or un-stressing any of the syllables). Just let it flow organically.

Once you feel comfortable with those few lines, try that whole process with the sonnet in its entirety:

> Shall **I**/ com**pare**/ thee **to**/ a **sum**/mer's **day**?/
> Thou **art**/ more **love**/ly **and**/ more **tem**/per-**ate**:/
> Rough **winds**/ do **shake**/ the **dar**/ling **buds**/ of **May**,/
> And **sum**/mer's **lease**/ hath **all**/ too **short**/ a **date**;/
> Some-**time**/ too **hot**/ the **eye**/ of **hea**/ven **shines**,/
> And **oft**/en **is**/ his **gold**/ comp-**lex**/ion **dimm'd**;/
> And **eve**/ry **fair**/ from **fair**/ some-**time**/ de-**clines**,/
> By **chance**/ or **nat**/ure's **chan**/ging **course**/ un-**trimm'd**;/
> But **thy**/ e-**ter**/-nal **sum**/mer **shall**/ not **fade**,/
> Nor **lose**/ pos-**ses**/-sion **of**/ that **fair**/ thou **owest**;/
> Nor **shall**/ Death **brag**/ thou **wand**/-er'st **in**/ his **shade**,/

When **in**/ e-**ter**/-nal **lines**/ to **time**/ thou **grow'st**:/
So **long**/ as **men**/ can **breathe**/ or **eyes**/ can **see**,/
So **long**/ lives **this**/ and **this**/ gives **life**/ to **thee**./

Isn't that beautiful? Mr Shakespeare sure knew how to cultivate the feeling of romance through his weaving of words.

However, what makes his collection of 154 sonnets so intriguing (aside from its mysterious dedication to 'Mr W. H.' at the start) is the contrast between the overtly romantic sonnets like the one above, and those that explore the more controversial themes (at the time) of lust, misogyny, infidelity and homoeroticism – to name a few. In this collection, beauty and joy are but a hair's breadth away from pain, grief and tragedy, echoing Lysander's famous line from *A Midsummer Night's Dream*: 'The course of true love never did run smooth.' Ain't that the truth.

Sometimes love is hard. Sometimes love is painful. But the real problem is that in trying to resist the hard parts of love, we often wind up closing ourselves off to the good parts, too. (If you've ever had your heart broken and are terrified to open yourself to love again, you'll know what I'm talking about.)

None of us can know where a love story is going to take us. As I write these words, I'm preparing to marry the love of my life, my soulmate and best friend. Even so, I can't possibly know everything that's in store for us. The work we've done on ourselves gives us good odds that we won't lose this union we've created due to infidelity or betrayal. But life is life; anything is possible. Would I ever regret having opened myself to a love like this, should something awful happen and I one day lose it (which is inevitable, given that neither of us is immortal)? Not a chance. This adventure has been the most extraordinary one of my life, and whatever happens I'm just so grateful that I got to experience it at all.

So this is my advice to you, dear reader: go and order yourself a copy of Shakespeare's sonnets. Don't download it from the internet; get a proper *book* (ideally a second-hand one with slightly tattered and yellowing pages). Open it up and breathe it in. Commit to reading the whole collection, one sonnet a day, from beginning to end.

In doing so, you will affirm to yourself and to the powers that be that you are ready and available for the full spectrum of human experience. And, when you have read – out loud and proud – the final syllable of the fourteenth line of Sonnet 154, any fear you may have been harbouring around the most vulnerable, terrifying and magical human experience of all – that of falling and landing in love – will have been replaced by a quiet knowing that whatever ends up happening in your love story... you'll be all right. More than that, you'll be truly living.

VOLUPTAS

'I finally figured out the only reason to be alive is to enjoy it.'
RITA MAE BROWN

As the author Elizabeth Gilbert soon discovered at the start of her journey in *Eat, Pray, Love*, when it comes to feeling attractive, visiting Italy can be polarising. On the one hand, the country basically runs on sex. On the other, it also runs on the world's most delicious carbs, thus initiating one of womankind's eternal dilemmas: to gorge and feel short-term ecstasy, but long-term guilt. Or, to exercise self-restraint and experience major short-term FOMO, but still fit into your skimpiest set of underwear without your circulation being cut off.

I was faced with this predicament during a trip to Italy with Joe and his family a year after we met. As I was renowned amongst my peers for boasting a high pleasure threshold, you can guess which way the tide of temptation took me on this holiday. *All the way, bambina.* There were lunchtime Aperol Spritzes and late-night trips to the gelateria (double-scoops, dairy-*full*). A sun-soaked afternoon sipping Sangiovese at a local vineyard. An other-worldly seven-course dinner that included truffle-smothered, gluten-free pasta, and mounds of burrata so creamy that it melted on your tongue like butter on a warm crumpet.

It was eight whole days of pure, unadulterated indulgence, and as such was not without its consequences; consequences that mainly involved me standing naked in front of a full-length mirror every evening, pinching at my love handles and feeling ugly, ashamed and just plain wrong for the gargantuan nature of my holiday consumption.

Unlike the majority of people I know who are either very good at pleasure, or very good at moderation, self-control and discipline, I've always oscillated between the two as consistently as the swing of the pendulum in a grandfather clock. While some might call this balance, for a long time I believed my innate love of pleasure was a problem; as if the only thing that mattered in life was how much joy you were willing to sacrifice in the pursuit of success.

One afternoon during the trip, following a pot-luck lunch of Parma ham, melon and about twelve different kinds of cheese and meats all washed down with a glass of prosecco (OK, *three* glasses of prosecco), I went to my room to change for the beach. As I stood there observing my expanding silhouette in the reflection ready to launch into my usual body slag-fest, I remembered something a mentor of mine had said to me years ago (probably when I'd just returned from a holiday in Italy and was feeling frumpier than Miss Trunchbull from the movie *Matilda*). She'd said, 'A goddess's primary concern is pleasure, not perfection.'

The ancient Greeks and Romans appear to have felt the same way, given that they both celebrated a female deity who was the personification of pleasure, enjoyment, and delight: 'Voluptas' to the Romans and 'Hedone' to the Greeks (which is the root of the English word 'hedonism'). More specifically, this goddess was all about the pleasure associated with the senses (eating, drinking, bonking etc.). Clearly, those ancient civilisations didn't attach guilt and shame to carnal indulgence in the same way that we do today.

Scanning over my full-bodied figure in the mirror, I realised I had a choice: I could continue berating myself for my holiday consumption, pinching and scrutinising my wobbly bits, cellulite and lack of a thigh gap. Or I could lovingly observe these things as marks of my commitment and devotion to the goddess Voluptas (my new favourite deity), and say to myself, out-loud and proud: 'This is a body that, for a short period of time, has luxuriated in the simple pleasures of fresh, delicious food-fuel – Christmas-red tomatoes, the ripest of avocados, the creamiest of gelato. This is a body that has relished every sip of crimson wine gifted by the Montepulciano grape, and revelled in drunken twirls around the dance floor to real-live music created by real-live instruments. This is a body that has unapologetically prioritised pleasure over productivity, laughter over logistics, satisfaction over success. This is a body that has permitted its owner all the joy and liberation she desires, and precious time with those she loves and who love her back, regardless of her dress size. This is a body that went to bed late and slept in later. This is a body that may not feel so zen right now, may not have drunk her green juice or practised one single downward dog in a week, but by *goddess* does she feel alive.'

What makes us attractive is not how we look or how disciplined we are. What makes us attractive is how we choose to feel about ourselves and our choices, from moment to moment.

What are you choosing right now?

TRIVIAL PURSUIT

'Do not spoil what you have by desiring what you have not; remember that what you now have was once among the things you only hoped for.'

EPICURUS

n a lively beach reggae bar on Gili Trawangan, a small island off the coast of Bali, my friend Lucy and I are celebrating her thirty-first birthday in low-key style.

For most of the evening, the dance floor has been commandeered by a group of gorgeous Chilean girls whose confidence and sex appeal is akin to Shakira circa 2005 with those honest hips of hers. They seem to be having more fun than all the punters in here put together (bar Lucy and me, of course).

What strikes me most about these girls, who I'd guess are in their mid-twenties, is how present they are with one another. Although plenty of men (some really quite fit) have tried their damnedest to wheedle their way into the Chileans' saucy little circle throughout the night, the girls have refused them entry each and every time; they just aren't interested. This is *their* night, and the only outsiders permitted to enter their fold are other girls they can twerk and take selfies with, which, joyously, includes Lucy and me.

I'm sad to say, this is a far cry from how I used to behave on the majority of girls' nights out in my early twenties. Back then, if I hadn't ended up in a new lover's arms before dawn I'd render the night a failure, despite having spent the majority of it with friends I claimed to love.

One of the main reasons women come to me for love coaching is because of how much the thoughts and feelings surrounding their romantic life dominate and dwarf all other aspects of their existence. Like twenty-three-year-old me, their friendships, careers and even families often play second fiddle to whatever dating saga they currently find themselves in, and too much of their time is spent willing a man to fall out of the sky and into their DMs. In the meantime, these women torture themselves by trawling through the reams of engagement, wedding and couples' holiday pictures clogging up their social feeds. Understandably, this leaves them feeling frustrated, less than and wracked with shame that their romantic reality doesn't match up.

The first thing I tell these clients when they turn up at my virtual door is to stop beating themselves up for obsessing like this. With the advances in technology (and the 24/7 nature of it), it's near impossible *not* to compare our love life to that of every Sue, Jill and Sally these days.

The second thing I tell them is to *step away from the dating apps*, because if they are causing you to obsess and stress, they are not serving you. Dating apps, like all technology, are not bad in and of themselves. In fact, they can be a great tool to connect with potential partners – *if* you're feeling good about yourself and your life, that is. If you're not, if you're using them for validation and to escape your pain, and if you don't have healthy boundaries around your usage of them, then they will only exacerbate the wound. (In any case, remember that human beings managed to procreate for tens of thousands of years without the help of dating apps. They are useful in the modern world, but they are not a compulsory component to attracting love.)

The third thing I tell them is that when it comes to finding a romantic partner to share your life with, it's not about where they are that's important, it's about where YOU are. The reason I spent so much time looking for potential suitors on nights out with friends is because I was terrified I'd somehow 'miss' the love of my life. I'd be in the bathroom or looking the other way while he'd slip out the door, never to be seen again.

It took me years to learn that if I stopped pursuing the romantic love I felt I lacked and just started appreciating all the good stuff in my life instead, the more empowered, confident and attractive I'd naturally start to feel as a by-product. Ironically, the night I fully grasped this lesson is the same night I met Joe. Funny how, when you stop prioritising a potential hook-up over the people who *actually* love you, when you stop looking for love, you give it a chance to find *you*. No need to endlessly trawl through dating apps. No need to obsessively analyse every glance, every text, every conversation. No need to manipulate and manoeuvre a love story to play out in the way you think it should. Because when you let go of the trivial pursuit of love, all it takes is a chance head-turn at the right moment for your entire world to change in an instant.

So, if you're single right now and don't want to be, take a leaf out of the Chilean girls' book and channel your adoration towards the friends who *already* adore you, devote your time to the family who *already* want to hang out with you, and invest your energy in the passions that *already* fill you with joy. And, instead of going out to try to meet a man, go out and see how many new girlfriends you can make on dance floors or in grizzly pub toilets. You'll never feel disappointed by not meeting the love of your life on a night out (or on holiday, or at a wedding) if that was never your priority in the first place. Better still, you'll create space for romantic love to show up when you (genuinely) least expect it.

PURA VIDA

'One day your life will flash before your
eyes. Make sure it's worth watching.'
GERARD WAY

In Costa Rica, they have an expression. This expression is incorporated in everything, from conversational greetings and farewells to every conceivable manner of branding and advertising associated with the country. The expression is *pura vida*, which means 'pure life' or 'simple life'.

It was first coined in the 1956 Mexican movie *Pura Vida!* – the words used by the protagonist of the film who chooses to remain optimistic, despite a host of unwelcome circumstances that surround him – and by 1970, the term was being used nationwide.

In Costa Rica, *pura vida* really is a way of life: a mindset, an attitude, an emotion. It's applied to how people work, how they interact with one another, how they approach their money and finances, their relationship with time. (Literally everything seems to run late here – punctuality is regarded as strange and even rude in some cases!) It's evident in how they decorate their homes and even how they dress; I didn't see *one* pair of heels or high-end designer label for the entire duration of my five-week trip there in early 2019. Minimal effort and maximum comfort is how they roll, whatever the occasion.

The Costa Rican people (or 'Ticos') don't stress or worry over things the way many of their visitors do, which is why Costa Rica has quite rightfully been deemed one of the world's happiest countries. Personally, I think this may have something to do with the fact that while Catholicism is the official religion of the country, the Church has not exerted a powerful influence politically or socially. Nor does Costa Rica have the temples or overtly spiritual vibes that can be found in places like India, Nepal or Bali. Instead, with its deserted, rugged beaches, luscious jungles and rainforests, as well as the diverse and exotic wildlife that can be found here, it's actually nature itself that the people seem to worship and build their lives around (which makes sense, considering that this tiny country is estimated to host 6 per cent of the world's plant and animal species)!

For Costa Ricans, the majority of their downtime is spent surfing, skydiving, trekking through the mountains, white-water rafting, horse-riding or doing something positive for the environment. I think it's fair to say that their relationship with nature is as (if not more) important as their relationship with anything else. This explains why Costa Rica is one of the most eco-friendly places in the world, with 27 per cent of the country's landmass devoted to national parks and reserves, and sustainability being a huge focus for both the government and its people.

During my time there, the sanctity of nature and the culture of *pura vida*-ism combined seemed to do as much good for my mind, body and spirit as a good yoga retreat (if you overlook my daily sunset piña colada). It also taught me to understand on a whole new level that our attitude to life, and the energy we emanate as a result of it, is the most powerful commodity we own.

If you come from a savagely ambitious place like London as

I do, you may not be aware just how much the busyness and intensity of city life influences the energy you give off, especially in relation to your love life. All too often, I see stressed out city-dwelling women so consumed by the 'GO! GO! GO! ACHIEVE! ACHIEVE! ACHIEVE!' Western mentality that finding a life partner has become yet another item to be ticked off the never-ending To-Do list. I get this. I was one of them.

Turns out that this approach to finding love isn't all that sexy. *Who knew?* So if you're swiping and scrolling all your free time away across half a dozen dating apps (just to hedge your bets) as rabidly as a coked-up Wolf of Wall Street pumping and dumping penny stocks, you're not doing your love life any favours.

What changed the dating game for me entirely was one simple sentence spoken on a Facebook Live by Canadian writer Danielle La Porte, several months before I met Joe. It epitomised everything I've since come to learn about the *pura vida* approach to living your (love) life:

> *The journey has to feel the way you*
> *want the destination to feel.*

YES OR NO?

'Luck is what happens when preparation meets opportunity.'
SENECA

ere's a checklist to help you get an idea of how ready you really are for love:

1. Do you speak to and about yourself with less reverence than you would your best friend?

2. Do you spend more time (negatively) comparing your love life to those of your peers than you do celebrating all the things that *are* working well for you right now?

3. Do you feel like, without a romantic partner, you and your life are incomplete?

4. Do you constantly deflect compliments and praise?

5. Do you play mind games/hard to get with potential partners out of fear that just being yourself would bore (or be too much for) them and make them run a mile?

6. Do you say yes to friends, family and dates when you really mean *hell no*?

7. Do you pretend you're just 'up for a bit of fun' when dating someone new, rather than tell them that you want a committed relationship?

8. Do you invest the same time, energy and finances into

achieving your romantic goals that you do in your other life and career goals?

If you're *actually* ready to attract a life partner, at least five of your answers will have been 'NO'.

9. HOW TO BE AN EXCEPTIONAL DATE

THE SHOW

'Once you are Real you can't be ugly, except
to people who don't understand.'
MARGERY WILLIAMS BIANCO, *THE VELVETEEN RABBIT*

'Just be your authentic self, babe!'
'All we want to see is the real, authentic YOU!'
'Ugh, she's so fucking inauthentic.'

This is the sort of nauseating jargon that gets regularly tossed around the wellness community these days, like a very irritating salad dressing. Every time I hear people spout such words, it grates on me like fingers down a chalkboard, because the insinuation is that authenticity is something you can just switch on and off, willy-nilly.

However, I get the meaning intended, having spent much of my romantic life trying to be the person I believed the guy I fancied wanted me to be, rather than who I actually am. It was exhausting.

Faking it like this is only sustainable for so long. Sooner or later you're going to be found out, and then the relationship will fall apart anyway. But the common advice to just try to 'be your authentic self' in a romantic context (or any context) doesn't help. Because if you're having to try, then you're putting on a show. If you're putting on a show, then you're not being yourself. It's a Catch 22.

Here's what I recommend instead: next time you're on a date, virtual or IRL, instead of 'trying to be yourself', simply take notice of whether or not you *are* being yourself. If you are, great. Continue on with the dynamic and allow it to evolve organically. If you're not, move on. Create space for the real deal, where being authentically you isn't just some naff Instagram caption but a state of being, no effort required.

MEISNER

'The only gift is a portion of thyself.'
RALPH WALDO EMERSON

'You're hating this,' he smirks.

'I'm hating this?' I reply, taken aback by the accuracy of his observation.

'You feel exposed.'

'I feel *exposed*?'

'And vulnerable.'

'*And* vulnerable!'

'But you've never looked more beautiful.'

His words throw me so off guard that I lose all recollection of what we're supposed to be doing, let out a nervous giggle, then look down at the peeling purple varnish on my fingernails. I know we aren't meant to break eye contact, but I'm feeling suffocated by his stare and can't stand the intensity of it a moment longer.

It's 2009. Somewhere around half two in the afternoon in a studio at my drama school in London. I'm sat opposite Tim, a fellow student on my Master's course, as the rest of our classmates observe our dynamic and scribble notes in their journals.

'Yes!' says Giles, our teacher for this session.

He pushes himself away from the ballet barre he's been leaning against and turns to face the rest of the class.

'See how he disarmed her by calling out the truth of what he was perceiving, instead of just focusing on the bullshit façade she

155

was hiding behind to feel in control. That was powerful because his focus was one hundred per cent on *her*, not himself.'

We're in the middle of the 'repetitive exercise', a technique developed by American theatre practitioner Sanford Meisner, which helps an actor learn how to be more truthful in his or her performance by actively listening and paying attention to the observations their stage partner is making about them.

Meisner once said of his pioneering approach to acting: 'To be an interesting actor – hell, to be an interesting human being – you must be authentic, and for you to be authentic, you must embrace who you really are, warts and all. Do you have any idea how liberating it is to not care what people think about you? Well, that's what we're here to do… Act before you think – your instincts are more honest than your thoughts.'

Reminiscing about those Meisner acting classes I took over ten years ago, I realise how they were, unbeknownst to me at the time, the perfect training ground for improving my love life, and then eventually helping other women do the same.

A decade on, the world has changed a lot. As the ever-increasing usage of social apps like Facebook, Instagram and Snapchat goad us into casting ourselves as the stars and celebrities of our own lives, we've arguably grown far less generous in our interactions with others. Especially when it comes to romance.

I'm the first to admit that for much of my dating life I spent too much time talking and not enough listening. Regretfully, I was (and can still be) guilty of *feigning* listening, when in reality I'm just looking for my cue to start talking about myself again. Not my finest trait, and one I see mirrored in our society all too often these days. Is it any wonder that *Time* magazine in the US aptly dubbed millennials the 'me me me generation', or that, according to the National Institute of Health, narcissistic personality disorder is nearly three times as high for people in their twenties as for the generation that's now aged sixty-five or older?

Technology has dominated our romantic experience to such an extent that we think nothing of swiping left and right for a potential life partner as though they were a new pair of shoes, a convenient vehicle for achieving our romantic goals (marriage, mortgage, babies), rather than a human being who, by dint of their birth right, deserves our respect and full attention, not just our likes on social media. We demand and expect these transactional dynamics to somehow make us feel deeply, deliriously happy – and to do it fast. When they inevitably fail to, it's but a brief hop, swipe and a jump before we're back online, scoping out our next prey. The cycle of dating doom continues.

With the romantic landscape being branded, packaged and commodified so meticulously, it's almost impossible to spot the one major flaw in this approach to dating and relationships: real love isn't created through algorithms, but through connection. And, as inspirational speaker Simon Sinek says, *there ain't no app for that.*

So, with all this in mind, here's a radically alternative approach to dating inspired by Sanford Meisner's work: STOP MAKING IT ALL ABOUT YOU. *Your* insecurity about whether or not this person likes you. *Your* anxiety that your garlicy breath will stop them wanting to kiss you. *Your* obsession with where this is (or isn't) going. Instead, pay attention to the other person. Listen to the truth of what they're saying with their words and their energy, and let that inform your reactions, rather than giving a contrived and polished performance of what you *think* they want to see from you. Cast aside any preconceptions of who you assume this person to be based on their digital imprint. Allow the moment, the unedited, unfiltered, imperfect moment, to reveal who they really are. Let that be enough.

SAY WHAT?!

> 'If you do not tell the truth about yourself
> you cannot tell it about other people.'
>
> VIRGINIA WOOLF

'But they'll freak out and run a mile!!' is what pretty much every coaching client I've ever had says when I tell them what I'm about to tell you. But before I spill those proverbial beans, some context...

While technology has made it so much easier for us to 'put ourselves out there' and connect with potential love interests – lots of them – it has also turbocharged our anxiety around romance for this exact same reason. There's just so much *choice* nowadays – not only in terms of people to date and places to date them, but also with regards to how we cross the threshold from casual dating to committed relationship. Do we play it cool and aloof to try to keep them on their toes? Do we date a bunch of other people at the same time so that we don't seem too keen or put all our eggs in one basket? Or do we put all games aside and be unapologetically direct from the outset about what we're really looking for in a partner and relationship?

The most effective way of dealing with this conundrum, in my experience, is to ask yourself a very simple question: what kind of romantic dynamic do you actually *want*? Because, if what you're after is just to 'win' someone's attention, then the first two options may very well do the job. However, if what you truly desire is a healthy, committed, lasting relationship, then my advice is to gravitate more towards option three: being honest about where you're at and what you want from the outset. Even if you don't get as many matches. Even if it gives you an almighty vulnerability hangover. Even if the other person ends up rejecting you for it (they were only going to do that further down the line, anyway).

I know how terrifying that sounds, given that from day dot our culture conditions us to believe that playing it cool and aloof with the people we're dating will somehow result in them falling madly in love with us. The problem with that course of action is that by definition, it requires us to hide who we really are.

I can't tell you the number of women who DM me asking for tricks or tips on how to 'play' a man to get him to stick around. The last thing they want to hear is that the only tip I'm willing to advocate is called 'Say It Like It Is'.

This is hard-earned advice from a woman who wasted far too much time doing the opposite. In the past, whenever a guy I was dating told me he wasn't looking for anything serious, I'd often hide my disappointment and pretend I was just up for 'a bit of fun', too. You can guess how those love stories panned out.

The reason we're all so terrified of being honest with the people we date is that we're afraid we'll be rejected if we do so. But, ironically, it's the lack of honesty that often leads us to being rejected, not the other way around. You can't blame a guy for ghosting or flaking out on you if you weren't honest with them in the first place. Remember: no one ever falls in love with a person through deception and game-playing, or because the object of their affections is so dazzlingly cool and aloof. We might fancy them or become infatuated, but it's certainly not love. And, it's love – *real LOVE* – that I want for you, not just a short-lived imitation.

To be clear, I'm not suggesting you ram your relationship goals down the throat of every person you casually meet for a drink. What I *am* encouraging you to do is share your truth with your date in a calm, mature, non-pressurising way when the conversation organically steers in that direction (and it will at some point – usually around the time you ask each other when your last relationship was). Whatever their response, you can't lose: either they'll want the same things you do, in which case you can keep on dating and see where it leads. Or, if they don't want those things (or aren't ready), you'll have respectfully given both of you the opportunity to step back before you get too emotionally attached, creating space for someone more compatible to show up in your life when the time is right.

RENDEZVOUS

Firstly…
Keep it in the date,
Ground yourself in the present moment –
In the experience of the date itself –
Rather than mentally skipping your way
Down the aisle towards this human
You've barely known two minutes.

Ready yourself for spontaneity:
If the vibe in the restaurant's shit
Suggest a picnic under the stars instead;
Follow your instinct not your logic
Heart over head, always.

Listen before you speak
(It's Not All About You) –
This alone will set you apart
In a world that's long forgotten how often
Empty vessels make the most noise.

When inspiration nudges
Be vulnerable;
Share something with your date that no one else knows,
Giving them permission to do the same,
Not through your words but your example.
(Tell the truth, always.)

Honour the space between the two of you:
Don't rush to fill the silence with futile words

About your cat's haemorrhoid problem or your boss's
latest snipe –
Silence is golden
And those brave enough to surrender to it
Disarmingly sexy.

Always leave them wanting more
(As they say in The Biz);
Not to fool them in to wanting *you*
But because courtship is better for both when savoured,
Not gobbled down in a grasping gulp.

Don't pretend you're busy when you're not,
But don't drop pre-made plans to prioritise this person
Who should not yet be a priority;
Cultivating a vibrant, exciting life for yourself
Aside from romance
Should be your priority.

(As my friend Fleur once told me –
Don't play hard to get, *be* hard to get.)

Allow the entire experience to flow and unfold organically
As a collaborative waltz between two untethered souls,
Rather than trying to mould it
To fit your agenda and timeline.

Rinse and repeat this process
With every potential partner you rendezvous with,
From the first point of contact to the very last
Then somewhere along the way

Love will align for you.

And when it does
Remember to apply this same approach
To your ever-evolving relationship too…

Because that's when it really stops being
All About You.

10. HOW TO GET YOUR SOULMATE

SURRENDER TO THE FESTIVAL

'Life is now, this minute, it's all we have. It's all we need.'
RAYNOR WINN, *THE SALT PATH*

Time to take you back to the start.

In the six weeks leading up to Wilderness Festival in the summer of 2015, my business partner Joanne and I were determined to get the first draft of *The Inner Fix* finished so that we could celebrate this milestone at the festival in style.

By this point, I'd been single for a year and a half. While this might not sound like long, for someone who'd bounced from relationship to relationship (usually overlapping) for as long as she could remember, this was no small feat.

Following my catting for co*k saga at this same festival the previous year, I'd ended my summer fling, and then gone on to have two separate stretches of four months at a time where I wasn't getting so much as a text from a man. I made no attempts to initiate a new love affair, either. Winning the book deal for *The Inner Fix* had made it undeniable how much I needed to put my money where my mouth was in romance and focus all my energy into improving my relationship with myself at a deeper level, so that I wouldn't need to use a man to validate me ever again.

In between those stretches of four months, I'd dated two other guys that I'd really liked. One was The Gentleman, who'd gracefully dumped me when an ex came back into his life. The other was a guy who I mention in the last chapter of *The Inner Fix*, with whom I called it quits when I realised he just wasn't as available for a committed relationship as I was.

While neither of these short romances had worked out the way I'd hoped at the time, they'd provided the perfect opportunities to practise all the new healthy behaviours I'd been learning about via self-help books, therapy and Sex and Love Addicts Anonymous. I'd been clear about my boundaries and spoken up when they were crossed. I'd been honest about what I wanted in a relationship, rather than pretending I was just up for a bit of fun so as not to scare them off. And, most importantly, I'd used these experiences to become more focused and specific about exactly what type of partner and relationship I wanted to attract, instead of just settling for whoever came my way.

By the time the festival rolled around in August, I was in a good place. The best I'd ever been, in fact. And it had nothing to do with a man. The reason I was feeling so good was because in those six weeks that my business partner and I were working on *The Inner Fix*, I was solely focused on living out the message of the book to 'focus on the insides and let the outsides take care of themselves'.

Every day, I'd wake at around 5.30 am and meditate, journal, eat a healthy breakfast and do some yoga, before spending the morning writing. At lunch, I'd take our family dog for a walk in Richmond Park, and would then write all afternoon. Finally, I'd eat a healthy dinner with my family and read or play my guitar in the evening. At the weekends, I'd catch up with friends and make the most of the nice weather, before returning to my routine on the Monday morning.

Those six weeks of dedicated, consistent commitment to loving and nourishing myself (while practising service to others through my work) were transformational for me. It was almost like being on an extended spiritual retreat of sorts. I'd never felt so calm, connected or present in my life. I'd also never felt so ready (like, actually ready) for the great relationship I'd always dreamt of having.

The last chapter I wrote before the festival was on love and relationships. In it, I explained how I'd been seeing a lot of butterflies recently, and how an old friend had told me that butterflies were a sign for the 'Twin Flame' relationship, and perhaps my seeing more of them was a sign that my Twin Flame was near.

While this was welcome information, it was also a warning that I'd need to be extra vigilant at the festival this time around, so that I didn't slip back into any sneaky old habits of scouring the fields, looking for a boy. Although I was open to meeting new people while there, I refused to waste one more second of my life in prioritising a potential hook-up above my sanity. The hedonism of festivals had always been a trigger and excuse for me to act out in the romance department, and I wanted to use this one as an opportunity to think and, more importantly, *behave* in a different way.

To aid me in this goal, I came up with a mantra for myself that would *hopefully* not only stop me catting for co*k, but would also help me be more present throughout the entire festival experience. The mantra was this: *Surrender to the festival, and let her take you wherever she wants to take you.*

I told myself to remember this saying every time I felt the impulse to judge, control or manipulate my festival experience into being anything other than what it was. While I did familiarise myself with what bands, workshops and banquets were on over the weekend, I hoped this mantra would prevent me from getting overly attached to going to any one thing or meeting up with other friends, unless it happened naturally and organically. It was almost like a mini-experiment for how I'd ideally like to live my life beyond the realms of the festival: choosing to believe that everything is playing out exactly as it's meant to.

What I hadn't bargained for was how this simple commitment to being present at the festival would go on to initiate a love story far better than I could have imagined (let alone engineered) myself. Because the moment I realised it was not my job to force love to come or to stay, everything became infinitely easier, infinitely simpler. And in environments of ease and simplicity, magical love stories are woven together, like a tapestry.

TURN AROUND

'Your whole life has been a long road
leading directly to this moment.'
JAMES REDFIELD, *THE CELESTINE PROPHECY*

One of my favourite parts of Wilderness Festival is 'The Valley': a big, messy, after-dark rave in (you guessed it) a valley, which is situated at the far edge of the festival site.

On Friday, 7 August 2015, long after my and my business partner's workshop has finished, I march our little festival crew towards the entrance to The Valley, only to discover an absurdly long queue spiralling up and down on itself a good few hundred metres away from the entrance. While this deters a few of our friends, who take it as their cue to call it a night, my friend Louisa and I decide to stay and ride it out.

Thankfully, the wait is much shorter (and more fun) than anticipated, and before we know it we're dancing under the stars in the middle of the rave, as bejewelled acrobatic mermaids twist and twirl inside huge metallic spheres that are suspended above our heads. The energy is almost otherworldly.

Sometime later, as we make our way closer to the front of the space where the DJ is located, I start to feel The Itch. It creeps up like an unwelcome shadow, goading me to try to catch the eyes of one of the beautiful, glitter-speckled men that are shimmying and swaying on every side of us.

As you'll know all too well if you remember the blistering hell of chicken pox, an itch demands to be scratched. It takes all of my willpower to resist opening Pandora's box, but somehow I manage to and I redirect my attention towards my 'surrender to the festival' mantra instead. I signal to Louisa to stay where we are, then I close my eyes, throw my arms in the air and ground myself into the present moment. As I do so, the music swells to a rousing crescendo and I feel a jolt of electricity coursing through my core that makes me spontaneously throw my head backwards and open my eyes to the star-studded sky above.

What I feel right now I can only describe as euphoria, like the feeling you get half an hour after you've popped an ecstasy pill and are starting to come up. Except I haven't popped a pill; I'm riding high on my own supply (ok, there may have been a *few* glasses of cabernet thrown into the mix this evening, too). The point is that I feel whole. Alive. Like nothing could make this moment any more complete than it already is. Because for once, I'm dancing just for *me*.

This is exactly the feeling I've spent a lifetime chasing via a thousand stolen kisses from boys who were as ill-prepared for the love I silently demanded from them as I was.

It's now, when I've finally released the compulsion to scratch The Itch, when I've finally let go of the struggle and surrendered to the festival, that another, much calmer instruction takes over my consciousness.

Turn around, it says.

JOEY WILDERNESS

'So many factors play a part in you being here today:
a delayed train, an extra cup of tea, the number of
seconds your parents took to cross the street.
This is chaos theory.'

UNKNOWN

turn around.

There before me stands the most gorgeous, green-eyed man I've ever seen in real life. He's wearing a black bowler hat with a couple of coloured pheasant feathers and a Jack of Hearts playing card tucked into one side. A glittery purple paw print adorns his left cheek, and he's holding a long wooden stick wrapped in fairy lights in one hand, and a can of Thatchers cider in the other. He smiles at me and says nothing.

'Who are *you*?' says Louisa, as my eyes lock on to his. We both ignore her and take a step towards one another. He's a full foot taller than me and I have to strain my neck to maintain eye contact. We share what I can only assume is an incredible first kiss. I wish I could remember it.

For the next hour, myself, Louisa and this mystery man frolic around The Valley until we're too hot and tired to dance anymore. At one point, as we're making our way through the revellers, I let go of his hand and consider whether to lose him in the crowd. After all, we haven't shared anything yet except saliva – for all I know he could be a total weirdo. We catch each other's eyes again, and I'm almost certain he's wondering the same about me. But, for some reason, one that we'll spend hours deliberating over in the future, we reach out and recover our grip.

A while later, he offers to walk Louisa and me back to our tent. I make it clear that no funny business will be happening. He laughs and says he wouldn't have made that assumption, anyway.

After Louisa's gone to bed, we spend some time chatting and getting to know one another. He's so kind and friendly, I feel like I've known him for years. He's also incredibly good-looking and a bloody good kisser, leagues ahead of all the late-night hook-ups I've encountered over the years.

When my mouth starts to feel sore from rubbing against his beard stubble, I decide it's time to part ways.

'Best get some beauty sleep,' I say with a wink.

He asks for my number and saves it as 'Persia Gorgeous' in his Nokia 3210 (his 'festival phone' due to its Spartan-like battery life). Then he puts his number into my iPhone, saving it as 'Joey Wilderness'.

With one last kiss, he tells me how excited he is to hang out again tomorrow, before disappearing into the sea of tents in the yonder. Like a mouse into a hole, I squeeze myself through the tiny flaps of the one-man tent I'm sharing with the now sleeping Louisa, and wonder if I'll ever see Joey Wilderness again.

SATURDAY MORNING

Joey Wilderness
11.02, 8 August

Hey Persia, had a really amazing time with you last night. Fancy meeting by the lake later? xx

Persia Gorgeous
11.48, 8 August

Helloooooooo! Yes, def up for a swim. Gonna head in soon for coffee – let me know when ur in xxx

TURN AROUND AGAIN

'The best preparation for the future is
to live as if there were none.'

ALBERT EINSTEIN

While my friends and I are queuing for the Portaloos in the blistering afternoon heat, I check my phone for a third time in as many hours. Still no reply from Joey Wilderness.

I feel the familiar onset of disappointment start to slink its way up on me as we make our way back to the main stage. *It seems my festival fling has flung itself out a lot faster than I'd hoped*, I think to myself, as I subtly look around for him among the swarm of gyrating bodies that surround us.

The finality of this thought swiftly jolts me back towards the promise I've made myself not to let this festival experience be hijacked by my man obsession, as it was last year. I refuse to fall back into the trap of believing that the fun and good times are to be found anywhere other than exactly where I am at this moment, with whomever I happen to be with.

Surrender to the festival, and let her take you wherever she wants to take you, I remind myself. If that's back into the arms of Joey Wilderness, then great. If not, then maybe Friday night was all I was ever meant to share with him. That's fine, too. It's still a memory I know I'll cherish going forwards, because it represents such a shift away from my usual interaction with men, having come about without any manipulation on my part.

With renewed conviction, I recommit to having all the fun I can muster with the friends I'm here with. While there is still the odd occasion where the impulse to scan the crowd for Joey Wilderness resurfaces, I quickly pull my attention away from the fantasy and back to reality, where it belongs.

That evening, my friends and I are watching a bizarre musical spectacle on the main stage, when halfway through the group of them decide to venture off super-early to The Valley so as to avoid the long queue. Not wanting to miss the end of the spectacle, and not feeling ready for the intensity of The Valley so early into the evening, I decide to stay behind with some old friends I've bumped into and meet up with my group later.

When the show is over, the group of us wander into the Peacock Bar tent to grab a drink. The last thing on my mind right now is Joey Wilderness. I'm midway through a conversation with a guy I briefly dated while in sixth form, who is dressed as one of the 118-118 brothers – wearing marathon running gear, a black frizzy wig and handlebar moustache – when last night's instruction emerges at the forefront of my mind, as out of the blue as it had been then.

Turn around, it says again.

KISMET

'There's nowhere you can be that isn't
where you're meant to be.'
JOHN LENNON

My grandma Banna (so called because when we were little, our cousin Leanne couldn't say grandma), was nine years old when she and her family returned to their home in Kingston upon Thames to find all their windows smashed and the pink curtains in the living room shredded.

It was during the Second World War, and the Germans had dropped a bomb on nearby Kingston hospital, where I was born decades later. Quite a few people were killed. Meanwhile, her father, a soldier, had been captured as a prisoner of war while fighting in Europe. Somehow, he managed to escape to Italy where he was kept hidden by a family who took pity on him. He was eventually reunited with his family in England, and never spoke of what had happened to him during the war again.

At a similar time, Joe's maternal grandfather, William, had been serving in the war effort in France. William's troop were responsible for placing dynamite on bridges to stop the Germans from advancing any further. One day, while they were on a train to their next destination, two German bomber planes flew overhead. The commanding officer of the troop ordered all his men to stay aboard, certain that the bombers were en route to London.

Being an engineer, William knew that the train was filled with explosives and ammunition. While disobeying a commanding officer was never a wise idea, neither was staying on a literal ticking time bomb. Along with five of his friends, William followed his instincts and jumped off the train. They ran as fast and as far away from it as they could. When they eventually turned back around, they saw the two German bomber planes circle back around and drop several bombs directly on to the train. Everyone on board was killed.

A couple of years later, William met and married Joe's grandmother, Eileen. With him being an engineer and her a communications major, prior to their meeting they had both volunteered for secret missions. Eileen had been due to go to Malta and William to Arnhem in the Netherlands. However, being newlyweds, they both decided not to go. They later learnt that all of William's troop had been killed at Arnhem. Once again, luck was on William's side.

This luck seemed to extend to Joe's grandparents on his paternal side, too. His great-grandfather, Alfred, had joined the army in 1912 as part of the Gordon Highlander Royal. Alfred was one of the first soldiers to be sent out to France right at the very start of the First World War. Thirteen days after setting sail from Southampton port in August of 1914, he took a bullet to the chest during the Battle at Le Cateau.

Alfred lay wounded in no man's land for three whole days, before being picked up by German troops, who took him to a nearby German field hospital. Here, he was treated by a Swiss nurse called Lena Tenude. Alfred and Lena fell in love and were married on 31 August, 1917. A year later Joe's grandfather, also named Alfred, was born.

That single bullet – the reason Alfred met his wife Lena and therefore the reason Joe's grandfather, father and Joe himself are alive today – was lodged so close to Alfred's heart that it could never be removed. If ever there was a symbol of how love stories and lineages are so often born out of seemingly unrelated or inconsequential moments, that bullet has to be it. It reminds me of Steve Jobs' 2005 Stanford commencement address, when he said: 'You can't connect the dots looking forward; you can only connect them looking backward. So you have to trust that the dots will somehow connect in your future.'

When I met Joe, I had no idea how many dots had had to connect in order for us to be stood in the same spot, at the same time, amidst thousands of other people. *Twice*. These dots did not just span the few days prior to us meeting, they spanned decades – centuries, even.

This is the case with all love stories. Yours included. You may not have met your soulmate yet, but your love story together is already being written. And one day, the two of you will be able to connect the dots of it, as Joe and I have.

JURASSIC PARK

'Call it coincidence, luck, fate, destiny, randomness.
Some would call it the hand of God. I wasn't sure
what to call it. What I did know is that this was a huge,
blinking neon sign I couldn't ignore or dismiss.'

DANI SHAPIRO, *DEVOTION*

turn around again.

There, striding out of the Peacock Bar tent, stick in hand and glittery purple paw print still visible on his left cheek, is Joey Wilderness.

Without a second thought, I bound over to him as though he's a long-lost friend. As soon as he sees me, his face lights up like a dog whose owner has just returned from three weeks abroad.

'Why didn't you reply to my text?' I ask him, not even attempting to water down our reunion with feigned aloofness.

'What?' he responds, whipping out his Nokia 3210 and showing me the text messages. 'You never replied to my message this morning about meeting up by the lake!'

Evidently, our most recent messages didn't make it past the shitty signal here. And yet the festival had found a way to bring us back together, regardless.

The rest of the evening is hands down the best night I've ever had with a man. Joey Wilderness and I venture around the festival like naughty schoolchildren, allowing it to carry us from one tent and experience to the next.

Eventually, at about three in the morning, we sit down by a campfire alongside all manner of weird and wonderful creatures, including a topless, middle-aged woman dressed as an elf, intermittently reciting passages from Tolkien and showing us her pouch of five hundred Valium that she's selling, 'Three for a tenner'.

As we snuggle into each other for warmth (and protection from the benzoed-up elf), we discover that we have a fair amount in common. Like me, Joey Wilderness also has a past mottled with messy self-destructive tendencies. He tells me he was at this same festival last year, too, but not in the best place in himself (perhaps that's why our paths didn't cross until now). Recently, he's embarked upon his own spiritual quest, which is to take him to Bali in a fortnight for a few months of adventure and soul-searching.

While he's asking me about the book I'm writing, he notices my dinosaur necklace hanging over the top of my jumper. I tell him that my friend and business partner, also nicknamed Joey, bought it for me for my most recent birthday.

'*Jurassic Park* is my favourite film, you know,' he says, twirling the necklace through his fingers. 'I actually wrote my dissertation at music college on the theme tune.'

I sit bolt upright and turn to face him.

'*Jurassic Park* is literally my favourite film! OF. ALL. TIME! I've always said that when I get married, I'm going to walk down the aisle to the theme tune.' Now, there's a sentence that'll determine how into you a guy *really* is.

The following evening, Joey Wilderness and I are wandering around the festival with Louisa and a few of his friends when we see a huge swarm of people gathered in front of one of the main stages. An entire orchestra fills the space, playing songs from well-known films as scenes and montages from those films are projected onto a huge screen behind the musicians.

Even before they announce the final song, I already know what it's going to be. While those first few familiar notes begin to play and the screen shows Sam Neill looking up at the Brachiosaurus for the first time in one of the most iconic moments of cinematic history, my happy little heart does a somersault, as Joey Wilderness pulls me so close that I can hear the thumping beat of his.

THE HOKEY-COKEY

'Sex is an emotion in motion.'
MAE WEST

Sexual health used to be about as important to me as dental health, which is to say, not very.

Despite my secondary school's attempts to impress upon my peers and me the vital importance of wearing a condom during intercourse, asking your lover to bag up in a moment of passion just wasn't the done thing. For, as any lusty teenager battling through the assault course that is puberty will tell you, having street cred always trumps being responsible.

Which is why it became a kind of rite of passage to be sat in The Magic Roundabout, our local sexual health clinic in Kingston upon Thames, at 4 pm on a Monday afternoon with a handful of other possibly knocked-up girls from the surrounding schools, all of us waiting to be doled out a morning-after pill and token scolding from the nurse on duty.

However, while we all did our best to present ourselves as being scared, embarrassed and full of remorse (as was expected of us), internally we were high-fiving ourselves and the friend we'd brought along for moral support; for we all knew what our presence in this waiting room *really* meant: we were now the top of the social food chain, because we were having SEX. And this simple fact was respected by all of us way more than our actual bodies seemed to be.

Unfortunately, this lackadaisical approach to bonking did not mature as I did. In fact, in my early twenties, I was even more careless in my sexcapades than I was as a teenager, which is really saying something. I behaved as though I believed a young woman had only two options when it came to her sexuality: she could either be the Madonna and earn a man's respect, or she could be a whore and command his desire. Out of the two, I'd choose the latter every time, being that it was faster and easier. And I was all about those fast and easy wins back then. Anyway, where was the upside to delaying gratification? I couldn't see one! It never occurred to me (or Freud, apparently) that respecting oneself can be the most powerful aphrodisiac of all, for both parties.

Living solo in central London, I was partying to the extent of blackout at least three times a week, which was often coupled with a one-night stand that I was usually too anaesthetised to even regret. It had felt like my body was constantly on rent to men who couldn't care less that every bone in me ached with loneliness. I never felt more alone than when I woke up next to a man I knew had zero capacity to love me, nor I him.

It became obvious something had to give when one such casual liaison ended up leading to a death threat. The week after one of my many trips to visit my Russian boyfriend in Moscow post-drama school, I received the following text from him: *There is red points on my penis. Explain him.*

If there is one piece of advice I really *can* give a woman, it is this: in your life, if at all possible, try your very best *not* to give the son of a Russian KGB general chlamydia. It doesn't tend to go down well.

I ignored what must have been at least thirty missed calls from him and a deluge of messages informing me: '*U R SLUT*'. And: 'MY DADDY WILL HAVE U KILLED'.

He was right, I *was* slut – and his daddy probably *could* have me killed, should he be so inclined.

In all seriousness, The Russian's messages were the kick up the backside I needed to make a long overdue appointment at the STD clinic. Here, I learnt that I did, indeed, have the clap. No big surprise, really; a city like London is riddled with it. And given that I was chucking myself in and out of bachelors' beds like I was the left foot in the hokey-cokey, it's a wonder I hadn't been riddled with it too years earlier.

When the nurse asked me if I wanted the clinic to contact the men I'd slept with recently and let them know they needed to get checked out quick-sharp, I told her this wouldn't be necessary as I must've got it from my boyfriend, since he was the only person I'd slept with since my last check-up. I was *that* ashamed of my sexual promiscuity that I palmed off the responsibility for it on to its primary victim. (Plus, I couldn't remember who I *had* slept with, and even if I had done, I was terrified the nurse would judge me for it. For me, that was a fate worse than the clap itself.)

This appalling episode was capped off by me successfully getting The Russian to forgive me, having explained that I'd only cheated on him the one time – because *I'd missed him so much*. Poor guy.

When I started reining in my promiscuity, I created a nifty little sex deterrent for myself whereby I wouldn't tidy my nether regions before a date, the idea being that this would prevent me from putting out prematurely. Sometimes, it worked. Other times, one gin and tonic too many would see me excusing myself to the bathroom of whichever gentleman I'd ended up going home with, frantically searching for a razor (his or an ex-girlfriend's would do). A mad minute of vaginal topiary later, and we'd be between the sheets before you could say 'shaving rash'.

A lifetime later, I met Joe. While our chemistry and attraction to one another was palpable from the moment of meeting, the years of work I'd done to heal from all the sexual abuse I'd caused myself had given me something I'd never had before at the start of a new romance: boundaries.

From my years working as a love coach, I've seen a pattern emerge whereby women tend to take action in the areas of romance better suited to being driven by the man (e.g. wooing, setting up dates etc.) and stay passive in the areas where it would serve them well to speak up: setting and communicating boundaries, right from the get-go. Especially with regards to sex.

When our kisses several days into meeting became so electric that I panicked I was about to let rip in lusty excitement (a very real issue for me when the sexy love butterflies take hold at the start of a new courtship – as is accidentally waking me and my new guy up with a fart), I knew it was time to let Joe in on the standard I now had for myself when it came to sex with someone new.

'I'm really attracted to you, Joe, but I don't do casual sex. It just doesn't feel good to me,' is what came out.

He looked both confused and panicked, probably thinking I was about to reject him.

'OK, I understand, I think,' he replied. 'So, what does…?'

I could see he had not a clue how to finish that sentence, because he'd never had a girl say to him what I just had.

'It's like this,' I said. 'In order for me to enjoy having sex with someone, I need to know that while we're sleeping together, they're not sleeping with anyone else. Vice versa, too, of course.'

'Why would I want to sleep with anyone else?' he said, as he leaned into kiss me.

Later into the evening, we got chatting about our past relationships and where we were at now, romantically speaking. I told him how much I valued transparency when it comes to dating.

'It makes everything a hell of a lot less complicated,' I explained.

I told him that he should probably know that while I wasn't currently sleeping with anyone else, I was still open to dating other guys and wasn't willing to commit to one person unless we were both on the same page about wanting a serious, long-term relationship – one that would hopefully lead to marriage, maybe kids, one day (the technical term for this is 'rotational dating').

I finished off by saying something along the lines of: 'Obviously, I've just met you so have no idea whether we're even compatible. I just wanted to give you a heads-up about where I'm at, so I don't waste either of our time.'

I said all of this as breezily as if I were telling him what I'd like to have for breakfast tomorrow morning.

Having tried to put similar boundaries down with the last guy I'd dated (and made a total dog's dinner out of it, given that it was the first time I'd ever put a boundary down prior to sex; 'the first pancake is always shit', as the saying goes), I was genuinely detached from Joe's reaction. If my truth scared him off now, he'd have only ended up ghosting me later on anyway – when sex would have already bonded me to him, and the sting of rejection would be that much more acute. I was more committed to respecting my body, my time and my desire for a healthy, committed relationship than I was to presenting myself as the aloof girl who's 'just up for a bit of fun'. I'd exhausted that role, played it every way it could possibly be played, and it only ever left me feeling hurt and disappointed.

Because I'd been so direct about my boundaries before Joe and I made the beast with two backs, he was under no illusion that bonking and bouncing was acceptable behaviour. Not only was he clear about what sex between us would mean for me, my honesty from the outset made him actually *respect* me. He just seemed so relieved that I had abolished any need for game-playing between us, and rather than this diminishing his attraction to me, it heightened it.

If you're going to allow a man to quite literally join his body with yours, an act so powerful it creates actual *human life*, having his respect should be a bottom-line necessity, not a 'nice-to-have'.

It's fascinating, the reaction I get when I share this story with the women I coach. Mostly, they tell me they're afraid that if they were to be that direct, they'd scare the guy off or come across as super needy – or they think it's unsexy. (Isn't it crazy that we live in a world where lying about our romantic desires is considered a more effective way to go about making them a reality than just *owning* those desires?)

There is nothing sexier than a person who knows who they are and what they want. The catch is that it takes time to grow yourself into a woman who can own who she is and what she wants, unapologetically. I'm writing these words now so that it doesn't have to take you the four and a half years it took me to get there.

SLIDING DOORS

'Life, uh, finds a way.'
IAN MALCOLM, *JURASSIC PARK*

Over the next two weeks, Joey Wilderness and I spend more time getting to know one another, seeing as he's about to head off to Bali for six weeks. We both just want to be sure that the synchronicity around our meeting at the festival is as significant as we hope it is. We don't have to wait long for an answer.

A week to the day after we first met in The Valley, we go out to dinner in East London. As we get in the lift to leave the restaurant, the doors are sliding shut when a man puts his arm out to stop them, and jumps inside.

Joey Wilderness nudges me and gestures towards the man with his eyes. I look up at this man's face. It's Sam Neill; the lead actor from *Jurassic Park*.

PART THREE:

COMMIT

'It is a terrifying thing when love finally works.'

JH HARD

Swimming with sharks never made it onto my bucket list. Not even lightly pencilled in. Given that I've had a fear of open water, confined spaces and man-eating fish ever since I can remember, the idea of my voluntarily getting into a metal cage in the middle of the ocean as hungry great white sharks circle around it seemed about as likely a scenario as my winning a Nobel prize. However, in January 2018, several years into my relationship with Joey Wilderness, that's exactly the scenario I found myself in (swimming with sharks, not the Nobel prize).

The two of us were halfway through a once-in-a-lifetime trip around the world when the opportunity presented itself. Not only did it present itself, it did so at zero cost to us because Joe happens to be related to the head honcho of the Rodney Fox Shark Expedition boat we were to be sailing on. Considering that a two-day trip like this usually costs around £2000, this left me in a real conundrum.

You see, while I've always been terrified of the undisputed rulers of the sea (to the point where I wouldn't swim in the deep end of the swimming pool as a kid, because I thought Jaws might get me), I've also been peculiarly fascinated by them – for the same reason that T-Rex and raptors have always intrigued me: because dangerous things are exciting things. Perhaps this explains my former pattern of dating addicts, drug dealers and narcissists.

I've watched most shark films out there (except, thankfully, the one where Mandy Moore gets in a steel cage in the open water, only for it to plummet to the bottom of the ocean when the cord connecting it to the boat gets severed). But despite my penchant for virtual shark viewing, not one part of me had ever felt inclined to float in their turf myself, steel cage or no steel cage. I was perfectly content respecting and admiring these colossal beasts from afar, so long as there was a computer or TV screen separating their reality from my own.

My apprehension stood in stark contrast to Joe, who, as an advanced diver, was overjoyed that he'd be privy to an even more intense rendezvous with the sharks than myself. The Rodney Fox Shark Expedition boat is the only one in the world that offers ocean-floor cage dives, in which the punters and a dive professional descend twenty metres below the surface, all the way to the seabed itself (unlike Mandy Moore's cage in *47 Meters Down*, though, this one is firmly attached to the boat above by three separate cords). As the group of divers are lowered down, the bucket of foul-smelling tuna gills inside of the cage acts as a bait to lure the hungry sharks towards them, giving the divers front row seats to an experience you literally could not pay me a billion pounds to endure myself.

Like most things I dread having to do (hello, tax returns), I put off thinking about the cage dive until the eleventh hour, i.e. the day of the dive itself. To buy myself some time (I'm not sure what for), I feigned graciousness and stepped aside so that a family of six could do the surface cage dive before me. Meanwhile, I observed two members of the crew baiting the sharks with the dead tuna from the safety of the stern, while another informed me that Rodney Fox developed these shark cages after surviving a near fatal shark attack in 1963. Nutter.

Unexpectedly, as the vast grey silhouettes began circling the cage, my curiosity was piqued. Now that they were within spitting distance, I somehow felt less afraid of the sharks than when we were separated by a screen. I made my way to the deck above, squeezed myself into my scuba gear like reverse human toothpaste, and headed back down towards the cage.

Sus, Joe's cousin and the second-in-command of the boat after the skipper, had kindly agreed to do the dive with me. Clearly, she could tell I was bricking it. She spent some time showing me how to breathe through the regulator, since I'd never used one before (talk about throwing myself in the deep end!) and then led me to the surface-level platform that the cage was attached to, leaving me exposed to the open water on both my right and left-hand sides.

This was the moment I'd expected myself to freak out and bail on the whole thing, given that the night before I'd had nightmares of a shark breaching out of the ocean and grabbing me in one fell swoop while I was preparing to get into the cage. But freak and bail I did not, miraculously. Often the monsters we imagine in our head are so much more frightening than any we encounter in reality, great white sharks included.

Once on the platform, Sus placed the weighted-belt around me to stop me from floating up to the surface once inside the cage. When we were both in, she asked me to dip my face into the water and practise breathing through the regulator.

'Yup, fine,' I said, taking it back out.

'Sure?' said Sus.

I nodded my head as I placed the salty regulator back into my mouth, eager to get this whole ordeal over with as quickly as possible.

Sus slowly lowered her shoulders and head into the water, signalling with her hand for me to follow her, which I did promptly.

Then, within seconds of my head going under, I panicked.

A word of advice: if you happen to be claustrophobic, acutely afraid of both the sea and sharks, don't let the first time you try scuba diving be simultaneous with the first time you get into a cage in the middle of the ocean, surrounded by great whites. It's a lot to take on board all at once.

I shot out of the water and tried to heave myself out of the cage like a terrified seal escaping a, well, *shark*.

'Ahhh!' I gasped weakly after spitting out the regulator. 'I can't!'

Sus came back to the surface a moment later, as the dreaded symptoms of a panic attack began to take a hold of me.

'Don't worry, Pers, let's get you out; you don't have to do it,' she shouted over the top of my whimpering gasps for air.

A wave of relief washed over me as I considered retreating back to the sanctuary of the boat.

But then something unexpected happened.

Being given permission to get out of the water flicked some kind of switch inside me, and suddenly everything felt different.

I'd had this experience many times before. It always seemed to happen the moment after I'd decided to bail on my relationship with Joe as a result of feeling overwhelmingly scared, vulnerable or trapped; the moment after I'd told myself, 'Right, that's it, *love is just too hard*. Get Out Now.'

On these occasions, the flicking of the switch would jolt me backwards, like an elastic band being pulled taut. It was always accompanied by a single, simple command: *Stay*.

A beat, then: *There's more for you here, so stay.*

These words were not a suggestion; they were an order. And

ignoring them, I instinctively knew, would have more wretched consequences than conceding to them.

But staying when I wanted to leave was not a familiar course of action for me. I'd always been a runner, an unanchored, fair-weather floater, who'd spent most of her life drifting, sometimes bouncing, from one hopeless romance to the next. I'd never stayed in any one story long enough to know what real love felt like. Once the initial infatuation had burnt itself out, I mentally and emotionally abandoned ship, even if I still appeared to be there in person.

However, by the time I met Joe, having worked through the root cause of my love avoidance (my childhood, like it is for most of us), I was finally ready to board a new vessel. The skipper guiding this boat did so in an entirely different manner to the last one – an impulsive, fickle bellower, who steered us into rocks and icebergs on pretty much every voyage, leaving our home in tatters and making me overwrought with anxiety and self-doubt at every turn.

This new skipper, though, I trusted her. She was direct but kind, firm but flexible, and, most importantly, she did not rush or hurry our expedition; she insisted that we take our time and savour it. I'd never allowed myself to savour anything before, especially when it came to love. Every encounter had been frantically gulped down so that I wouldn't have to feel the terrifying vulnerability of being still.

Which brings us back to the terrifying vulnerability of being semi-submerged in a steel cage in the middle of the ocean, surrounded by the world's most feared predator. Because those two experiences felt remarkably similar to me. In both cases, where there had been an uncontrollable urge to Get Out Now, there was suddenly a stronger impulse to remain.

As Sus went to help lift me up out of the cage, I shook my head and stopped her.

'No,' I whispered, as I prepared to put the regulator back in my mouth. 'One more go.'

'Sure?' said Sus again, looking understandably sceptical.

I nodded.

It was as though all the yoga, meditation, breath work, journaling and Twelve Step meetings (as well as dozens of other tools I'd picked up over the years to keep me sane and growing) had been preparing me for this one specific moment. In isolation, the effectiveness of these tools had been significant. Right now, they seemed to have accumulated together to transport me from being mortally terrified to uncharacteristically calm in the blink of an eye. This, I suppose, is why implementing such tools is often referred to as having 'a practice'. The daily repetition of them prepares us for the unaccredited exams of life: for situations such as this one that put you face to face with your own mortality; that cause you to experience, at a primal level, what it is to be alive.

Clamping my mouth around the regulator, I closed my eyes, took three deep breaths, then slowly lowered myself back into the cage. Sus helped me climb down the ladder to the bottom of the steel structure and led me around to the front for the best view, as though she were an usher at a theatre showing me to my seat in the stalls.

The wind had picked up by this point, making the cage clunk around so heavily in the water that we had to hold on tightly to the metal bars to keep ourselves from being jolted back up to the surface. It felt as though we were inside a gigantic washing machine on a spin cycle.

As I tried to maintain steady, focused breathing, I scanned the surrounding area to see if we were being watched. The coast was frustratingly clear.

After what felt like an eternity (but was probably less than a minute), Sus pointed towards the bottom right-hand side of the cage. Five metres or so below us swam a great white shark, seemingly oblivious to our presence. It was far enough away for me not to freak out, but not quite close enough to feel like I'd had the full underwater shark experience I'd been compelled to get back in the water for. However, as I glanced back towards the front of the cage, I saw an immense shape barrelling towards us from only a few metres away. Several rows of razor-sharp teeth were exposed, which made it look like the shark was smiling at us. Without even realising what I was doing, I instinctively pushed Sus in front of my trembling body. I may have got back in the water, but I was still no Crocodile Dundee.

Unable to stifle my curiosity, I peeked over Sus's right shoulder just as the shark took a hard left and glided past the corner of the cage. It was so close that if I'd been foolish enough to extend my arm out, I could have stroked its back.

It was hands down one of the most extraordinary moments of my life. Where I'd expected to feel terror, what I actually felt was more like connection: not with the shark; with myself.

As soon as the great white had disappeared back into the shadows, I signalled to Sus for us to go back up. We couldn't have been down there for more than five minutes – nearly half an hour less than the family who were in the cage before me. I didn't care. There was no point trying to match other people's experiences, because we'd all been brought to this divine appointment for different reasons. I already understood what I'd got back in the water for, and it wasn't the sharks. I'd got back into the water because, in that moment, I knew there was more for me to gain by staying, than by running.

11. HOW TO MAKE SPACE FOR LOVE

BAD HAND

'A wonderful gift may not be wrapped as you expect.'
JONATHAN LOCKWOOD HUIE

Not all love stories start out as perfectly as they appear to. Especially not ours.

An hour or so before Joe and I first met, something happened to me that could very well have stopped our romance before it even started. To be honest, I'm surprised it didn't.

Having spent our first half an hour in The Valley dancing like it was 1999, Louisa and I were busting for a wee. We couldn't spot any Portaloos, so we made our way up the far bank and found a tree that was reasonably hidden from all the ravers and couples getting jiggy. Relieved, I stood against the tree, pulled down my pants, and got straight to business. Alas, it was more business than I was expecting.

All the red wine we'd been drinking had obviously played havoc with my gut, because the consistency of the number two was almost indistinguishable from the number one, which is why a gentle push was all it took to release the floodgates to my arse.

This was a real problem, given that I'd forgotten to pack both toilet roll *and* hand sanitiser. Schoolboy error.

'FUCK, I think I just pooed!' I stage-whispered to the squatting Louisa, who was midway through the Alabama shake against the tree opposite mine.

'SHUT. UP!' Louisa replied, before erupting into laughter.

Then, out the corner of my eye, I saw some toilet roll on the ground a few feet away. Instinctively, I picked it up. Almost immediately, I realised it was already covered in shit. Someone else's shit. Gagging, I threw it back on the ground, but it was too late; I now had a shitty arse *and* a shitty hand to deal with.

'Louisa,' I gasped as she was doing up her jeans, 'get some foliage! QUICK!'

With that, Louisa (still laughing) scurried into a nearby bush and returned a few moments later with two hands full of dry bracken and leaves. It would have to do.

I did my best with the tools available, but the stench of poo on my right hand was going to require a lot more than a leaf.

'Let's get some hand sanny from the bar?' Louisa suggested, before placing her palm over her nose and stifling a wretch. I offered her my good hand and let her lead me back into the crowd.

As we joined the queue for the bar, I heard someone call my name. I turned around to see a group of my sixth-form boyfriend Andy's mates waving at me from further along in the queue. Forgetting about my shitty hand, I waved back.

'Persia, put your hand down! It *stinks!*' said Louisa, pulling down my arm.

After what felt like yet another hour of queueing, we finally reached the bar.

'Could we have some hand sanitiser and two gin and tonics please?' said Louisa to the barman.

'We're not allowed to give out hand sanitiser,' he replied as he started to pour our drinks. (This would never happen post-2020.)

'PLEASE!' Louisa leaned in and whispered to him as she pulled up my arm and pointed towards the offending hand. 'Her hand is covered in *human* faeces – have a heart!'

I don't know whether it's because he felt sorry for me, or because he could smell that Louisa was telling the truth, but, after handing us our drinks, he gestured for us to meet him around the back, where he squirted a huge dollop of industrial-sized hand sanitiser into my cupped palms.

'Hope that helps,' he said with a smirk, before returning to the bar.

I rubbed my hands together rigorously, lifted them to my nostrils and took a whiff.

'I can't tell,' I said.

'I can,' said Louisa, grimacing. 'Still smells of shit. Drink this and let's just go and dance and forget about it.'

With that, she handed me my gin and tonic and led me through the crowd towards the stage.

A short time later, I met Joe and forgot all about my shitty hand. He didn't seem to notice it, either – maybe because the smell had faded by then, or maybe because his attraction to me was more powerful than the smell, I don't know. What I *do* know is that when I share the story of how we first met, I tend to leave out the poo-tastrophe part. It kind of ruins the romance. (Also, I was saving it for the right time – like this book, or our wedding day).

Having coached many women through the early stages of a new courtship, I can confirm that *no* love story plays out as perfectly as Instagram would have you believe, particularly at the beginning. His shoes will turn your stomach. You'll make a twat of yourself when you first meet his friends. He won't say 'I love you' in the exact way you pictured him to. Your hopes and expectations will *not* be met in a myriad of different ways, because no love story is without its fair share of flaws and obstacles (not even in Disney). But if there is love… does it matter?

FOUR SEASONS

'There are snakes that go months without eating,
and then when they catch something, are so
hungry that they suffocate when eating it.'
DON DRAPER, *MAD MEN*

I t's three days since I met Joe at Wilderness, and I'm sat eating
spag bol with Joe, his Aunty Louise and Uncle Nigel at their
twelfth-century farmhouse a few miles down the road from the
festival.

I appreciate this is fast moving for a new love story, even for
me. However, having not washed for four days – on top of getting
soaked through in a torrential downpour as we were packing up
our tents earlier – there was no way I was going to turn down
Joe's offer of a hot shower and meal within half an hour. (The real
reason, of course, is that we're already smitten and aren't ready
to part ways just yet, especially considering we haven't left each
other's side in the last thirty-six hours. And, NO, in case you're
wondering… we haven't done anything but kiss at this point.)

The Johnson family home is a veritable snuggle-fest, if ever
I saw one, and the ideal place to clean up and dry out after a
soggy festival. The last few days have been filled with so many
unexpected delights, I feel like the universe is winking at me.

Here, she seems to be saying, *have some more magic.*

The magic continues when, moments after arriving at the

Johnsons', Joe's cousin, Tom, asks us if we fancy watching the new *Jurassic World* film. Given the synchronicity of the orchestra playing the *Jurassic Park* theme tune at the festival last night, I take this as a sign that Joey Wilderness and I have been gifted a few more hours together, and I'm not one to look a gift horse in the mouth.

After a much-needed shower, Joe takes me to the pub around the corner from the Johnsons' for a welcome feed and cheeky G & T (seeing as this pub is home to around three hundred different types of gin, it would be rude not to).

With bellies full and hearts even more so, we return to the house, watch *Jurassic World* with Tom (who, I discover, had persuaded Joe to come to Wilderness at the very last minute, so is largely responsible for us meeting), and pass out for a good few hours on what feels like the world's comfiest sofa. After three incredible but exhausting days adventuring through a festival, this is bliss.

By the time we wake up, Joe's aunt and uncle have returned from work. Surprisingly, they don't seem the least bit put out to find that their wayward nephew has brought home some random festival girl, whose face is still covered in flecks of glitter and hair has bits of grass and straw matted into it. (I later discover that the Johnsons are used to having visitors show up to their door unannounced.)

I assume their arrival is our cue to leave. However, excited for me to get to know some of his family, Joe offers to make us all dinner, and Tom asks his parents if it's cool for us to spend the night in the spare room.

'Sure,' says Aunty Louise with a smile, as though she's just been asked whether she fancies a cuppa. 'There are fresh towels in the cupboard on the landing.'

I've always prided myself on hitting it off with the parents of a new boyfriend, but this has to be some kind of record. It feels like we're three months into a new relationship, when it's actually just three days into a courtship.

Considering my past habit for falling hard and fast into a love story that I had no business being in, on the drive back to London the next day I voice my concern to Joe that perhaps we should slow down.

He nods his head as he takes in my words, his eyes remaining fixed on the road.

'I hear what you're saying,' he says, 'but bear in mind that I *am* going to Bali for six weeks in ten days' time.'

He has a point, and I guess we're just trying to figure out what this thing is between us before he leaves. Either way, the next day, while sitting at my desk and procrastinating over editing *The Inner Fix*, I decide to hit up Google (for better, or worse) to see if it has any helpful insights around this dilemma.

I come across an article on the lifestyle site Elite Daily, in which the writer, Scott Spinelli, explains that when we rush into a relationship, we miss out on the crucial things that make our new partner who they are – things that aren't going to be listed on their online dating profile, things that take time to reveal themselves, and, most importantly, things that may make us question whether or not we're a good match for one another in the long term.

'People say you don't truly know your significant other until you've lived with them,' he explains. 'I think I've come across a quicker – and more all-encompassing – method to help you understand your boyfriend or girlfriend: date them for a full year and experience all four seasons with them.'

What he's basically saying is *take your time* when it comes to making any big decisions in a new relationship, e.g. moving in together, getting engaged, having a kid, etc. I believe it's crucial to have this same attitude when considering whether or not to commit to a new relationship in the first place, because who we choose to give our heart to (and, it *is* a choice, remember) will impact our experience of life more than any other decision we are bound to make. Which is why I'm all for embracing the courting rituals of ye olde days.

According to the *Oxford Dictionary*, courtship is described as 'a period during which a couple develop a romantic relationship before getting married'. Historically, with regards to a formal engagement, it was understood that it was the role of the man to actively 'woo' or 'court' the woman, therefore helping her to understand him and determine her receptivity to a marriage proposal.

Nature displays various modes of courting, too. However, it's typically initiated by the male making a remarkable presentation to the female, sometimes through distinct sounds, sometimes through aggressive behaviour, and sometimes through dance. The female then decides which suitor takes her fancy. Quite right. Some social scientists believe that this is not all that different to human courtship, which is arguably more controlled by the female of the pair (in that she decides whether or not sex is on the table, so to speak), while the male battles for her favour and attention through various modes of solicitous behaviour.

What makes traditional courtship seem worlds away from modern dating is that it's a process that requires time, patience and effort. And for all its benefits, the one thing the technology of today has undoubtedly eroded is our ability to be patient, causing us to forget (or never even learn) that the best things in life often require space in order to flourish.

While I'm not against couples getting speedily engaged, hitched or shacking up together if that's genuinely what works for them, I do think it's worth questioning this insatiable need of (many of) ours to bulldoze our way through these romantic rites of passage. Social media and online dating have clearly shortened the amount of time we bestow on the process of getting to know potential partners. Sure, there may be the *illusion* of a courtship by going on a handful of dates (before jumping into bed together). But this is not the same as developing a deep and nuanced connection and appreciation of one another. That only comes with time.

In my own life, I can see how I've rushed through the early stages of a new romance out of fear I'd somehow 'lose' my paramour unless this thing was locked down. Sometimes, the rapid hurtle towards commitment was born out of such intense desire and passion that we couldn't prise ourselves away from one another long enough to consider whether or not we were actually a good fit. (We never were.)

You need only look to the great love stories throughout the ages to see why we're so reticent to slow down, engage our brain and take a good while getting to properly know and understand the person we're dating: Romeo and Juliet meet, fall in love and tragically die side by side in the space of four days. Richard Burton and Elizabeth Taylor were married within a year of meeting on the set of *Cleopatra* – despite him being married for fourteen years and Taylor being on her fourth husband at the tender age of twenty-nine. And don't even get me started on Henry VIII. So, although a slow courtship may have been best practice back in the day, true romance has always been associated with drama, speed and a whole lot of bad decisions. After all, what fun is a rollercoaster without the ups and downs?

In the early days of new love there is an explosion of neuro-chemicals in our brain that creates an intense experience of happiness and desire within us. But no matter how great that spark feels at first, no matter how much you convince yourself it'll last forever, that (typically highly sexualised) infatuation is only a short-term phenomenon that results from the insecurity and newness inherent in the relationship dynamic. As psychologist Susan Heitler puts it in a post on the *Psychology Today* website: 'Love is blind while you are in the initial infatuation stage. After that, clarity about reality tends to emerge. Continuing to love someone is likely to depend on how suitable that person is as a partner in the project of living.'

A year after meeting Joe, I'm once again sat with his Aunty Louise in her kitchen, this time discussing how I'm to be moving in with her nephew in a few months' time. I've been living with one of my best friends, Jess, for the last six months, having lived at my parents' house for the first six months of mine and Joe's relationship. While I've obviously stayed at Joe's flat a lot during this time, we decided to wait just over a year before committing to full cohabitation – mainly because it will be the first time I've officially lived with a partner, and I want to be sure we're both ready to take this next step in our relationship.

By this point, we've experienced each other's biggest flaws. We've had a few gargantuan fights – and survived them. We've both continued to cultivate rich and exciting lives outside of our relationship. We've been away together a fair few times and not wanted to throttle one another (for the most part). We've gotten better at navigating and resolving conflicts. We both know exactly where we want this relationship to go (marriage and probably kids one day – with lots of travelling solo and together thrown in, too). But most importantly, we aren't making this commitment while still in the starry-eyed honeymoon phase; we are making it even though we are now very much aware of one another's various failings and foibles. And, despite them, we still choose each other.

So, although we may have fallen in love fast, when it comes to sharing utility bills and deciding whose turn it is to scrub the shit-splattered toilet bowl, we've taken our sweet time.

RESPECT AND PROTECT

Joey Wilderness
10.04, 9 September

Sorry about the slight drunkenness last night, gorgeous. I remember you saying tomorrow you'll wake up and send some big text apologising, so here it is.

I know a lot of that conversation was very deep, but I'm excited beyond words that I've met you. If anything scares me it's the fear of getting hurt, as I never open up like I have with you. But I feel safe with you, I feel that I want to share myself with you and I want you to totally share yourself with me.

I find you the most incredible, enchanting person I've ever met, Persia. I was drawn to you when I first set eyes on you without words even being said, and then when we finally spoke, it all made sense.

Great and wonderful things will happen with you and I. Going away has been a good thing, because it's given me a real chance to allow my feelings to grow and think about what this all means to me.

I miss you more than anything, but it's not affecting the experience I'm having here. The way I see things is, I'm on a permanent level of excitement. For my time out here, the things I'll do, people I'm going to meet along my journey, but then my returning home and holding you in my arms again, and how amazing that will feel. Pure natural rush.

I'll call you once I've done my meditation class.

Sleep well, mon amour xxxxx

Persia Gorgeous
16.27, 9 September

Thank you for this message JW ;) I know you were drunk so don't worry about it – I was being a bit mean! I just want to use my head with this (for the first time!) as well as my heart and gut, because I want it to be sustainable. Respect and protect.

Like you, I do have some fears I need to talk through with you face to face, but I'm so grateful that I feel safe enough to open up to you and be myself, warts and all! And I do accept you for who you are – I love that you wear your heart on your sleeve, I just want us to help each other out by giving the needed space around work stuff.

Will try and call you later, have a beautiful day & meditation! xxx

THE ELASTIC BAND THEORY

'Stand together, yet not too near together:
For the pillars of the temple stand apart,
And the oak tree and the cypress grow
not in each other's shadow.'

KAHIL GIBRAN, *THE PROPHET*

The first time Joe tells me he loves me is mid-sex, several hours after stepping off the plane home from his six-week lads' trip in Bali.

Because he's in between flats and I'm living with my parents (and have been for the last four years), I've saved up to book us a room at the Dean Street Townhouse in Soho so that we can spend the entire weekend making up for lost time (i.e. bonking like rabbits) in the heart of the city, a luxury I've never been able to afford until now. However, since Joe came into my life, a lot of other great things have come about, too – including a new tutoring client that requires a lot of my time, and whose family is willing to pay generously for it. It's as though my bank balance has magically tripled in size overnight – a phenomenon, I'm delighted to report, that many of my future love-coaching clients will experience themselves when their own love lives are in a good place. The better it gets, the better it gets, as they say in Twelve Step rooms.

It's obvious Joe has been planning this moment for a while.

Unfortunately, though, it hasn't quite gone to plan… Sharing hotel rooms with his mates clearly hasn't afforded him much 'alone' time over the past six weeks in Bali, so the most romantic, significant moment of our courtship so far went something like this:

Four thrusts into sex…

> Joe (looking into my eyes):
>   'Persia, can I tell you something?'
> Me: 'Yeeeees…'
> Joe: 'I love you.'
>
> *[Pregnant pause]*
>
> Me: 'I love you, too.'
> Joe: 'Oh… God!'

THE END.

Later that evening, after he's taken me out for dinner and then on to The Comedy Store in Leicester Square (my ideal city date), he asks me to be his girlfriend.

'Let me think about it,' I tell him.

He looks like a puppy who's just been kicked, so I explain where my head is at.

'I'm crazy about you, Joe,' I say, 'but I also know that I want my next relationship to be with the person I'm going to marry and possibly have kids with one day, so I need a little more time before making this commitment.'

He raises his eyebrows, smiles and then shrugs.

'Take as long as you need,' he replies, before planting a kiss on my cheek and jumping off the bed to run a bath.

The following day, Joe goes back to his parents' home in Worcestershire, and I use this time apart to find out whether a committed relationship with Joe is the next right move for *me*. After a week spent meditating, journaling and going to my regular Al Anon meetings, my gut gently informs me that it is.

This entire journey, from our first meeting at the festival to officially becoming boyfriend and girlfriend two months later, is the healthiest, most conscious and enjoyable entrance into a romantic relationship I've ever experienced (my only anxiety being that I'm not used to it feeling this good or easy!). It has also taught me a very specific strategy around how to effectively relate to men, one that has enabled my relationship with Joe to continue to thrive and evolve with every year that passes.

This strategy is called 'The Elastic Band Theory', and it's from a young adult novel by Louise Rennison called *Angus, Thongs and Full-Frontal Snogging*. The theory goes something like this: picture a large rubber band wrapped around the guy you're dating or in a relationship with. When you feel him pulling away, your natural instinct as a woman tends to be to move closer to him and try to close the gap between the two of you, which means that the imaginary elastic band connecting him to you goes all slack.

One of the main differences between the way men and women respond to love and dating is that, for men, romantic desire most often develops in the space – not in the closeness, as it tends to for women. It's also in that space that a man works out whether he feels you're a compatible mate in the long term, whereas women tend to determine compatibility through spending time with their potential partner.

In my early twenties, I was always anxious that the guy I was dating was on the brink of performing a vanishing act. To try to prevent this from happening, I clung to their most precious commodity – their time – with ferocity, convincing myself that the more hours we'd clock up together, the deeper they'd fall in love with me and the harder it would be to leave. But the more I'd clutch, the further I'd feel them slip away. Having been in their shoes many times since, I understood why: there's nothing less sexy than feeling cornered by a lover's insecurity and neediness.

As I learnt the hard way, the greatest gift you can ever bestow on a romantic partner is to allow them the freedom to be, do or have whatever their heart is calling them towards. Because the truth is that no matter how hard you try to make them follow your agenda, humans will always follow their own in the end (and if they don't, you can bet your bottom dollar that there will be a whole heap of resentment coming your way soon enough).

So, now imagine this scenario: you spend some quality time with your partner or date. You feel connected and bonded to him. His natural desire for space after this intimacy drives him to pull away from you. However, rather than panicking and trying to close the gap between the two of you, so that you can experience that closeness with him again, you do nothing. You stay still. And, instead of moving towards *him*, you move more deeply into yourself and allow that imaginary elastic band around him to be stretched as far as he requires it to be.

This is *not* about just sitting around and waiting for him to come back to you. It's about understanding that a relationship between two people is just a heightened reflection of the relationship each partner already has with themselves. It's about respecting his need for space, in the same way you would want him to respect *your* needs, whatever they might be. It's about flipping the narrative in your mind that tells you that his pulling away means he isn't as into you as you are into him. It's about using this situation as an opportunity to spend quality time with yourself, friends and family – not merely to pass the time, but because time spent with other loved ones (yourself included) fills you up as much as your relationship does.

It's been my experience that soon enough, having felt no pressure or intrusion on his need for space, your partner will spring back towards you, because the time away has given him a chance to feel that desire for connection and intimacy with you once again. (And, if he doesn't? Well, I'm afraid you've got your answer: he's not springing back to you because he *doesn't want to*. I know that may be hard to hear, but I'm hoping it saves you a lot of heartache in the long run and frees you up to invest your time and energy into a guy who *will* spring back to you, without question.)

This romantic dynamic is something I've had modelled to me by my parents for as long as I can remember. One of the things that's helped my dad stay sober for so many years is trekking in the mountains. He'll go away on trekking trips the other side of the world for weeks (often months) at a time. And my mum happily lets him, which is pretty radical, considering his trips have nothing to do with his work. When Dad returns (or meets up with Mum after his trek in India, her favourite place in the world), their joy in being reunited is palpable. It's like being around a pair of love-struck teenagers. This is because they've had a chance to actually *miss* each other, meaning that their desire for one another is heightened, and it feels like they're falling in love all over again.

Eventually, having spent years working on my insecurities, I began to model my parents' dynamic in my own romantic relationships. When Joe was in Bali for those six weeks at the start of our courtship, while of course I missed him, I wasn't counting down the hours until he returned. I used this time to get the second draft of *The Inner Fix* finished, hung out with my friends and family and continued to enjoy an active social life.

Four years later, Joe and I went to Costa Rica for six weeks. Towards the end of the trip he was given an opportunity to stay out there for a further two weeks, while I had to return to London for work. He later told me that one of the main reasons he proposed shortly after that trip was because of how chilled out I was about his decision to stay, even though we'd planned to go back home together. He said he was excited to marry a woman who was so secure in herself and the relationship that she didn't need to guilt-trip or manipulate him into sticking with the original plan. (He can thank my parents for that!)

This is the key to successfully implementing the elastic band theory: you first have to build a solid relationship with yourself and the rest of your life so that when he inevitably pulls away, it feels like a gift to be savoured, not a chore to be endured. After all, whatever may happen in your love life in years to come, you're going to be in a relationship with you until the end.

NEW DOORS

'Look on every exit as being an entrance somewhere else.'
TOM STOPPARD, *ROSENCRANTZ AND GUILDENSTERN ARE DEAD*

t's a sad day when you turn to your own self-help book for help. But a year into my relationship with Joey Wilderness – and a few short months after the publication of *The Inner Fix* – here I am, turning the pages of that same book, looking for answers to questions that were penned by my own hand. The irony is not lost on me.

Yesterday, my friend and business partner, Joanne, sat me down in her local park and told me she felt it was time to walk away from Addictive Daughter, the positive lifestyle movement we've spent the last four years building together. I knew she was right. I wished she wasn't.

We are at the top of our game at this point, and I've been lapping up the feeling of success like a kid with an ice-cream cone on a hot summer's day. Our book has received multiple features in mainstream press, we are represented by one of the top three UK talent agencies for both literary and presenting, and we have four different production companies interested in turning our book into a TV show. We've even signed a six-month, first-look deal with one of them.

I know I've been getting a little too wrapped up in all this media attention. It's hard not to when you've spent the majority of your life setting the stage for it. A born high-achiever, I've been dreaming of this level of professional recognition since childhood (certainly since my days as an unemployed actress working in a strip club to try to make ends meet). Success is like sugar to me: the more I have, the more I crave. But, like sugar, the hit from success is fleeting and not without consequence.

Our main message of *The Inner Fix* is what my dad shared with me on the beach in Thailand (more than five years ago, now): *Focus on the insides and the outsides will take care of themselves.*

Clearly, when it comes to my career, I needed to learn this lesson all over again (never trust a self-help author who isn't brought to their knees and forced to practise what they preach on at least an annual basis).

This fork in the road isn't just about me being served up a necessary dose of humble pie, though. It's also a wake-up call to the reality that mine and Joanne's personal and professional relationship is no longer working as it used to.

The two of us met at drama school in our early twenties, our instant bond born from a mutual obsession with boys of the bad variety. Different as we were, the volatility of our love lives had always been the one constant in our dynamic. This hadn't always worked in our favour, though; one of us was usually in heartbreak just as the other was falling in love afresh. Joanne even got engaged two weeks after I got dumped (if you want to gauge the strength of a female friendship, that situation will give you a pretty accurate overview).

By the time *The Inner Fix* came out, Joanne had been married for a year and I was nine months into my relationship with Joey Wilderness. While both of these romances had their challenges, we knew we were in them for the long haul. Break-ups and bad boys were now a thing of the past, and with them went the common ground our friendship had once been founded upon.

Historically, I've struggled with friendship break-ups nearly as much as romantic ones. I find it hard to accept that you can be so closely intertwined with someone one minute, and practically strangers the next.

When I was little, I had countless 'best friends'. I revelled in feeling like my companionship was superior to that of others; like we had a bond and understanding of one another that no one outside of our little unit could touch. While such friendships had no sexual dimension to them, the level of intimacy was so potent that when the dynamic drifted or ended, the space their absence left in my life felt seismic.

A famous anonymously penned poem states that people come into your life for a reason, a season, or a lifetime. I instinctively know that mine and Joanne's decade-long friendship came about for a reason: to prepare me for the lifetime assignment of my relationship with Joey Wilderness.

Soon enough, the dots of synchronicity connect and confirm this to be the case (to me, at least). Not only does Joey Wilderness share the same first name as my business partner (whose nickname is Joey), he also happens to have lived around the corner from Joanne and her husband, Luke, in London since a few weeks after returning from Bali. However, as soon as we decide to walk away from Addictive Daughter, their flat (which has been on the market for some time) sells and they move to the other side of London – in the same month I move into their former neighbourhood with Joey Wilderness. Life has a funny way of facilitating the opening of a new door just as the old one closes.

While we are still friendly and love one another, it's time to accept that mine and Joanne's place in each other's lives has changed. Significantly. A new horizon is beckoning each of us, separately, and resisting this change will only delay the inevitable. Just like a break-up.

Sometimes the lesson is to stay and learn how to navigate a new dynamic in an old relationship. But sometimes it's to gracefully let go of what's no longer meant for you.

Having given myself permission to grieve the ending of this chapter of my life, I pick myself up, dust myself off, and walk into the next part of my story.

SLEEP SWIMMING

'No man was ever so much deceived by another as by himself.'
FULKE GREVILLE

One of the most unexpected perks of committing to a relationship with Joe was that it helped liberate me from the things in my life that were no longer serving me.

Although the early days of our love were peppered with all sorts of challenges, I've never once questioned the validity of Joe's feelings towards me. I've never once felt shamed by him, or emotionally unsafe in his presence. So why on earth had I felt obliged to put up with feeling like this in so many of my previous relationships? Why had I wasted a gargantuan portion of my life contorting myself into boxes that didn't fit me, or I them?

One such box was church. This was a tricky one for me, because since I was a child I'd experienced as many pros from attending church as I had cons.

In my first year of secondary school, during Mum's first spell in rehab, I went to the school's Christian Union camp that my sister had been on for the last few years. She loved it, so I guessed I would, too. I was right.

The worship songs and hymns we sang as a group every night were my favourite bit. When I sang, I forgot myself. I felt a rush of love come over me not dissimilar to my first experience of taking ecstasy years later. Only this had no awful comedown.

During the evening talks at the camp, I learnt more about the theology of Christianity. I was still not particularly fazed by the supernatural concepts that lots of my friends could never get past: the water being turned into wine, lame people being healed – even the resurrection. *Weirder things have probably happened,* I thought.

Life at home was hard and believing in a loving God made it bearable. It was as simple as that. I didn't even care if it was all in my head; that's where I needed it most. And since no one could actually *prove* if it was true either way, I resolved to err on the side of optimism.

Over time, I became more and more drawn to the historical character of Jesus, the people's champion, who didn't spend his time hanging out with the religious leaders of the day, but with the underdogs – the scum of society: prostitutes, tax collectors and lepers. I liked that he was an actual *man*, something tangible and physically touchable (once upon a time), not just an esoteric concept beyond my comprehension. I liked that the twelve men he had chosen to be his closest disciples and friends were always messing up, yet were still encouraged by him to do some pretty radical things. I liked that he turned up to his public unveiling as the Messiah on a donkey, a celebrity entrance that even Lady Gaga couldn't trump, in my opinion. And I liked that my church youth group was held on a Sunday, the day when the chaos of the rest of the week would otherwise wither into a depressing grey haze set to the tune of *The Antiques Roadshow*.

I knew that Christianity had been responsible for countless wars and atrocities, but I selectively numbed myself to the things I didn't want to see, a strategy I applied to most areas of my life. In other words, I took what I liked and left the rest. It was moral relativity through and through, and my perspective frustrated (even offended) other Christians. As did the fact that while I was more than happy to talk about my belief in God, I had no desire to convert or evangelise, which made me a really rubbish spokesperson for the Kingdom.

Essentially, it was the *relationship*, not the religion, that I wanted to be a part of; and as long as I could talk to this invisible man and feel I was being heard, I was happy to accept that, for me, Jesus was my pipeline to God, without having any issue with other people accessing God in whatever way worked for them.

However, although I continued to go on the Christian Union camps every year, I soon started to feel like a fraud. I was now leading the vocals in the worship set, but, behind closed doors, I was drifting out of my spiritual connection and into boys' beds more and more frequently, as I tried to numb the pain of my turbulent home life with a faster fix.

While my faith itself never wavered, my reliance on it did. As sex and Smirnoff became as regular for me as the Sabbath, in swooped guilt and shame. And, totally missing the point, I started turning away from the beautiful simplicity of the relationship that I'd known as a child. I no longer saw God as a friend and confidante, but as a judge who now deemed me and my behaviour as not good enough for His holy companionship.

By the time I arrived at university at eighteen, I had stopped my side of the relationship going, in that I stopped conversing. More importantly, though, assuming that God would no longer answer the prayers of the lustful liar that I'd become, I stopped listening.

Then, in my mid-twenties, my whole world fell apart in a single week. As I've mentioned earlier, I suddenly found myself without a boyfriend or job, and back living with my parents. This was painfully humbling for a former hedonistic nomad.

It often takes a catastrophe of sorts to realise you've been sleep-swimming your way into perilous waters, and that something needs to change. Fast. That week from hell was the wake-up call I needed to recommit to my Twelve Step programme for friends and family of addicts and alcoholics, Al Anon. It was also the reason I said yes when a mutual friend of mine and my (very recently) ex-boyfriend's invited me to attend a Sunday service at her ritzy central London church.

Before I knew it, I was once again attending church every Sunday, as well as a weekly Bible study group and the annual church camp, just as I had done a decade before. After the gaping, miserable hole hollowed out by heartbreak, church had given me a new community, and with it the opportunity to rebuild my life and identity on more salubrious foundations. I got to stand on stage and sing, which made me feel seen. I got to volunteer at my church's soup kitchen, which made me feel useful. I got to flirt with the handful of good-looking bad-boys-turned-holy in the posh pub after the Sunday evening service, which made me feel like I still had my edge. Basically, I got to curate an entirely new version of myself – the best version, the version of me which got to succeed in all the areas where I'd failed so spectacularly up until this point. And therein lay the problem: it wasn't real.

It's funny how the moment I gave up acting professionally, I assumed a role that required as much skill and focus as any I'd played in my days treading the boards. What happened to my persona when I crossed the ecclesiastic threshold felt strangely similar to what happened to it as I emerged from the wings onto the stage during a theatrical performance: I went into character. I may have still looked and sounded like myself, but really it was a consciously constructed appropriation of me, designed to fool everyone that I fitted in here, myself included.

There were moments in church when I'd be chatting to one of the very sweet members of the congregation and I'd mentally zoom out of my body and observe myself acting out this bullshit production, as though I were a director reviewing the rushes at the end of a day's filming. This is exactly what I felt like on most dates, too: I wasn't *in* the experience, I was performing it. I was auditioning for a part in the other person's play at the same time as questioning whether or not to cast them in mine.

I'd silently acknowledge the tell-tale giveaways that this was performance, not truth: the affected voice – softer and more high-pitched – so as to stay in tune with the women I gauged as being the most popular and respected here. The constant mental editing of what I was about to say before I said it, so as not to offend or reveal who I really was, which made everything that came out of my mouth feel contrived. The way I carried myself – slightly hunched and slow of pace – so as to appear modest and unassuming (and, most importantly, not a threat). For a bolshie extrovert who's renowned amongst her friends for her complete lack of conversational filter (once even being given the nickname 'Inappropriate' during an acting job in China), this was an exhausting role for me to uphold.

When I thought to question why the majority of women at my church seemed to present themselves in such a similar way, I needed to look no further than the Bible itself, littered as it is with diatribes about why women should remain silent and submissive in church.

The Bible's attitude to women has never sat right with me. I won't bore you with the reason for this – the blatant misogyny speaks for itself. What I'm more curious about is why, despite my disdain for any patriarchal system that seeks to exclude and control women, I felt so compelled to a) attend church in the first place and b) twist myself into a pretzel to try and fit in. The answer to the first question is that I believed going to church would help fix my broken heart, as it had done when I was a child.

During that hellish week in my mid-twenties, when all the markers of validation were extracted from my life in one fell swoop, finding ways to feel safe and loved again became my number one priority; hence attending church and Al Anon.

In my Al Anon meetings, I was surrounded by people who understood the negative effects addiction can have on your relationships at a deep level, because they had experienced them, too. The way the meetings and fellowship as a whole are structured means that there are no issues or question marks around gender or power politics. The purpose of Al Anon is laid out clearly at the start of every meeting: the fellowship exists to 'help families of alcoholics by practising the Twelve Steps set out in Alcoholics Anonymous, to welcome and give comfort to families of alcoholics, and to give understanding and encouragement to the alcoholic'. The simplicity and directness of this opening preamble – which is maintained throughout every single touchpoint and teaching in the Al Anon programme – has taught me that in order to feel safe in a relationship or group dynamic, I require full transparency about the nature and intention of that dynamic. I need to know I'm not being lied to, and I need to know it's safe to show up as I actually *am*, not as you think I *should* be.

These were not boundaries that could be met in church. However, having just had my heart and ego smashed to smithereens, a need emerged that was even more pressing: I needed to feel like I *belonged* somewhere. In hindsight, I can see that what I really needed to belong to was myself. But, at the time, I thought I needed to belong to a new community and set of friends, because they would take up the space my ex and acting career had once occupied. This isn't the healthiest reason for reinserting oneself back into church life. What's even unhealthier is that I wanted to belong in this particular church because my ex had brought me to a carol service here prior to breaking up, so it helped me feel connected to him.

This church was also known for the pedigree of its congregation: good-looking, successful professionals, with a fair few celebrities thrown in for good measure. In my delicate state, I latched on to the false belief that if I hung around this place long enough, their shine would rub off on me. But, as anyone who's ever attempted to infiltrate a clique under the radar will tell you, it ain't all that easy. In church as it is in high school, herd mentality often makes it as hard for an established group to open its circle to someone new as it does for that new person to open themselves up to potential rejection by that group.

Realising that I probably wasn't going to be welcomed into the main clique of shiny happy people, I swiftly swapped tactics and gravitated towards the group of church renegades instead. (There's always a clique of renegades in every institution. They are the ones sitting at the back, making a show of the fact that they're sat at the back — and you're not.)

Thankfully, with this group I wasn't required to shine through my virtue to feel like I belonged. In fact, the reason they'd thrown open the invisible doors to their pack and ushered me inside so quickly was that the ringleader, a Lebanese criminal lawyer called Sam – the most big-hearted bad boy I'd ever met, had heard about my sordid past from a mutual friend and was intrigued to see if I lived up to the legend. It was a huge relief to know I could just drop the act of trying to be shiny and sink into my loud, vulgar, inappropriate self like I was sliding into an old pair of slippers. My former Jezebel-style glory was welcome here – celebrated, even.

Inevitably, it didn't take me long to fall into a relationship with Sam. He was leader of the renegades, after all: how could I resist? After a typically bumpy start to our love affair (owing to the same old story that he was already dating someone else when he expressed interest in me), we had a solid year of relative romantic bliss before the cracks of our incompatibility started to show.

When we broke up in the spring of 2014, I left our church so that I could more easily maintain the 'six months no-contact' rule I'd set for myself, and started attending another parish closer to home. But without my motley crew of renegades granting me permission to show up as my real self, it wasn't long before I was back to my old theatrics, back to trying to razzle-dazzle like the shiny folk; back to telling one story on the inside and another on the outside.

In the year and a half that passed between the break-up with Sam and meeting Joe, I tried my damnedest to make church work for me, and I for it. I really did. But it was getting harder to kid myself that coming here was still about spiritual healing and growth for me, as it once had been. The truth was that I was coming here to be seen, an impossible feat since I spent so much energy hiding the bits of myself I didn't think fitted in. As I'd learnt from so many of my previous romantic encounters, if you're having to work really hard to make a dynamic fit you, maybe this is a sign it's time to try on another size.

Joe was that other size for me. Meeting him felt like unbuttoning my jeans after a Sunday roast: I could just let it all hang out without worrying he'd judge me for being 'too much' – a term I'd been branded with by friends, lovers and even family members ever since I can remember.

Ten days after we met, we were road-tripping from London to Joe's parents' house in Worcestershire when we somehow got on to the subject of religion. I filled him in on my vacillating relationship with the church and Christianity. A minute or two after I'd wrapped up, he punctured the silence with a most unexpected question.

'What's your favourite Bible verse?'

'Uh… let me think…' I stuttered, scouring through my mental library and finding diddly squat. 'What's yours?' I said, diverting the spotlight back to him.

'Ezekiel, twenty-five, verse seventeen,' he replied, his eyes remaining fixed on the road. 'The path of the righteous man is beset on all sides by the inequities of the selfish and the tyranny of evil men. Blessed is he who, in the name of charity and good will, shepherds the weak through the valley of the darkness. For he is truly his brother's keeper and the finder of lost children. And I will strike down upon thee with great vengeance and furious anger those who attempt to poison and destroy my brothers. And you will know I am the LORD when I lay my vengeance upon you.'

I didn't know whether I was turned on or terrified that I'd unknowingly been hooking up with the most unlikely zealot in the history of religion.

He'd make an excellent spy, I thought. *No one would suspect him in a month of sunny Sundays.*

He let the awkwardness hang in the air for a moment longer than I would have liked, and then turned to me and winked.

'Samuel L. Jackson in *Pulp Fiction*,' he grinned.

It took a moment to register that he'd obviously been joking and I wasn't driving to an undisclosed location with MI5's best-kept secret, for which I felt relieved. After all, I had once dated the son of a KGB general when I'd lived in Russia, so it didn't feel totally implausible to be falling in love with a spy.

Joe then started telling me about his own experience with the church. Like me, he'd been mainly drawn to the social aspect of it, after his neighbours had invited him to a service when he was fourteen. However, where I'd been attending your bog standard Church of England services, he'd been part of the much more niche Christadelphian group, a community that was first established around 160 years ago, and who have a modest global following of approximately 50,000 based in 120 countries. Their aim is to get as close as possible in faith and practice to the early Christian Church. There are no priests or central leaders, and they base their beliefs solely on the Bible, so reject the concept of the Trinity and the immortality of the soul.

The idea of Joe attending *any* church was hard to get my head around, but the fact he'd once possessed a knowledge of the Bible that was akin to Dot Cotton's from *Eastenders* was completely mind-boggling to me. He was the most straightforward enigma I'd ever met.

He went on to explain how, at age sixteen, he'd been ousted from the Christadelphian community after being caught bonking one of the pretty young members of the congregation. Godly *and* reckless? Now I was *really* smitten.

Following Joe's lead, I opened up about how I felt I'd never really fitted in at church, and how I'd spent most of my time there putting on a performance so that I wouldn't be outed for being a fraud (or a once-upon-a-time borderline Jezebel).

'Why do you go, then?' he asked. I didn't have an answer to that question, and it hung over me like a cloud for the entirety of our first year together. Still, I continued to attend.

I feel it's important to acknowledge how sweet and kind the leaders and many members of the congregation were to me during this time. They always invited me to social events, asked me to sing at special services; and they even let my business partner and I host our book launch for *The Inner Fix* in the beautiful church hall – free of charge. They weren't the problem. Given that I was putting on such a good show of everything being fine and dandy, how were they supposed to know I was struggling? People aren't mind readers (a useful thing to remember when it comes to dating and relationships, too).

The problem was that church was no longer the right solution for me, and I was too afraid to admit that to myself because, once again, I was worried what others would think if I chose to follow my own truth. This is exactly why I stayed in so many relationships way past their sell by dates, and why, to make staying more bearable, I lied and cheated. My life became one big game of smoke and mirrors, and I was tired of it.

Then, one day shortly after *The Inner Fix* book launch, I stumbled across some uncomfortable information involving a few key members of my little church crew. Although it wasn't really any of my business, the fact that I – along with the rest of our group – had been lied to for several months dented my ego considerably. I wasn't bothered about the actual incident so much as I was hurt and humiliated that I hadn't known about it earlier. It was like checking your partner's phone while they're in the shower, only to discover they've been doing the dirty on you for months; you knew something wasn't right this whole time, but you pushed it to the back of your mind until the niggle became a roar. When your suspicions are confirmed, you're as angry at yourself for having ignored your gut as you are at the person who deceived you in the first place.

This scandal in my crew, like discovering your partner's string of naughty text messages, served as the perfect excuse to extract myself from a dynamic that hadn't been right for a long time.

What was even better – I didn't have to take any responsibility for my decision, because it was all *their* fault.

Failing to own my part in the whole experience meant that I went on to harbour an unreasonable amount of resentment towards the church for several years, much like after a break-up. Church became the ex-boyfriend who'd never really loved me, and I the jilted damsel who couldn't understand where it had all gone so wrong.

I felt the bitter sting of separation for several years. In that time, I relied on other modalities for spiritual sustenance – Al Anon, Sex and Love Addicts Anonymous, therapy and coaching. All of them helped me continue to grow and work through the various challenges that came up in my fledgling relationship with Joe and my career pivot into love coaching. But it was years before I felt ready to rifle through the emotional debris left in the wake of my hasty departure from church.

Then Joe proposed in May 2019, and I was surprised to find myself visualising us marrying in his family's local village church in Worcestershire. Surprisingly, it was Joe – who'd up until now been set on us getting hitched in the woods (*Robin Hood, Prince of Thieves* starring Kevin Costner is one of his all-time favourite films and he wanted to recreate the wedding scene at the end) who suggested we go and check the local church out the day after the engagement.

The moment I stepped inside the thirteenth-century building, I noticed how the veil of bitterness I'd been holding on to had melted away and in its place was appreciation: appreciation for the hope, love and support that church had given me as a child. Appreciation for the new community church had provided me with when I was heartbroken and needed a fresh start. Appreciation for the many, many lessons I'd learnt from church (directly or indirectly) throughout my life. It was like being reunited with an ex-lover years after parting and realising that, even though you weren't destined to spend a lifetime together, the experience moulded you into the person you are today; who knows where you'd be now without it.

So, even though I'm not sure I'll ever be a full-time ecclesiast again (although never say never), church will always hold a special place in my heart, along with all the other loves who came into my world for a time, and left it richer than they found it.

12. HOW TO KNOW IF HE'S THE ONE

THE LIST

'When you reach the end of what you should know, you
will be at the beginning of what you should sense.'

KAHLIL GIBRAN, *SAND AND FOAM*

It's a month since I met Joe, and I'm sitting on a plane to
Morocco next to my friend Jess, reading her a list of all the
reasons I should be in a relationship with Joe, and all the
reasons I shouldn't. This is not uncommon for me at the start of
a new romance.

In years to come I'll often be asked by my love-coaching clients
why I think the dinosaur signs kept showing up for Joe and myself
in such coincidental ways. (Joe even worked on the locations for
one of the *Jurassic World* movies, and in 2020 we bought our first
house together in a village in Surrey where dinosaur bones had
recently been located.) I'll tell them that, for me, they served a
very important purpose: they made it nearly impossible for me
to run away, as I was prone to do whenever I was treated well
by a man. I'll be forced to look at this pattern in a year's time,
when Joe and I attend a plant medicine retreat together in the UK

that is so confronting, I'll very nearly shit myself (the incident I shared at the start of this book).

When our worlds collided at Wilderness that first night, I was certain that Joe would be nothing more than a fun story to relay to my friends; a short-lived festival fling at best. I should've guessed he wasn't on board with this assessment of our connection, considering that he took me back to his aunt and uncle's house just three days after meeting. When a guy is really into you, they tend to do things like that.

In the weeks since, I've felt trapped between the ease and flow of our dynamic, and the scrambling panic this has stirred in me because it feels so alien. Despite my being in the middle of writing a book about trusting your intuition, dating Joe has incited a very real battle between my heart and my head, which has tried to talk me out of the relationship in any way it can. It all just seems too easy, and a lot of me still doesn't really believe I'm deserving of a good man – or relationship, given my past.

It doesn't matter that my new man is good-looking, fun, kind, spiritual, emotionally available, solvent, has a great job that he loves and wants the same things I do in a romantic partnership; or that this is the cleanest, healthiest start to a love story I've ever had (mainly because it's the first time neither myself nor the guy I'm dating is already in a relationship). It feels so foreign to me that we may as well be courting on Mars.

I can still pinpoint the exact moment we came dangerously close to tumbling off the cliff of our blossoming romance. Prior to leaving for his Bali trip, Joe and I were en route back to his family home in Worcestershire to make the most of the free house while his parents were away in Italy. Being on a strict writing deadline for *The Inner Fix*, I decided to capitalise on the three-hour car journey by reading through the draft I'd printed off and making notes in the margins. After twenty minutes or so, having grown bored of the silence, Joe asked me to read some of the book out to him. Never one to shy away from the opportunity to hear the sound of my own voice, I turned back to the first page, cleared my throat theatrically, and began.

Sharing my story with a man I'd just met wasn't new for me. Having been both actress and over-sharer for the majority of my life, I was well accustomed to revealing intimate things about myself in a dating context, a not-so-subtle method for hoodwinking men into falling for a version of my identity that existed several layers above the truth. But what I realised in the car that day was that it's not so much *what* you share that initiates intimacy, but when, how and who you share it with.

When I was with Joe, there was no space or possibility for roleplay. My usual bullshit games just didn't work, because a game requires two consenting players – and he had zero inclination to don a mask of any kind. In the simple transparency of this dynamic, stripped of the intensity I was so used to experiencing with a new lover, there was nowhere for me to hide. As a result, I felt gut-wrenchingly vulnerable, and it took every ounce of self-restraint I had not to ask him to pull into the nearest service station so that I could go and lock myself in the neutral space of a toilet cubicle for a bit. My mind was clambering around for an exit strategy from the very person and relationship I'd been so devoted to manifesting only weeks beforehand.

This is what we do: we obsess over finding real love with someone who will stay, but the moment we do, our first impulse is to run from it as fast as we can. The truth is that even though we *say* we want commitment and intimacy, if we've never actually experienced them in our love life in a mature and healthy way, we will subconsciously rule out potential partners that could be a great fit for us, because the ease of such a dynamic feels so out of our comfort zone.

We humans will always gravitate towards what is familiar to us over what is unfamiliar, even if what's familiar is an emotionally unavailable guy who brings nothing but drama and chaos to our life; better the devil you know, than the devil you don't.

I've seen this time and time again with women. We tell ourselves we don't really fancy the nice guy we're dating, that they're not our type, *that they're boring.* We nit-pick over the most trivial of things, using them as an excuse to keep the unfamiliar sensation of reliable romance at arm's length.

The reason I've been feeling so conflicted about Joe coming home from Bali is that I know he will ask me to be his girlfriend as soon as he does. I also know this will be the last time I'm ever asked that question.

'Want some honest feedback?' says my friend Jess on the plane when I've finished reading out my list to her.

'Not really, but how else are we gonna kill the next few hours of the flight?' I reply, as I crack open my packet of overpriced Easy Jet olives.

'It won't take long,' she says, nabbing an olive and tossing it into her mouth. 'All the positives you've listed are about how good Joe makes you *feel.* All the negatives are pretty superficial: they're mainly about what you're worried others will think of him or you as a couple.'

I look at the list again. She isn't wrong.

There, I guess, is my answer.

In years to come, I'll look back and wonder how my life would be today had I let that loud, fast, fearful voice in my head override the quiet, slow, loving voice in my gut that told me to stay. That told me Joe had just the right combination of qualities and imperfections that would help me heal at an even deeper level, so that we could evolve into the people we are meant to be together.

To the one who may have met The One but wants to RUN... listen: maybe you *are* just meant to be friends. Maybe you won't ever want to rip his clothes off. Maybe this person isn't The One, after all. But take it from me: stay open to the possibility that they *could* be.

So don't walk away before you've given it a chance. Don't walk away because even though it *feels* good, it's not perfect and doesn't look how you thought it would. Don't walk away before you've listened – really *listened* – to what your gut has to say on the matter. It knows more than you give it credit for.

SIX SIGNS

'Love does not consist of gazing at each other, but
in looking together in the same direction.'

ANTOINE DE SAINT-EXUPÉRY

The problem with falling in love is that it's such an overwhelming experience, we often get confused about whether it's real, genuine love we're feeling, or just infatuation that will soon burn itself out.

Over the past five years of love coaching women, I've discovered six signs that healthy, long-lasting, 'real love' relationships exhibit right from the start:

1. IT'S EASY TO BE YOURSELF AROUND YOUR NEW LOVE INTEREST

I've spent far too much time on dates (and even in relationships) trying to be the person I believed the object of my affections wanted me to be, rather than who I actually am.

The reality is that faking it like this is only sustainable for so long; sooner or later you're going to be found out, and it will inevitably affect the dynamic of the relationship in a negative way.

When it's real love, you instantly feel you can be yourself around the other person, which means that if they do fall in love with you, it's the authentic you, not an idealised version.

2. YOU CAN SEE THIS PERSON IN YOUR FUTURE

In our culture of instant gratification, we've grown accustomed to getting what we want *now*, with little thought of how this fits in with who we want to be and where we want to go in the future.

When it's real love, you can't stop yourself from picturing your future together, because it feels so exciting and expansive.

On the other hand, if it's not a good match, you avoid thinking about the future because you know the relationship probably has an expiry date. This inconvenient truth means you'll have to endure a break-up at some point, which is why you tend to dismiss the voice for so long.

3. YOU'RE NOT INTERESTED IN DATING OTHERS

Infatuation is a fickle beast; one minute you're certain that no one could ever bring you as much happiness as your new lover does. However, it doesn't take long before they start to irritate and annoy you, or they fail to match up to your idealised perception of them. This inevitably leads your eyes and attention to wander off to greener pastures elsewhere.

When it's real love, your focus remains solely on the person you're with, because even in the rocky phases, you know they're the right person for you.

4. YOUR FRIENDS AND FAMILY APPROVE OF THEM

My loved ones have always been spot on when it comes to calling who is (and isn't) a good match for me in the long run.

Sometimes we're so blinded by our infatuation with a new partner that we cannot see how totally wrong they are for us.

Our friends and family can be far more objective, however. First, they are not emotionally invested in the relationship like we are, and second, because they *know* us, and so have a legitimate perspective on who is likely to make us happy.

While your opinion is ultimately the most important, don't shun advice from loved ones who really do have your best interests at heart.

5. THEY INSPIRE YOU TO BE A BETTER PERSON

If the connection between you and the person you're dating is a healthy one, you're more drawn to their inner qualities than their external markers of success, which inspires you to become a better version of yourself as a result.

When I met Joe, I was struck by how many great qualities he had that seemed to come so naturally to him. For example, he doesn't care what other people think of him, which makes him easy to be around because he's not trying to be someone he's not. Being a chronic people-pleaser, this was not a quality that came so easily to me. But the more time I spent with him, the more motivated I became to try to let go of other people's opinions of me.

So, although I felt major resistance in the early days of dating, our relationship feels much better than I ever imagined a relationship could. As a result, I'm far more available, giving and successful in every other area of my life, too, because I'm not wasting my time and energy obsessing over someone who'll never be able to give me what I want, or hurting someone because I know I'll never be able to give them what they want.

6. THEIR WEIRDNESS FITS YOUR WEIRDNESS

One night early on in our relationship, having returned home from a night out with friends, Joe turned to me and said (deadly serious): 'Shall we watch *The Little Mermaid*?'

If I didn't know before that he was the one for me, I did then.

MUST LOVE DOGS

How to know if he will be a good life partner:

Look at how he is with animals.
Look at his dynamic with his mother and sisters.
Look at how he talks to the waiter.

Is it with adoration, reverence and respect?
Or is it with aggression, contempt and distain?

No one is ever going to be 100 per cent
compatible with us.

However:
If he doesn't have a grating baby voice
That he uses solely to speak to dogs…

… He ain't The One for me.

13. HOW TO NAVIGATE NEW RELATIONSHIP PITFALLS

THE TAMING OF THE SLOO

'You don't develop courage by being happy in your relationships every day. You develop it by surviving difficult times and challenging adversity.'

EPICURUS

I n the summer of 2010, the most dysfunctional year of my life, I bagged myself a significant acting job. I was to take on the title character in an outdoor production of William Shakespeare's play *The Taming of The Shrew* (or 'The Taming of The Sloo', as my friends whose nickname for me is 'Sloo' dubbed it).

As an English Literature and classical acting graduate, Shakespeare was my forte. As a lost, angry and misunderstood hedonist, the shrew was a role I was eager to catapult myself into as a distraction from my recent rapid weight gain and increasingly chaotic love life.

The main plot of the play centres around the courtship of the foul-tempered and quick-witted Katherina (aka 'The Shrew', or 'Kate') and Petruchio, a wealthy young (and equally boisterous) bachelor who is unapologetic about his intention to marry Kate so that he can get his hands on her father's money.

From the outset, Kate has no interest in engaging in the relationship. However, as the plot unfolds, she's left little choice. Petruchio subjects her to various psychological and physical torments, such as keeping her from eating, drinking and sleeping, until she finally acquiesces and transforms into the obedient and covetable bride he desires for himself.

Kate's seemingly happy and willing submission to her husband in the final act has led many people to dismiss the play as being wildly misogynistic and offensive. Others have argued that Shakespeare is presenting a striking critique of his own patriarchal society, and is seeking to champion women's rights.

However, playing the role of Kate during my tempestuous, rather shrew-like summer of 2010, I was drawn to the third (and least respected) interpretation: that this is, in fact, a love story about two lost, angry and misunderstood people whose attraction is instant, but who have to go through an extremely unpleasant 'training' process in order to make it possible for them to have an equal, healthy and sustainable relationship in the future.

The crucial element in this interpretation of the play lies in Petruchio's likening of the taming of Kate to the taming of a falcon. During the sixteenth-century, falconry was an expensive sport reserved for those of noble prestige. The methods of taming a falcon included depriving the bird of food to the point of starvation, and of sleep to the point of exhaustion, until the bird's behaviour changed from extreme wildness to extreme obedience, meaning that the falconer could trust the hawk to hunt out in the field without flying away.

Most significantly, though, throughout the entire process the falconer had to undergo the same extreme deprivation, being forced to watch the falcon constantly and to take care of any injuries the bird may have acquired. So, although undoubtedly a baptism of fire, it was one that both parties had to endure simultaneously; kind of like when you make the foolhardy decision to merge your life and your baggage with your lover's life and *their* baggage in what's commonly known as a 'committed relationship.' (Please note that I am IN NO WAY condoning physical or emotional abuse of either animal or human; it's just a metaphor, k?)

Frankly, I think Shakespeare is a genius for understanding that in order for two human beings to live together in relative harmony, some uncomfortable work needs to happen. You wouldn't expect to do well in the Olympics with no prior training, so why on earth would you expect the emotional and romantic equivalent to be any different? Committed love requires discipline. You may not be deprived of food, drink or sleep, but you sure as hell will be deprived of sanity at times. Because, when all's said and done, it's not the courtship that's hard (unless you happen to be dating an emotionally unavailable arsehole). It's the bit that comes after.

For me, the first three months with someone new were always magical, but the moment the passion and excitement started to wear off, I mentally and emotionally checked out of the relationship, certain that real love would be waiting for me in the arms of someone else. This is a pattern I've seen time and time again in my love-coaching clients, too.

The truth is that all of us are as wild as Kate and as controlling as Petruchio when it comes to love. We might not want to admit it, but we are. It's the natural, animal instinct within us that on the one hand wants total freedom to be, do and have whatever the fuck we like... And, on the other, is willing to compromise our independence so that we can experience the savage beauty of long-lasting love. Even when we know there's a big risk our partner could fly away, never to return, or control and smother us into taking flight for good ourselves.

In Matt Haig's book *How to Stop Time*, he writes that 'a blade of grass is not dull until you see a flower'. Before I learnt that commitment is a process, not a one-time event initiated with the words 'I do…' (want you to be my girlfriend/want to move in together/take you to be my lawfully wedded husband/want to have this baby), I considered it to be dull as ditch water. Like Kate, I defended my freedom with ferocity, convincing myself that long-term monogamy would never, ever feel as exhilarating as those early electric kisses with someone I probably shouldn't be kissing. So, if being in a committed relationship meant that I'd have to deny myself the pleasures to which I'd become accustomed (flirting/sleeping with whomever I wanted, whenever I wanted), then there were only two options, as far as I could see: end it before it got too serious, or lie. I tended to favour the second option; it took less courage.

The journey I had to go on from that head and heart space to where I am today – engaged to my partner of nearly six years in a relationship that both parties want to be inside of in equal amounts – has been excruciating at times. And euphoric at others. Where love once felt to me like a frenzied tango, with both partners hell-bent on leading, it's now evolved into more of a jumbled, sloppy waltz in which toes are regularly trodden on and egos get momentarily bruised, but in which we soon fall back in step with one another just long enough to feel like we're floating. Have you ever felt like you're floating in love? I'll tell you one thing: it's far from dull.

LOVE COACH

'We only have what we give.'
ISABEL ALLENDE

Romantic love has always been my North Star, my pain and panacea in equal measure. So when my business partner, Joanne, and I decided to walk away from Addictive Daughter and pursue our own individual passions in work, I knew straight away I'd be focusing on love: the area where I've struggled the most, but also where I've experienced the biggest transformation.

Having met the man I wanted to spend the rest of my life with, I believed that being a love coach would help stop me from sabotaging our relationship, like I had done every time before it. Because not only would I stand to lose Joe if I cheated on him, I'd likely lose my career, too.

'Don't make it too easy for yourself to leave,' my mum once told me when I asked for her best piece of relationship advice. 'For a romance to work long term, you need skin in the game.'

The social accountability of being a love coach was that skin for me, particularly in the early days of Joe and me, when my old compulsion to cut and run felt most acute.

But that was just the tip of the iceberg of benefits I've experienced from my career transition into love coaching. What has been most profound and inspiring is reading my clients' own stories of transformation, and seeing myself in all of them – like this one, from Abby:

> I came into Persia's programme after four years of being single. Prior to this I'd had one relationship that I thought was the only one I wanted, and when it ended my world fell apart.
>
> I fled to the other side of the world and used the bodies of a lot of unsuitable men to help me feel worthy. I liked the power that casual sex gave me, and when I got back from travelling I thought I could carry this on. But we all know that doesn't end well.
>
> So I was using dating apps and going out with guys who didn't want me, I think because I wasn't really ready to be wanted. I chose men who wouldn't ever commit to me, because I was scared of commitment.
>
> I came to Persia's programme sick of this cycle and ready to do the work that would let me be at peace until I found my partner. It wasn't even about finding 'The One', I truly just wanted to realise that I was enough.
>
> So I did the work and I waited. Somewhat impatiently, but I waited, during which time ALL my friends were married/living with/got kids with their partners – and it really upset me, until I found that switching my view of it really helped. So, instead of being like 'I'm so jealous of what

they have', I changed it to 'I'm so excited for what I have to come', and if people asked if I was seeing anyone I'd answer along the lines of 'I will be when I find someone who deserves me' – which helped change my mindset on it, too.

And then along came J. He is everything I asked for and everything I thought I didn't deserve. He is kind, funny, sensitive, protective, empowering and hot as hell! We can talk about a future that before would've terrified me. Now, it only excites me, because I know it's attainable and I deserve it.

Five months later and we've just made it official. Five months would've felt like an eternity to the old me, the one that thought she was desperate to feel loved and find a man. But, to the me that's done the work, it felt natural and right to wait that long. I've learnt that love cannot be rushed – and, with the right person, slow feels amazing.

It's taken a lot to learn to let go of my negativity and self-doubt around relationships, but once I started to value myself, I found a man who valued me too. I am so grateful for everything that brought me to Persia and her wonderful GYS group. You've changed my life.

WITHDRAWAL

'Sex is a team sport, sugar.'
CHERISE SINCLAIR, *BREAKING FREE*

Throughout my sex life, my most consistent mode of birth control was screaming at whomever I was bonking at the time to pull out before the fatal moment: aka, good old-fashioned withdrawal.

While this method worked for me (in that I've never been with child), it sure wasn't great for my peace of mind. Like many of my friends, I didn't have the good sense to back up my danger-bonks by keeping tabs on my period cycle. In fact, because I had no idea when to expect it, every period was a surprise: welcome on the one hand, because it meant there was no proverbial bun in my oven, infuriating on the other, because – of course – it would always come on the one day of the month I'd worn white, or wouldn't be in reach of a tampon for at least three hours.

When Joe and I fell in love, given my age (twenty-nine) and the fact we both saw a future together, it occurred to me that if I got pregnant, I'd have little excuse not to keep it. Having felt conflicted about the prospect of motherhood since I accidentally left my Tiny Tim dolly out in the rain as a child, I knew it was finally time to start taking my reproductive abilities seriously.

While I'd tried a variety of different birth-control pills over the years, I had yet to find one that didn't give me back-ne (back acne), which is why I always resorted back to withdrawal a few months in. Because of this, I decided to try something different with Joe, and the Mirena coil seemed the lesser of lots of apparent evils: although it was a hormonal device and the insertion was reported to be notably unpleasant, the benefits tended to include shorter, lighter and, in some cases, NO periods (#boom). Also, the Mirena coil can stay up there for a solid five years before it needs to be re-inserted, which meant that I wouldn't have to face my fears around motherhood for at least that long. Or so I thought.

With a heady combination of excitement (for the outcome) and trepidation (for the process involved in getting there), I jacked myself up with a heavy dose of painkillers and took me and my uterus on down to the local GP.

I'll spare you the details (you'll see why in about fifteen seconds), but needless to say, the procedure was no picnic. Nor were the two weeks that followed it. However, once that bit was over, sex between Joe and I took on a life of its own – ironically, because we were no longer worrying about the act of it creating life.

Then, a year or so in, I accidentally pulled out the coil, thinking it was a tampon. I think this warrants a back story.

There had been several occasions in the past where I'd had sex with a partner, forgetting that I already had a tampon in. Inevitably, this didn't facilitate a great sex session. I hasten to add that I've had a number of women tell me they've done the same thing (we obviously had a lot on our minds that day), so at least I'm not a lone plonker.

The day of Coil-gate, I was nearing the end of my period when Joe and I got down to a bit of belly-bumping. Afterwards, having spotted a box of tampons on the bedroom dresser, I couldn't remember for the life of me if I'd accidentally had one in during intercourse, like I had before.

Panicking, I ran to the toilet and spent a good while rummaging around in my nether regions, convinced that Joe's had unknowingly rammed the tampon so deep into my uterus that if I didn't extract it immediately, then some poor junior doctor was going to have to do the honours. (I'd read about such a scenario in a magazine once. It did not sound fun.)

Squatting on the bathroom floor like a convict mid-strip search, I eventually located what I assumed must be the end of the tampon string and gave an almighty yank. You can imagine my surprise when what emerged was not a tampon at all, but a bit of white plastic that looked like the letter 'T'.

The rest of the evening passed in a flurry of tears, hysterical laughter, WhatsApp messages to girlfriends, and gin. Thankfully it was a Friday, so at least I had the weekend to get over the shock.

Poor Joe was not so grateful. Perhaps it was the sudden lack of hormones circulating around my womb, but everything he (and other men) did that weekend enraged me.

'Babe, I know you're sore, but please don't shout at me. I'm only trying to help,' Joe said after I criticised the temperature of the hot water bottle he'd made me.

'It's not you, it's the patriarchy!!' I wailed as I lay curled up in the foetal position on our sofa, ramming another chunk of Dairy Milk into my mouth.

It was the first time that I'd fully taken stock of just how unfair it is that both a man and a woman get to enjoy the sexy bit of sex, but it's only the woman who has to deal with the physical consequences of it. I don't know why, but that had never quite landed for me before.

The patriarchy aside, natural or divine law once decreed that only the female of the species would be gifted (or burdened, depending on how you look at it) with pregnancy and birth. You can rant, rail and bury your head in the sand about this all you want, but it won't change the reality of it. If you've been blessed with the gift of fertility, then you have a responsibility to take ownership of this reality – for yourself, and your potential offspring.

So, ghastly as this whole experience was for me, it did present me with a new opportunity to practise self-love in the reproductive arena, something I'm embarrassed to say I'd never taken seriously until now. After all, if I wanted a man to respect the sanctity of my uterus, I first needed to respect it myself.

I decided that my first port of call was to familiarise myself with my menstrual cycle so that I'd at least have some idea what the hell was going on inside my body – especially given that I still had up to twenty years' worth of periods ahead of me. Which is why I downloaded 'Clue', an app that's designed to make tracking your fertility accurate, fast and friendly, enabling you to keep tabs on your monthly cycle by entering data about your period, pain, mood and sexual activity on a daily basis.

The second thing I did was book a check-up with a private doctor on the Monday (the NHS couldn't see me for another week), to make sure I hadn't damaged myself in the yanking-out process. I know not everyone's in the financial position to do this, but it occurred to me that if I'm willing to spend a fair bit of money on eating well and exercising to care for my body (or on a festival ticket to bring joy to my soul), then why shouldn't I invest in my reproductive health in the same way?

The third thing I did was as much a step (in my mind) for womankind, as it was for me personally: I asked Joe to pay half the cost of this check-up, 'as a gesture for women everywhere!'

It wasn't that I was short of money; I just wanted him to acknowledge that this was a shared responsibility – not with his words, but with his wallet. After all, heterosexual intercourse is a two-player game; without a man's participation, there'd be no need for birth control. If our sex life one day resulted in me getting pregnant, Joe would expect to share the cost of bringing up the baby, so why shouldn't he share the cost of keeping me baby-free? Also, considering I'd had a piece of hormone-secreting plastic lodged in my womb for over a year for our mutual pleasure, I figured it was the least he could do.

A few weeks after the incident, it was time to evaluate how we wanted to move forwards with birth control. One option was to have the coil re-inserted (that got a hard NO from me). Another was to get the injection, but I hate needles. The implant was a no for the same reason. There was always condoms, but who were we kidding; we were more likely to opt for celibacy as a method of contraception.

It looked like the pill was our only option, so I shared a post on my social media, asking women about their experience of taking different contraceptive pills. The reaction infuriated me, because many of the women who responded seemed to feel it was their place to tell me what to do with my own body (as opposed to just sharing their own experience with contraception, as I'd asked), one commenting that if I went back on the pill, I was a 'fucking idiot'.

Womankind hasn't come this far in gaining control over our bodies only to be judged or criticised by other women for our choice of contraception. Our bodies are all different. Our lives are all different. What's right for me probably isn't right for you, and vice versa. And, like most things in life, our birth control choices evolve as we do. What worked for us a year ago might not work for us today.

Five months after Coil-gate, Joe and I would be setting off to travel the world for six months, an adventure we'd been saving up for since the early days of our relationship. If you hadn't already noticed, we like to have sex. The last thing I wanted was to get knocked up while in some remote village in India or Nepal, so it looked like getting back on the pill (at least until the end of our travel stint) was the best of a bad bunch of contraceptive options.

Was I happy about this? FUCK NO. No one actively *wants* fake hormones stuffed down them every day, do they? But, sometimes, sexual needs must, and back then I was more up for the potential side-effects than I was the potential of pregnancy. I just wasn't ready (jury's still out on that one, by the way).

All in all, contraception is only ever going to be a compromise at best. There is no ideal course of action; there's just whatever the preferable course is for you and your partner at any given time. But my one suggestion is that whatever you *do* opt for, ask your man to pay half of the cost involved. He owes you that much.

MESSY JOE

'You don't love because: you love despite; not
for the virtues, but despite the faults.'
WILLIAM FAULKNER

Most mornings start the same in our home. Joe, who chooses to arise precisely two minutes before he has to be out the door for work, whizzes through the flat like a tornado. As soon as he's satisfied that testicles, spectacles, wallet and watch are all aboard, he rushes over to the bed where I'm still lying prostrate, trying to work out which day of the week it is, and plants three quick kisses on my unwashed mouth.

When he's out the door, I take a couple of deep breaths and ready myself for the next segment of my morning ritual: clearing up the trail of destruction my calamitous lover has left in his wake. It typically takes me around half an hour to bring the flat back to an acceptable order. It then takes another half hour of yoga and meditation to diffuse the resentment I feel at having to spend my first thirty waking minutes in this way. Such are the joys of OCD.

Having left him home alone this past week while I've been in Spain with a girlfriend, I knew I'd be returning to a bit of a shit-hole. But the bout of insomnia I experienced on holiday, coupled with raging hormones from my new contraceptive pill, has not helped matters.

On entering the flat, I can tell Joe has used the old trick of burning incense to mask the lingering accents of curry, tobacco and boy that have clearly been wafting about for the last six days. While he's attempted to do the washing-up, all of the plates, pans and cutlery are covered in a thick layer of grease and have been precariously heaped on to the drying rack, threatening to topple over at any moment. The living-room rug is scrunched up and wonky; I can tell he's spilled something on it, then chucked it into the washing machine and back under the coffee table, hoping I wouldn't notice. Clearly, he's forgotten he lives with Monica from *Friends*.

This isn't the worst scene I've come home to in our short time dwelling under the same roof. But, given my exhaustion and fluctuating oestrogen levels, I lose it.

Why is he so INSENSITIVE! I groan to the empty flat. *Couldn't he have made a BIT of an effort, JUST FOR ONCE?*

When he arrives home, he bursts into the kitchen full of the joys of spring, as I'm stood at the sink rewashing cutlery like it's eternal winter in Narnia.

'Hello baby! Welcome back!' he gushes.

'Hi,' I reply, without turning my head.

'Are you… OK?' he says.

I let out an exasperated sigh and turn around.

'Well, no, as it happens; I'm not really OK, Joe, no.'

I then launch into a full-blown tirade of how I am not interested in living in a student flat at the ripe old age of thirty-one, and how devoid of love and comfort this place felt when I walked in earlier. I fail to see the irony in my words, and I fail to remember that a loving home is established through the dynamic between the people in it, not the sanitation levels.

Messiness has always been a trigger for me. A big one. When I was growing up and my parents were struggling with addiction, impending bankruptcy and my mum's Hepatitis C diagnosis and chemotherapy, our family home was often in a state of disarray. Because of this, I came to associate a messy house as being synonymous with an unhappy one.

At university, I had a mini panic attack every time I came home from a lecture to find the house I shared with five girls to be an utter shambles, with clothes, make-up and paperwork cluttering every surface. To manage this anxiety, I'd spend at least an hour trying to restore order, or I'd lock myself in my room so that I didn't have to sit with the others in the mess, pretending I wasn't fazed by it.

I also put an unbelievable amount of pressure on myself to be perfect in every area of my life. This was no small feat, considering that I kept on falling into relationships with extremely messy men; meaning that my OCD had to work overtime to maintain the illusion of perfection I thought I needed to uphold so as to be worthy of love. Their untidiness was a source of most of the fights in these relationships, mainly because I wasn't afraid of shouting at them about the state of their flat, like I was with my female housemates (nothing worse than being ostracised from a girl clique because you're unbearably anal).

When I moved in with Joe, the messiest person I'd ever met by a long shot, it was inevitable that my OCD gremlins were going to surface. To be fair, I had been warned right at the start of our courtship, when my childhood friend, Shell, saw a picture of Joe on my Facebook page and said: 'Oh my God, Pers, are you dating MESSY JOE?'

Turns out, Shell had been in the same halls as Joe at Oxford Brooks University, where his messiness was almost legendary. All those thousands of men in the Wilderness Festival Valley that night we met, and I had to stand in front of the one so messy, he'd earned himself a nickname for it.

After my rant about the state of the flat, Joe and I sit watching TV in silence for an hour, my righteous smuggery about as subtle as the layer of grease covering the kitchen counter. But you can only sit in passive aggression for so long before you realise that, as much as you may be punishing the other person, you're mainly punishing yourself. No one is winning here.

'I'm sorry I was a twat,' I say, looking down at my peeling pink nail varnish. 'I'm just really tired, didn't sleep again last night and all I wanted was to come home to a nice clean flat. But I know it's not OK to speak to you like that.'

'The thing is, babe, I'm struggling at the moment, too,' he replies. 'My new boss is treating me like shit, and all I wanted was to come home to the one person who usually lifts my spirits, especially since I haven't seen you for a week. But the moment I walk in, you speak to me like I'm useless. I know I'm never going to be tidy or clean enough for you, but I'm doing the best I can. It just feels like no matter how hard I try, nothing will ever be good enough.'

His words burn through me, like fire on snow. I fling my arms around him and melt into his shoulder, horrified that I've triggered the same feelings of inadequacy in him that have plagued me all my life. I am ashamed of myself.

The painful truth about relationships is that we're programmed, at a cellular level, to attract the people whose teeth fit our wounds, and vice versa. But rather than a curse, we can choose to see this as a blessing, for it's only by confronting the wound that we can ever hope to heal it. While this is a searingly painful process in the moment, like having antiseptic rubbed into a fresh cut, this is how we stop the infection from the wound spreading any further.

I know I didn't attract a messy man by accident. Throughout our relationship, he continues to hold up a mirror to my perfectionism time and time again, showing it to be a sham: it is my self-hate masquerading as self-respect. It is a lie. And if I don't stay and heal this with him now, I know I'll only attract someone else later on whose teeth fit the same wound.

Either way, our respective wounds will not be healed through judgement, force or manipulation. We only grow through love. So, instead of shutting down and closing my heart when I'm feeling triggered in our relationship, I want to use it as an opportunity to love myself and him *more*, not less.

Because there's a lot to love about Joe, when I'm not choosing to obsess over his messiness. If I'm down or going through a shit storm, he's the first to comfort and cheer me up. The first to buy a round of drinks in the pub. The first to offer a bed and home-cooked meal to any friend or family member going through a rough patch.

While he's not for everyone, to those that love and get him he's a legend: a raw, rambunctious, woodland-dwelling, fairy-light-stick-wielding, green-eyed delight of a man, who's taught me more about what it means to be a spiritual, loving person than all of the self-help books I've read put together, and whose love and loyalty have healed me to a greater depth than a thousand therapy sessions ever could. I can't believe I get to spend the rest of my life with him.

Over the years, our relationship has made me realise that there is no such thing as the wrong partner or relationship. We each attract the person who provides the maximum opportunity for healing and growth at any given moment. Whilst not everyone we attract is going to be our life partner, no romance, however short, is ever a waste of time. (Not even the brief ones with emotionally unavailable ghosters, because they teach us not to abandon ourselves in order to stop the other person from running away.)

However much your heart may have temporarily broken after a love story imploded, you always have the choice as to whether or not you want to learn the lesson it was there to teach you, so that you can go on to become the person you need to be for your future lifetime partner and relationship.

Every apparent fuck-up, every mistake and bad choice in my romantic life eventually led me to be standing in the middle of a rave at a festival, right in front of the man that is now my fiancé. Looking back, I wouldn't change a single thing in all the love stories that came before ours, because otherwise we may never have met. And I wouldn't change a thing about my messy man, because it's inside of his mess that I'm slowly learning how to love without condition.

JACKPOT

I think we hit the jackpot baby
Though you're the messiest person I've ever met –
You leave the bathroom soaking wet,
You live your life without regret,
And you're teaching me to do the same.

I think we hit the jackpot, baby
Though I can't cook and you can't clean;
You're like Ronnie Wood at seventeen –
You work so hard to live your dream
And you're teaching me to do the same.

I think we hit the jackpot, baby
Though I sometimes fear that this won't last
Because we fell in love so very fast,
But for us you say you'll take the chance
And you're teaching me to do the same.

14. HOW TO COMMUNICATE AND CONNECT

MUCH ADO ABOUT NOTHING

'What a lover's heart knows let no man's brain dispute.'

ABERJHANI

There aren't enough words in the English language to describe the torrent of unnecessary shit that's resulted from my inability to effectively communicate my feelings and boundaries with a romantic partner, and from their inability to do the same. Here's one of my most absurd examples.

Joe had just returned from his Bali trip and moved into his new flat in Queens Park. One morning, having gone to work early and left me alone in his flat for the first time, I felt compelled to have myself a good old snoop-athon.

Wandering into the spare room with my freshly poured cup of Nespresso, I spotted a large plastic box on top of the bed that Joe had yet to unpack. Peering into the box, I could see a picture frame containing an image of Joe wearing a cowboy hat with his arm around a blonde girl wrapped in a pink feather boa – the kind of mise-en-scène you get from a novelty photo booth at weddings. My immediate thought was that the picture was of him and I, which made no sense, given that we'd only recently started going out and had never been to a wedding or fancy dress party.

Naturally, I picked up the frame for a closer inspection and discovered that the picture wasn't of me at all; it was of his ex-girlfriend from several years ago. (I'd already had a stalk of Joe's Facebook photos and was so clued-up on his romantic history that I'd have probably aced a pub quiz on the subject).

Even though I questioned why he still had a framed photo of an ex-girlfriend (conveniently failing to remember all the pictures and letters from my own exes still stuffed away in my bedside cabinet at home), I instinctively knew that it was harmless; he'd simply forgotten he had it. Though we were fairly new lovers, I felt secure enough in our dynamic not to ascribe any significant meaning to this picture's presence in his flat; I took it as a sign of his absent-mindedness, not his duplicity. If only I'd have also trusted my initial gut feeling over what I found next.

As I was about to place the photo frame back into the box, I noticed a small packet of prescription pills that had been lying underneath it. Unable to stifle my curiosity for a second time, I picked up the packet to read what it said:

15 X ACICLOVIR 400MG TABLETS
TO TREAT CURRENT OUTBREAK OF HERPES.
JOSEPH GOULD.

If ever there was an unwelcome revelation to discover about a new partner, this had to be it – especially considering the date on the box was a few weeks ago.

I opened the packet. Empty. And yet, despite this insanely incriminating evidence, my first instinct was that there *had* to be an explanation, and that I should call Joe immediately to find out what it was. Instead, though, I allowed my logic to overrule my gut. After all, what possible explanation could there be for the fact he'd lied to me?

Joe was one of the few men I'd been with who I'd felt was having sex *with* me rather than *at* me, and, because I'd felt so safe and respected by him between the sheets, we'd been bonking like it was going out of fashion. We'd bonked first thing in the morning, last thing at night, and every time we had a spare ten minutes. We'd bonked in his bed, on the sofa, in the car – and a few other places too inappropriate to mention here. If what I was reading on this packet was accurate, and there was no reason to believe it wasn't, then I hadn't only contracted a genital infection (for life), I'd also been deceived by the man I'd recently come to believe I was going to spend the rest of my life with. A decent man. A good man. This was way more painful to me than the fact I now had herpes (which, to be fair, a few friends of mine had contracted themselves and told me it really wasn't such a big deal these days).

When the initial shock began to subside, I did what any woman would do following such a revelation: I called two of my closest girlfriends. The polarity of their responses took me by surprise. One of them urged me to look at the facts. When I did, there was no denying that Joe had lied to me, which made me wonder whether he'd hooked up with someone when he was in Bali and contracted the infection there. This friend said that, if it were her, she'd wait until he was in front of her to confront him, so that he wouldn't have a chance to concoct a BS story. The other friend echoed my own initial reaction. Having met Joe herself, her instincts told her that although this situation did *not* look good, there had to be an explanation; Joe didn't strike her as an arsehole.

Unfortunately, their contrary opinions only served to exacerbate my pain and confusion, as is prone to happen anytime you consult more than one friend when a boy has done wrong by you. I did not want to shroud myself in denial around such blatantly incriminating evidence, as I had done so many times before when information about a boyfriend's shitty behaviour had come to light. But, in the same breath, I didn't want to lose faith in this man and our (up till now) magical love story.

Had I imagined it all – the mad synchronicities and coincidences, which I'd interpreted as signs the universe was conspiring to bring us together? Had I been kidding myself all along: the magic not magic after all, but evidence that my old addiction to fantasy and romantic illusion was back with a vengeance? Because, if Joe really did have herpes, given that he hadn't told me and had continued to sleep with me anyway, then I hadn't just mistrusted him, I'd also mistrusted myself. On an epic scale. And that was even worse than knowing there was no way I could stay in a relationship that had been built on lies.

In the end, my fear pipped it to the post. I decided to wait and confront Joe when he was home from work, meaning that I spent the entire day in purgatory, fretting over how my new genital infection (an infection I now had for LIFE) was clearly karma having the last laugh by smiting the very part of me that had caused myself and others so much grief in the past.

When I arrived back at Joe's that evening (to what I thought would be our break-up chat), I was as glum as Eeyore on a particularly bad day. The melancholy of my mood was instantly punctured, however, when Joe – happy as a Labrador whose owner has just returned home after a two-week holiday – materialised from the bathroom down the hallway, naked as the day he was born. It took everything in me not to laugh out loud at the absurdity of the situation.

'Joe, we need to talk,' I said as I stormed past him into the living room, trying my best to avoid direct eye contact with his duplicitous genitals.

'What's wrong, babe?' he replied as he walked towards the sofa I'd just plonked myself onto.

Still naked.

'Joe, *please* can you put some clothes on? I need to have a serious conversation with you.'

'Why can't I be naked?'

'Please, Joe!'

I've always had a weird thing about seeing the man I'm dating naked (until I've been with them a long time), but, given the context, this took it to another level. It felt like I was watching Bill Clinton insist on national TV that he 'did not have sexual relations with that woman'. Hiding in plain sight, I think it's called. Well, I REFUSED to be Hillaried!

Getting the hint that I wasn't messing about, Joe skulked off to the bathroom and returned wearing a towel around his waist. It was the best I was going to get for now.

Without saying a word, I rummaged around in my coat pocket for the packet of pills, and handed it to him. Confused, he took the packet, turned it over and read the label.

Silence.

Then, furrowed brow.

And, then…

'Fuuuuuuuuuck,' he said under his breath, while throwing his head back; then – was that a *LAUGH?*

A moment later, his tone switched. He held the empty pill packet out towards me and looked directly into my eyes.

'Persia, listen to me, I know how this looks – and I know guys say this sort of shit all the time, but I SWEAR TO GOD, this *really-isn't-what-it-looks-like.'*

He didn't need to say one word more, because I knew instantly that he was telling the truth. I just knew. But I'd be damned if I was going to let *him* know that just yet.

'Tell me, Joe, what is it then? Because what it looks like to me is that you've either had herpes this entire time and not told me, or you fucked someone in Bali and picked it up then. So, which one is it, exactly?' I replied in as condescending a tone as I could muster.

'It's neither,' he said standing up.

The towel fell to the floor and he was naked once again, but now the suspect was directly at my eye level, less than a metre from my face. This felt like a direct replica of the opening scene of the movie *Forgetting Sarah Marshall*, which, ironically, we'd watched together only a few weeks ago.

I put my head in my hands in a bid to look exasperated, though really I was trying to stifle a giggle. Meanwhile, the naked Joe walked over to the kitchen counter to pick up his rolling skins and tobacco, then plopped himself back on the sofa opposite me and started to roll a ciggie. When he'd finished rolling, he put the cigarette behind his ear, clasped his hands in front of his bare torso, leaned forwards, and continued.

'Babe, this is honestly the truth,' he said. 'We've had a lot of sex since we met, yes?'

I shrugged my shoulders and looked away.

'After a while, I started feeling really... sore... on my John Thomas.'

JOHN. THOMAS.

God, I love this guy, I thought.

He went on to explain how he'd felt too embarrassed to tell me about his sore willy so early on in our relationship; how he'd never experienced anything like this before, and how he'd panicked that, considering everything I'd told him about my sordid past, I'd maybe given him something, but he wouldn't ever dare ask me that out of fear I'd be livid and run a mile. So he'd hit up Google – and totally pranged himself out. Eventually, after hours tunnelling down the rabbit hole of pictures and testimonials displaying all manner of genital malfunctions, he'd convinced himself it must be herpes, and promptly ordered some pills off the dark web – pills he didn't even end up finishing.

'I know I should have told you. I'm so, so sorry, Persia, I just didn't want to lose you, and now I've fucked it up, anyway,' he said, his eyes watering as he lit his cigarette.

One of my favourite qualities of Joe's is his inability to lie. Like, he literally cannot lie for shit. As ridiculous as it sounded, I knew he was telling the truth right now. Sometimes the truth really is stranger than fiction.

My gut instinct was confirmed when we both went to the STD clinic to get checked out the following week. Turned out, neither of us were riddled with anything more than paranoia. Joe had every test under the sun – several times in fact, and the result was always the same: clean as a whistle. Talk about much ado over nothing.

We women tend to forget that the men in our lives can often suffer the same neuroses and spiralling negative thought patterns we do. They can also find it just as hard (if not harder) to voice those fears – especially if those fears could in any way bring into question their masculinity.

So, next time your mind starts to make some very big assumptions about your fella's integrity, even if the evidence seems overwhelmingly incriminating, remember Herpes-gate, and save yourself a heap of unnecessary stress: talk to your partner about the issue – as soon as it comes up. Listen to what they have to say in response. And, most importantly, trust your instincts over whether or not they're telling the truth. After all, if your instinct has the wherewithal to save you in life and death situations, it can certainly save your love life. Even if it doesn't give you the answer you were expecting or hoping for.

BACK POCKET

'What do we live for, if it is not to make
life less difficult for each other?'
GEORGE ELIOT

Here are three simple phrases to keep in your back pocket when you enter a new relationship. Use them often, and they will enhance the dynamic between the two of you exponentially.

1. 'HOW CAN I MAKE THIS BETTER?'

Much of the time in relationships, we're so focused on getting our point across or our needs met that we don't stop to consider what our partner wants or needs – particularly when we're in the middle of an argument.

Asking a simple and direct question like this when we're going through a challenging time puts the ball in their court, and demonstrates that we care enough about them and the relationship to do whatever it takes to make it right.

2. 'I APPRECIATE YOU.'

It's easy to take our partners for granted in the business of our day-to-day lives.

While the words 'I love you' are always nice to hear, they're a little generic; sometimes we need to try a more personal approach to cut through the noise so our partner can actually *feel* that love.

Try saying the words 'I appreciate you' instead – followed by some specific examples of what, exactly, you appreciate about them. Such as how much effort they make with your friends and family. How they always remember to pick up your favourite snack on the way home from work. Or their unrivalled scrambled eggs.

3. 'I WAS WRONG.'

If you're anything like me, apologising when you mess up is not fun. Our pride can lead us to concoct all manner of reasons or excuses as to why we made an error – if we're even willing to admit that we made a mistake in the first place.

But rather than getting defensive, playing the victim or projecting our guilt onto the other person to try to save face, simply owning that we were wrong (without trying to justify *why*) will resolve any conflict in a relationship so much faster. Not only does it create space for our partner to feel seen, heard and respected, it gives them the opportunity to forgive us. Then we can get on with the best bit about arguments: the make-up sex.

NICE

'I do not wish [women] to have power
over men; but over themselves.'

MARY WOLLSTONECRAFT, *A VINDICATION OF THE RIGHTS OF WOMEN*

n the grand scheme of history, we women have not had power over our lives for very long. We weren't even considered people in our own right until 1929. Nor were we granted equal pay for equal work, before a law was passed in 1983 (and we all know how respected *that* law has been). As if that's not enough to grate on your ovaries, how about this: marital rape wasn't made a criminal offence until 1991. That's *1991*, people!

When I was studying English Literature at university, it never failed to boggle my mind how much women have been shoehorned into assuming the idealised female identity of being silent, chaste and obedient throughout the course of history, and in the outlandishly biased writing that has documented it. If you look closely at the majority of texts that make up the Western canon (i.e. those considered 'high art' by – yep, you guessed it – *men*), you'll see the heavy price paid by any female character who dared challenge the stifling limitations of her patriarchal culture, whether intentionally or unintentionally: when Desdemona refutes Othello's wrongful accusation of infidelity, he bumps her off with a pillow. Miss Havisham from Charles Dickens's *Great Expectations* is branded a batty old crone, having suffered a mental breakdown after being defrauded and jilted at the altar by her horrible husband-to-be. Similarly, in *Jane Eyre*, Mr Rochester's first wife, Bertha, is locked away in the attic like a rabid dog for suffering from a mental illness that renders her incapable of playing out the wifely role required of her. She eventually takes vengeance by setting fire to Thornfield Hall, before throwing herself off the roof of the burning building.

Such violent ends were not uncommon for women, fictional or real-life, who failed to stay within the confines set out by the patriarchy. Take poor old Anne Boleyn, who lost her head for committing the exact same crime as her rotund husband. Unfortunately for Henry, the savageness of this punishment only served to immortalise his fiery wife as one of the most fascinating, brave and pioneering women of all time. (She even gives Henry a run for his money in the fame stakes.)

But what do these historical female figures and characters have to do with how modern women are showing up in our romantic lives, where – for the most part – getting our head lopped off for cheating on our other half is not of major concern? A lot, actually: they provide crucial context as to why many of us find it so difficult to be clear, direct and forthcoming when it comes to communicating – especially with the men we're dating.

The only hope women from earlier centuries had for steering their own fate lay in their ability to coerce and manipulate under the radar. And guess what? That compulsion is very much still alive and kicking today. If there is one reason I believe women can be prone to passive aggression, manipulation and playing the victim as a means of getting our needs or desires met, it's because we still harbour an underlying fear somewhere in the recesses of our psyche that speaking our truth, directly and unapologetically, equates to certain death. Not so much a literal death (although, shockingly, that's still a reality for far too many women today), but an intrinsic feeling that speaking our truth will result in us being shunned, rejected or exiled from our community – which to women from times gone by would mean literal death, anyway. Any woman who has resonated with the #MeToo movement will be all too familiar with the fear associated with speaking up, because the majority of rape or sexual harassment claims are still dismissed, even to this day.

Gervase Markham, an English poet from Shakespeare's era, published a book in London in 1615 entitled *The English Housewife, Containing the Inward and Outward Virtues Which Ought to be in a Complete Woman*. In it, he said that to be considered worthy and desirable, a woman must be:

> Of chaste thought, stout courage, patient, untired, watchful, diligent, witty, pleasant, constant in friendship, full of good neighbourhood, wise in discourse, but not frequent therein, sharp and quick of speech, but not bitter or talkative, secret in her affairs, comfortable in her counsels, and generally skilful in the worthy knowledge's which do belong to her vocation.

I wonder if the female *Love Island* contestants got the memo.

Seriously, though, while this exhaustive list may seem laughable to us nowadays, the modern woman is still raised to be what's essentially a blend of all these 'virtues' put together, and that is… NICE.

According to the *Cambridge Dictionary*, 'nice' is defined as 'kind, friendly or polite'. There's a subtle inference in our culture that 'nice' also means passive and conforming. Any indication that a woman is being anything other than 'nice', and she's often labelled a bitch (or, at the very least, *tricky*). Being a bitch immediately identifies you as an untrustworthy outsider, and, as we've already seen, being a woman cast out to the peripheries of society was once akin to receiving a death sentence.

Is it any wonder, then, that we fall back on old, familiar modes of passive communication when potential for conflict or tension arises? There are few among us who'd be happy to be labelled as a tricky bitch – and even fewer who'd welcome being rejected or outcast simply for holding an opposing view to the status quo. (You need only look at the crap that successful women at the top of their career have to deal with for daring to be as direct or ruthless as a man, to know it's a path fraught with obstacles and judgement.)

One of the main problems with stuffing down our truth in order to be considered a *nice girl* is that, soon enough, the repression can become so unbearable that we may find ourselves involuntarily launching into full-blown bunny boiler mode. Like Bertha in Rochester's attic, we'll wind up burning down the prison of conformity that's kept us incapacitated all this time, and though there will likely be collateral damage in the form of harassed ex-boyfriends/their new girlfriends, it's us who'll ultimately end up a broken mess on the floor.

So, what to do, then, when a cause for conflict arises in our relationship? We feel the fear of death that's steeped in the blood of our female ancestors, and we speak our truth, anyway. We learn how to assert our needs, our desires and our boundaries with grace, maturity and respect – and without apology. We remind ourselves that the people who are worth our time and energy won't disappear if we are brave enough to be vulnerable with them.

Here's what we *don't* do: we don't try to diminish our pain to spare another person from having to feel theirs. We don't hint or kid ourselves that the people in our life should just 'know' how we're feeling. We don't condemn or vilify other women for being more assertive or ballsy than we're currently able to be. We don't chastise ALL men for the patriarchal structure that is responsible for the suppression of women; many of them are victims of it, too. And, if we're serious about dismantling this patriarchal structure, then we must be brave enough to speak up in our personal lives as well as our social and political ones, because the personal *is* the political. Every time we effectively communicate our boundaries and preferences to any human we encounter, whether that's saying NO to a man that continues to cheat or verbally or physically abuse us, or simply turning down the invite to our friend's dinner party (without making up a BS excuse) because we don't feel up to it... we do our female ancestors proud. They didn't have a choice whether or not to communicate their truth. We do. We owe it to them and to ourselves to own it.

LOVE LANGUAGES

'Real giving is when we give to our spouses
what's important to them, whether we
understand it, like it, agree with it, or not.'
MICHELE WEINER-DAVIS

Eighty per cent of the time, my relationship with Joe is easy. The remaining twenty (the bit where I have to navigate my trauma around his messiness, and my fear of commitment, to name a few) can be excruciatingly hard. But this is where the growth happens, enabling our relationship to improve with every year that passes.

However, whatever trials and tribulations we've had to face throughout our time together, one thing neither of us has ever had to battle with is doubting our love for one another. This is because we happen to share the same love languages.

The concept of love languages is explored in the mid-nineties bestseller, *The Five Love Languages: How to Express Heartfelt Commitment to Your Mate*, by Gary Chapman. In it, Chapman outlines five ways we express and experience love; a theory he came to after years spent working as a marriage counsellor and in the field of linguistics.

According to Chapman's theory, each person has one primary and one secondary love language:

1. Gifts: 'visual symbols of love' – can be little or large.

2. Quality time: giving your partner undivided attention and doing activities you enjoy together.

3. Words of affirmation: verbal or written indicators of love such as compliments, encouragement etc.

4. Acts of service: doing things you know your partner would appreciate e.g. loading the dishwasher, driving you to your meeting or cooking a meal, etc.

5. Physical touch: kissing, stroking, cuddling, bonking – you get the gist.

Chapman says that to discover another person's love languages, you must look at how they are naturally drawn to expressing love to others. Also, listen to what they ask their partner for most often – and what they complain about. Chapman's experience has taught him that we tend to naturally give love in the way we prefer to receive it, and that the key to better communication can be achieved when you prioritise demonstrating love to your partner in the love language they understand.

From day one, it was clear Joe and I were naturally drawn to giving and receiving love via physical touch and quality time. The first two weeks of our courtship were mainly spent hanging out in forests and snuggling, like a pair of horny fifteen-year-olds. I didn't need him to verbally affirm how much he liked me, although he did anyway. I didn't care if he drove me around in his car or took me out for dinner, although he did anyway. And I wasn't bothered about getting gifts, although he brought me back lots of cute bits from his Bali trip.

I've found that when someone is really into you, they often (but not always) oscillate between *all* of the love languages in the first few months of dating, because it feels so good to express and receive love in all its glorious forms at the start. However, this is not sustainable for either parties in the long run. For a romance to thrive beyond the honeymoon phase – when each of your annoying habits have been unveiled (and the passionate sex has inevitably started to dwindle) – you need to know which two love languages each partner is most drawn to.

I know that my relationship with Joe is thriving when we prioritise sitting down together every day to play the guitar and sing. This isn't just quality time for us, it's quality *creative* time; meaning that not only does it connect us emotionally and romantically, it connects us on a more spiritual level, too – as does doing yoga or meditating together. Because we both favour physical touch, cuddling on the sofa to watch a movie after a jam or yoga session bonds us even more. (No fancy dinner required to tempt either of us into the sack!)

However, I've been in other relationships where my partner and I had totally different love languages. Looking back, I can see that my lack of effort to consistently express love in a way that my boyfriend could understand (and vice versa) was a significant factor in why we didn't work out.

So, whether you're single or in a relationship, my suggestion is that you spend a little time discovering what *your* two main love languages might be. And then – when you're in a position to – get curious about what your partner's are, also. If they happen to be the same as yours, like mine and Joe's are, then you probably won't have a hard time feeling loved by one another (although you'll still have plenty of other problems to contend with!). If your love languages *aren't* the same, you'll have the perfect opportunity to learn how to love in a way that might not come naturally to you, but will cause you to evolve into higher levels of compassion, generosity and creativity. Either way, you can't lose.

TEASE

'Love difficult people. You're one of them.'
BOB GOFF

Unless we're in a heated argument, I've always been good at speaking kindly to my friends. (My work there now is to ensure I always speak kindly *about* them, too.) However, when it comes to how I speak to a boyfriend, historically I've had a much less disciplined approach.

Aside from the imaginary arguments I'll often have with them in my head (my favourite pastime, as I always gets to win), I've never thought twice about nagging, making digs – and, on my worse days, flat out mocking my fella. When they object, I'll say my jibes are just harmless banter, and they need to chill out.

The truth is that I would never say to my friends what I sometimes allow myself to say to Joe (or to myself, for that matter). I can try to justify it all I want, but this is nothing more than plain old passive aggression tarted up as teasing, and by any other name would be considered gas-lighting.

What I'm starting to realise is that this habit, which is common in the women I coach, too, doesn't just negatively affect our relationship with our partner. It negatively affects our relationship with *ourselves*.

How we treat someone else is a direct reflection of how we feel about ourselves in any given moment. So, if we're committed to practising self-love, then we'd do well to remember that this also requires us to practise loving the person we share a bed with, too. Especially when they're doing our head in.

PHUBBING

'Technology is the knack of so arranging the
world that we do not experience it.'

ROLLO MAY

have a confession: I keep phubbing off Joe.

I phubb him first thing in the morning and last thing at night.
I phubb him when we're eating dinner. I've even phubbed him
when he's trying to open up and share something important.

What on Google Earth is phubbing? I hear you cry.

For those not down with the kids, 'phubbing' is a term coined
by Generation Y. It's an abbreviation of 'phone' and 'snubbing',
and refers to those moments (or in my case, sometimes hours)
when you choose to focus all your attention on your phone,
rather than the person you're with.

I've been on the other end of phubbing myself, so I know how
infuriating it can be. I'll be midway through a riveting story
about my day, and Joe will be nodding along, giving a token
grunt every now and then to indicate he's listening. Meanwhile,
his thumb swipes around his iPhone screen like he's warming up
for the Thumb War Olympics, indicating that he's absolutely *not*
listening.

Did you know that the average person in the UK spends just
under three hours on their phone a day? Or that eighty-six per
cent of people constantly check their phone while talking to

friends? How about this: one in five people aged eighteen to thirty-four has used their smartphone during sex. (Then again, that one makes a lot of sense.)

Elevating our smartphone's worth above our partner's (i.e. 'phubbing' our lover) means that we're destroying the real, intimate human connection that gives our romantic relationships meaning. But it doesn't have to be this way. Given that technology isn't going anywhere any time soon, our only choice of saving the sovereignty of real-life romantic connection is to create and commit to upholding personal boundaries around our phone usage.

Here are my boundaries. I cross them often, but progress is more realistic (and sanity-saving) than perfection:

1. No picking up my phone during a conversation with Joe, unless it's to show him something specific.

2. Admit and apologise whenever I accidentally phubb Joe (or anyone else).

3. Put my phone on flight mode as soon as I get into bed and don't turn it off until 8 am.

4. Put my phone in another room when eating dinner or watching a movie to remove the temptation to phubb. (At a restaurant, do NOT have phone on the table. Unacceptable!)

5. Don't have phones anywhere near us during sex. Unless it's to make ourselves a naughty little porno.

THE PAINTER

'The most significant conversations of
our lives occur in silence.'
SIMON VAN BOOY

A while ago, I was sat in a group coaching session when one of the members shared that her husband of thirty-five years had just died.

Having suffered a stroke, in the months leading up to his death he was only able to communicate one word: 'No.'

The woman had spent all day every day since the stroke caring for her husband in every conceivable way, and now found herself overwhelmed by all the freedom, time and space she'd once been so desperate to call her own.

'I could never see what was right in front of me,' she said midway through her story.

Her husband had been a painter of extraordinary talent and skill. Prior to his illness, he'd exhibited his paintings all over the world, and was highly revered for his work. But he was also a stoical man. Quiet and reserved, he was not accustomed to sharing his emotions with others – unlike his wife, who had always worn her heart very much on her sleeve.

'What are you *feeling*, though?' she'd often plead with him.

All she had ever wanted was just to feel included in his internal world, however melancholic it might be. His silence felt like exclusion, like a betrayal.

When her husband died, what was left was even more silence – silence and thousands upon thousands of his paintings, drawings and sketches. They filled practically every wall and corner of their home.

But, she explained, it was only when he – the artist – was no longer there, that she – his wife – was finally able to see him and his creations clearly. What she saw was a tidal wave of emotions and feelings, some light and hopeful, others dark and nebulous. Many, everything in between. What she saw was him, *all* of him, all that depth and connection and feeling that she'd been so hell-bent on extracting from him for all those years. The irony was that he'd been pouring it out right in front of her, all along.

What I learnt from the woman's story is that sometimes the problem in a relationship is not an absence of love, but our inability to see the love that's already here for us now, in this moment. It might not be in the form we hoped for, but it's all we've got.

It made me think of how I often mentally propel myself into our future, mine and Joe's – travelling the world together, buying our first home, our wedding – because I'm afraid of standing still in the beauty of what we have already created. I'm afraid that it's not enough; but I'm even more afraid that it's everything and I'm going to lose it, like the woman did when her husband died. Jumping into the fantasy of our future distracts me from the pain of this thought. But, in chasing things I don't yet have, what I'm really doing is running away from everything I *do* have, meaning I miss out on all the magic that can only be experienced *now*.

I also learnt from the woman's story that, sometimes, it's in the silence between two people that love is most fully expressed.

15. HOW TO ENVISION YOUR ROMANTIC FUTURE

HAM STRAIGHT

'For the two of us, home isn't a place. It is
a person. And we are finally home.'

STEPHANIE PERKINS

When I was younger, I spent around 70 per cent of my waking hours with horses.

The parents of my childhood best friend, Salena, owned the stables around the corner from my family home and the primary school that Salena and I attended together. Fortunately, the stables were also just ten minutes by horse from London's largest green space, Richmond Park, which was created in the seventeenth century by Charles I when he moved his court to Richmond Palace to escape an outbreak of the plague in London.

The most exhilarating (and, at times, frightening) part of all our Richmond Park rides was braving 'Ham Straight', a long stretch of gently sloping, sandy track that served as the perfect runway for a hearty gallop. And gallop we pretty much always did, for turning left onto Ham Straight meant that we were on our way back to the stables – and the horses knew it. Their ears would prick up, their eyes would widen, and they'd tuck their hindquarters under to prepare for the almighty race back home.

Until my parents got sober in my mid-teens, home was more of a place that I associated with wanting to run from, than towards. I felt the same in most of my relationships, too. But when I moved in with Joe more than a year after we met (the first time I'd officially lived with a boy), whenever I was on the bus or Tube en route back to our flat, I'd think of the excited anticipation the horses would feel the moment we turned them up Ham Straight… and I'd get it.

CALLING CARD

'Freedom is not the absence of commitments, but the ability
to choose – and commit myself to – what is best for me.'

PAULO COELHO, *THE ZAHIR*

A few weeks ago, Joe proposed.

Since then, I've had moments where I've been overwhelmed with gratitude, excitement and even a sense of relief that my future is en route to being officially hitched to his for the rest of this lifetime. I've had other moments where I've felt nothing short of terrified, for the same reason.

What if us bringing the government into our bedroom is a bad idea?

What if it isn't?

Who will I be with you in the years ahead?

Who would I be without you?

'Till death do us part' is a big commitment. And an uncertain one. Could mean five decades. Could mean five minutes. Who knows?

Why does no one ever tell you about the comforting dread of *forever* when it comes to crossing the threshold?

What I do know in my bones is that this dread – this sporadic, fumbling panic that comes in waves – has nothing to do with Joe. Or our relationship. I know he's my person; knew it from the moment our eyes met in the valley that night. (Well, my soul

289

knew it; my mind was a muddle from too much red wine.) I also know that I'd have felt like this with any partner I ended up with, because committing to marriage strips me of the one freedom my entire identity had once been founded upon: the freedom to flirt with any man I felt intrigued by.

Picking up men was my thing for as long as I can remember. I excelled at it the same way my ex-boyfriend excelled at making the perfect rollie, or my friend Lucy excels at witty comebacks. It was my calling card.

My success in seducing wasn't down to my looks, sense of humour or talent. I had friends who were prettier, funnier and more gifted than I was. But they couldn't always guarantee a hook-up the way I could. It's not that I could get anyone, but I could always get *one*. And one was enough.

It was all a turn-on to me: that moment you first feel their eyes on you from the other side of the room. The thrilling anticipation of waiting to see what excuse they'll come up with to spark conversation. The dizzying high from knowing you hold all the cards – and will do until you give it all up in the hope that love-making will somehow equate to you feeling loved.

It took getting engaged and becoming a love coach for me to realise that the reason I picked up guys so consistently was because I expected to. That's it. Expectation is a by-product of repeated success (or failure) in one area, and I was repeatedly successful at this game because I had to be. It was my lifeline, the one thing I could grasp on to when everything else felt so untethered.

Now I have no need to pick up a man to make me feel worth something. Now I know my worth. I also know Joe's worth, and I know what our relationship is worth to me. Now this is my calling card.

So, maybe the comforting dread is not something we need to fear or feel guilty about. Maybe it's just us grieving the old life we are leaving behind as we step through the portal into our new one. And, maybe, if the film *Moulin Rouge* is anything to go by (and it is), it's a sign that we are finally ready for the greatest thing we will ever learn: just to love, and be loved in return.

2020 VISION

'What is behind your eyes holds more power
than what is in front of them.'

GARY ZUKAV

Today was meant to be my wedding day.

Right now, I should be sipping fizz with my bridesmaids, while my former client (now friend) puts my hair in rollers. I should be reading through my speech one last time, and telling my Maid of Honour, Katy, to put on some reggae to calm me down. I should be asking my mum whether glitter on my cheeks is too much for a traditional church ceremony.

'Of course it is,' she'd say, 'but don't let that stop you. More is more.'

I should be getting ready to marry the love of my life. But I'm glad I'm not. I'm glad, because today was not our day, and 2020 was not our year. A few months in, a worldwide pandemic brought our economy to its knees. Shortly after, the knee of a corrupt white cop on the neck of an innocent black man brought global attention to the pandemic of racism that built and sustains the world's economy. Everything as we knew it has been turned upside down. How lucky are we that a postponed wedding is our biggest challenge, when other people's lives and livelihoods are crumbling around them.

Change only happens when the pain of staying the same

becomes more unbearable than the pain of learning to do things differently. What this year has taught me is that seeing and doing things differently is no longer an option, but a necessity.

Had the events of 2020 not come to pass and our wedding was still happening today, I'd have entered my marriage sleepwalking – despite all the work I've done on myself over the years to wake up. Now when I walk down the aisle, it will be with my eyes wide open, which means I'll be able to see my future husband as clearly as I saw him when we first fell in love: with 2020 vision.

The other day, I found the list of positive things about Joe and our dynamic that I wrote two weeks after we met. (I ripped up the page of negatives; I didn't need to hide behind them anymore.) Whenever we hit a wall in our relationship in years to come, I'll read this list to remind me that if I want things to get better, I have to start by seeing him – and us – through the lens of love, not judgement. If nothing else, I hope the events of 2020 have inspired enough of us to do the same. Here it is:

- Who you see is who you get
- Knows exactly who he is
- Kind
- Doesn't judge me or my past
- Sees the best in people
- Funny AF
- Plays guitar
- Generous
- Reminds me of Dad
- Calls me angel
- Honest
- Outdoorsy

- Loyal
- Family man (loves dogs!)
- Feels safe to be 100 per cent me
- FIT
- Has an actual job
- Great taste in music
- So positive and excited about life
- I feel seen and heard
- Amazing cook and looked after me so much when I was sick
- DINOSAURS
- Quite literally can't keep hands off each other
- Feel like a team already
- Have not doubted his feelings for me once
- Outgoing but not a thunder stealer
- Same love languages
- Best friend who I want to sleep with
- I love who I am around him
- Fun-est courtship I've ever had
- Open-minded, respectful, reliable
- Welcoming to new ppl
- Proper traveller
- Been through shit, come out the other side
- I know I'd never get bored with him
- These two weeks have been like a movie – the Saturday night at Wilderness was hands down the best time I've ever had with a boy
- Think I'm falling in love

LANDING

Sometimes love doesn't show up how you hoped it would.
It shows up how you need it to.

And it's better. Easier. More fun.

Since we met nearly five years ago
We've lived in five different homes in the UK
(Seven, if you include living with both our folks during
quarantine).

We've dealt with delayed flights,
God-awful Delhi Belly,
Being shat on by pigeons in Kathmandu,
Horrific PMT while trekking in the mountains
And the quagmire that is Kuala Lumpa airport
(Four times).

We've slept on cold concrete floors,
In tin huts and bamboo shacks with rats
Scratching around in the roof above our heads.

We've bickered, argued and sworn at each other
Under (you) and over (me)
Our breaths aplenty.

I've learnt to live with your messiness
And bedroom floor-drobe.

You've learnt to live with me constantly tidying up
after you
(Then forgetting where I've put your favourite trinkets
and treasures).

I've started to accept you'll never wash up or
make the bed
As well as I do.
You've started to accept that even though
I sometimes panic and push you away,
I'll always come back to you.

Because the truth is that
You are now my home.
I have no other key,
No back-up plan or safety net
Should I shut out you,
Or you shut out me.
There is only us
And what we've built together,
Between the walls of our two souls.

And whatever life throws at us
I know we'll always find a way through it.
Even if that means we have to move out of our flat earlier
than we'd hoped.
Even if we don't get to visit our beloved friends and family
Across the globe for months (possibly years).
Even if we don't get to marry for a second time
Because of this damned virus...

…It's all good.

This is just a different kind of festival for us to surrender to.

(And that, my love, is what we do best).

Who knew that landing in love

Could be even more magical than falling into it?

SPROCKET

'We find ourselves in the sacrifices we make.'
CAMMIE MCGOVERN

When I was ten, I started riding and looking after my friend Salena's former pony, Sprocket.

Sprocket was a little shit much of the time. But, boy, did I love her. It didn't matter that she'd landed me in hospital with broken bones on three separate occasions; still I rose and shone at six o'clock every Saturday morning so I could muck out her stable, wipe all the poo off her dappled white coat and get her looking and smelling immaculate for another ride in Richmond Park.

Every now and then, we somehow managed to win a rosette at a gymkhana. 'We did it!' I'd whisper into Sprocket's ear as I threw my arms around her in the stable afterwards. Such moments made all the hard bits worth it.

I sometimes wonder if my time with Sprocket might have prepared me, at least a bit, for the experience of motherhood. From what I'm told, babies – like mischievous little ponies – require a hell of a lot of upkeep. The hours are long, the cost astronomical, and the thanks you get for your pains, minimal. But, regardless, there you'll still be at the crack of dawn each day, grooming box in one hand, morning feed in the other, because the love you have for them far outweighs the brutal assault they wage on your body, your freedom and your bank balance.

Unlike many of my friends, I've never felt a strong desire to have a child; always felt I lack that elusive mumma-gene that seems to come so naturally to others. Growing up around addiction, I learnt how to protect and prioritise myself – often at the expense of those around me. I built walls to keep others out, but they ended up locking me *in* – to some very damaging beliefs about myself. One being that I'm far too selfish to ever be a mother.

I know I'm not the only one who feels this way. As my peers and I amble through our thirties and motherhood is no longer something we can so easily push to the back of our minds until our next decade (like we did in our twenties), we're now being called to confront two of womankind's most important questions: a. do I want to – and b. am I *capable*… of being someone's mother?

Thinking back to Sprocket as I write this, having just bought and moved into my dream home in my dream location with Joe, now my fiancé, and having just put a deposit down on 'Reggae', our very own cockapoo puppy (!), that second question has started to answer itself. It has said:

'Persia, you *have* been capable of loving and caring for something other than you. That something just happened to be horse, not human. And that still counts.'

I hope that still counts. I hope that if it felt natural to mother that pony and get a dog, if it (eventually) felt natural to commit to Joe despite my past, then one day it might feel natural to commit to mothering a human, too.

The truth is, I felt safer giving my love to something that may well break my bones, but would never be able to break my heart.

And it seems to me that in becoming a mother you risk both breaking the heart of your child, and yours being broken by them.

I know how fortunate I am to have witnessed my parents come out the other side of their addiction – together. It has not only taught me that transformation is possible, but that the journey we go on to heal those wounds between our parents and ourselves is what gives our life meaning; it's what enables us to love and be loved to a greater depth than we ever imagined possible.

As Shakespeare once wrote:

> Ruined love, when it is built anew,
> Grows fairer than at first, more strong, far greater.

Perhaps all children will break their parents' hearts at some point, and all parents will break their children's hearts, at some point. Because to birth is painful, and to be born is painful. But it's how we become alive.

EPILOGUE

'It is not the mountain we conquer, but ourselves.'
SIR EDMUND HILLARY, FIRST MOUNTAINEER TO SUMMIT EVEREST

The journey from Phaplu to Namache in the Khumbu region of the Himalayas is around 34.8 km as the crow flies. However, if you're trekking between the two places as Joe, my dad and I were back in October 2017, the mountainous (and at times treacherous) terrain you have to navigate nearly doubles that distance.

Twice along this route you get a clear glimpse of Everest, the world's highest mountain at 8,848 metres. Everest also goes by the name of 'Chomolungma' to the Tibetans and 'Sagarmatha' to the Nepalese, meaning 'Forehead (or Goddess) of the Sky'. Having been intrigued by this mountain ever since my dad trekked to advanced base camp on the Tibet side of it shortly after finishing rehab (which is still an impressive 6,500 metres), I was excited to see it up close.

While the first few days of our trek were far more challenging than I'd anticipated, by the third morning I'd found my mountain feet. For three whole hours, I zoomed past my dad, Joe and even our lovely Sherpa, Tenzing. No incline was too steep or demoralising for me, and I finally understood why Dad is so addicted to this alpine sport.

However, come lunchtime, inevitably, I hit a wall. My feet were swollen, my fingers chafed from the trekking poles, and I was struck by a horrific bout of PMT that caused me to feel irrationally livid at all men, for no reason at all. This is not ideal when you are stuck on a mountain with three of them for an entire week. It is also not ideal when you realise that two of those men, your father and boyfriend, seem to have morphed into the same person. And that person knows exactly how to push your buttons.

By the late afternoon, the intensity of emotion I was feeling – coupled with the physical intensity of the trek itself – was overwhelming me. I'd had enough. But the problem with trekking in this region is that no matter how fed up and exhausted you are, you have no choice but to keep going until you reach a guest house before it gets dark, and there may not be one for miles. Otherwise, it's just you against the mountain for the night, and guess who's more likely to win that battle.

Somehow, we made it to a guest house before nightfall, but my foul mood continued on well into the next day. What made the whole ordeal harder was that the further I withdrew into myself, the more loving and encouraging Dad and Joe were towards me. It's always been a pattern of theirs. And it's always been a pattern of mine to shut out the people who love me when I'm in a bad place.

The thing is, I find it painful to be loved. Mostly when I'm feeling like shit, but sometimes even when I'm feeling happy. I find it far harder to *be* loved than to give love, because the love you give away can never be taken from you. Even if the relationship ends, you can still feel the love you have for the other person; it's yours, no matter what. But when you're being gifted love, there's always the possibility that it could disappear at any moment. They could break up with you. They could take a job in another country. They could get sick. They could die. So, I push and push and push it away. Then I get to be the one to end it, before the other person has a chance to. It's why I cheated in past relationships. It's why I broke up with men the minute it became too serious. And it's why I shut out my dad and boyfriend when I'm feeling unlovable.

I'm not a love coach because I find relationships easy. I'm a love coach because I find them exceptionally hard. Yet something in me still longs to find a way to summit this Everest of mine.

Which is why I got a tattoo of a semi-colon in Kathmandu the day before we left for the trek. I'd seen this tattoo on a few people in Twelve Step meetings over the last year, so when Joe and I decided to go under the ink together for the first time, I hit up Google to find out its meaning:

> A semi-colon is used when an author could have chosen to end their sentence, but chose not to. The author is you and the sentence is your life.

This must be why so many addicts and people who've struggled with mental health have a semi-colon tattoo: it's a symbol of hope.

I got the tattoo on my wedding ring finger to remind me that, when it comes to the area I've struggled most in life – romantic relationships – I must find a way to keep going. Keeping going looks different, depending on the circumstance. Sometimes it means literally continuing to put one foot in front of the other (for example, when you're climbing a mountain but would rather chuck yourself off it than take another step). Sometimes it means asking yourself whether you're hungry, angry, lonely or tired, and dealing with those symptoms before you try to tackle anything else. Sometimes it means leaving a relationship that's not right for you, and persisting through the pain of the aftermath. And, sometimes, it means finding a way to stay in a relationship you know *is* right for you, but pushes you so far out of your comfort zone that leaving, even with all the grief and heartbreak involved in doing so, seems like the easier option.

Like Everest, love is confronting. It demands all of us. And, like climbing Everest, love doesn't always succeed. No matter how hard we strive to reach the summit of love's experience, not all of us will make it. Divorce happens. People betray, leave us or die. Bodies of those who gave their last breath seeking to reach the highest point on earth still lie near the top of Everest, frozen in time.

So, why bother even trying when success in neither love nor summiting is guaranteed? In the words of mountaineer George Mallory, who died when attempting to summit Everest in 1924: 'Because it's there.'

'Just five more minutes, Persia, and then you see the first view of Everest,' Tenzing the Sherpa tells me as he practically carries me up the steep hill towards the Everest viewpoint in the Sagarmatha National Park.

I look up to see that Dad and Joe are already there, and immediately resent them for getting to see one of the seven natural wonders of the world before I do.

Then, as I take my last few heavy steps, the song on my iPod changes from *The Little Mermaid's* 'Under The Sea' (desperate times) to The Verve's 'Lucky Man'. As the opening chords begin to play, I round the corner to see the snow-capped top of Everest peeking through the trees in the glistening midday sun, like an iceberg suspended in the sky.

Without saying a word, Joe and Dad put their arms around me. My anger instantly melts away. As we look out towards the top of the world together, I'm finally able to hold still and accept the love that's being offered to me.

Just because it's there.

RESOURCES

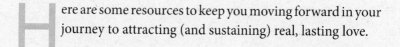

ere are some resources to keep you moving forward in your journey to attracting (and sustaining) real, lasting love.

1. Access your free *Love is Coming* bonuses at loveiscomingbook.com

2. If you found *Love is Coming* a useful resource, I'd be so grateful if you'd take a few minutes to write a quick review on Amazon. This will help the book reach and support more women who are struggling in their love life.

3. Find out more about Sex and Love Addicts Anonymous at www.slaauk.org

4. Find out more about Al Anon (for families and friends of addicts and alcoholics) at www.al-anonuk.org.uk

5. Connect with me on social media for regular (and free!) dating tips and please share your biggest insight from *Love is Coming* with me – I'd love to know!

Instagram: @persialawson
Twitter: @Persia_Lawson
Facebook: @PersiaLawsonLoveCoach

#loveiscoming

6. Find out how I can support you and your love life more powerfully via my programmes and 1-2-1 coaching practice at persialawson.com

ACKNOWLEDGEMENTS

I started writing this book five years ago, shortly after *The Inner Fix* came out. A lot has changed in that time, but the one constant has been my relationship with my beloved fiancé, Joe. This book would not exist without you, JW. I am grateful every single day for the mad synchronicities that brought you into my world, and for the many adventures we've shared together over the last six years (most recently getting Reggae, the best fur baby we could've hoped for).

Thank you to Rosie and her team at Book Printing UK for helping me bring this book baby to life. You've gone above and beyond to make me feel supported every step of the way (even when I'm being unbearably anal!).

Thank you to Sue Lascelles, my wonderful editor, for helping me separate the wheat from the chaff in these pages, and for being such a delight to work with.

Thank you to my team: mama bear Susan for talking me off the ledge too many times to count, Leila for putting up with my incessant voice notes and forgetfulness, Samara for making me feel calm and confident in front of the camera (for over fifteen years!), Jerri and Create and Elate for the brilliant book trailer, Ruthie for the Instagram magic, Rhianna for your excellent VA support, Claire for getting this book in front of the media and Dr Ness, for being the creative yin to my yang and understanding how my brain works better than I do. I'm so proud of what we've all built together (and we're just getting started...).

Thank you to my coach, Shaa Wasmund, for never letting me settle, for being as generous as you are fierce, and for inviting me to be a part of your brilliant mastermind, The Cartel (!). Who knew that business could be such a hoot?!

Thank you to the incredible women in my own mastermind, The Love Squad, for choosing me to be your guide. Getting to know you and watching your transformations has been one of my highlights of this last year. (Special thanks to Madeleine for your feedback on the book – you are an eagle-eyed diamond!)

Thank you to the life-changing Twelve Step fellowships (and all of their members): Al Anon, Sex and Love Addicts Anonymous, and most recently for me, Workaholics Anonymous. I honestly don't know if I'd still be here today if it wasn't for you.

Thank you to all my teachers and mentors from the last decade, including Suzy Ashworth, Gabby Bernstein, Marie Forleo, Elizabeth Gilbert, Glennon Doyle, Abraham Hicks, Boho Beautiful, Danielle La Porte and Matt Kahn, to name a few.

Thank you to Joe's location crew for being such entertaining and lovely legends (if only you'd stop warbling on about cable ties and generators all the live long day!).

Thank you to all of my girls: my beautiful bridesmaids (especially my bestie and MOH, Katy), The Sloos (especially my surrogate sister, Salena) and my work buddies Lucy K (big up the Kensal Rise Massive!), as well as Jody, Jess, Jules, Lauren, Lucy S, Mazzi and Sean for your ongoing support. Special thank you to Ashley James for the gorgeous foreword. I'm so happy our paths collided.

Thank you to my soul sisters, Noo and Fleur, for being an outstanding source of wisdom and support since the world went stark raving mad in early 2020. If it's true that you're the average of the five people you hang out with the most, then I'm extremely lucky, because you two are unparalleled. I don't know what I'd do without you or our meetings.

Thank you to Joe's family: Andy, Deb, Jethro and Elliot (plus Boo and Red!) for the most hilarious and fun first lockdown in the shire, where I finished Draft One of this book. Also thank you to the rest of Joe's insanely large family for being so generous and welcoming to me over the years (especially the Johnsons and the Wests).

Deepest thank you to my family: Mark, Jane, Evie, Toby and Baby Margaret. We've been on quite the journey as a family, but I wouldn't change a thing because where we are today has been worth it. Mum and Dad, thank you for everything you have done for us, for taking the road less travelled, and for showing me that the best really is yet to come.

Finally, thank you to the Soulmates: all the women I've coached over the years, and who are part of our amazing GYS community. Witnessing your own love stories unfold has been the privilege of a lifetime. I hope you've enjoyed reading this book as much as I have creating it for you.